BOUFFONNERIE MUSICALE

The Story of H. B. Farnie,
author, journalist, golfer, librettist, adapter, and song writer.
(1836-1889)

by
Keith Drummond Sharp

The Queme Press
in conjunction with
The Fife Family History Society
2010

Published in 2010 by
The Queme Press in conjunction with
The Fife Family History Society

The Fife Family History Society is a registered Scottish charity
(Registration Number - SCO25246) whose aim is to promote and
encourage the study of family history throughout Fife.

ISBN 978-0-9567090-0-4

British Library Cataloguing in Publication Data.
A catalogue record for this book is
available from the British Library

CONTENTS

ACKNOWLEDGEMENTS

I would like to thank Andrew Campbell who, some years ago, wrote an article, *Henry Brougham Farnie, the Cupar adulterer*, for the journal of the Fife Family History Society. Farnie was one of the characters he studied in research which culminated in his publication last year of *Cupar : The Years of Controversy : Its Newspaper Press, 1822-1872*. When I published, in 2001, *The Flow and Ebb of the Tide*, the story of the Farnie shipbuilding family of which Henry Farnie was a younger son, we realized that there was an overlap in our work and we began to share pieces of information. Andrew has generously allowed me to use material from his research concerning Farnie's days as a journalist in Cupar, Fife and given me a lot of encouragement, and I am very grateful to him. And my very special thanks to my cousin, Refna Wilkin, who, with her experience in publishing, checked my manuscript and was able to offer editorial suggestions and advice which have been invaluable to me. My thanks, too, to the staff in the reading rooms of the British Library and the Bodleian Library for their unfailing courtesy and help, and particularly the custodians of the John Johnson collection of printed ephemera at the Bodleian. Also to Kristy Davis, manager of the Mander and Mitchenson theatre collection, and the staff of the V&A Theatre Collection.

Pictures of the young Henry Farnie and James Farnie, his father, are reproduced by courtesy of St Andrews University Library. That of Henry Farnie as a young man by courtesy of the Vantage Press, New York, that of the mature Henry Farnie by permission of the New York Public Library, and the picture of Alex Henderson by permission of the British Library. Other illustrations are from my own collection.

Keith Drummond Sharp, Forest Row, 2010

Chapter One

LEVER DE RIDEAU

It was a bitterly cold Sunday, 1 May 1836, with a piercing wind from the north and occasional showers of snow and hail, when the Provost of Burntisland, a small town on the Fife coast of the Firth of Forth, led his family to St Columba's parish church where the latest addition to their family was to be baptized. Henry Brougham (pronounced 'broom') Farnie had been born on 8 April 1836, the second son and fifth child of a family of ten.

He later claimed that he had been named after Lord Brougham; Henry Peter Brougham the eccentric Whig lawyer and politician who had been appointed Lord Chancellor and created Baron Brougham and Vaux in November 1830, to whom Henry Farnie said he was distantly related. This claim, though unproven, is not impossible; Lord Brougham's mother was Eleanor Syme, the daughter of Rev. James Syme minister of the Church of Scotland at Alloa, Clackmannanshire, while Henry Farnie's mother was Margaret Cairns, daughter of Rev. Adam Cairns minister of Longforgan, Perthshire. The families of ministers were almost a class apart, being at once well educated but not well off, and they did tend to intermarry, so the families may well have been connected.

Henry's father the Provost, roughly the equivalent of an English mayor, was James Farnie, a shipbuilder. It was his father, also named James, who had first moved into the town. James senior had been born in Largo, son of a wheelwright, and had learned the trade of ship carpenter. He started constructing ships on his own account at Methil, some twelve miles east of Burntisland, where he had been so successful that he needed to move to larger premises. In 1803 he purchased a large property and houses adjacent to the harbour at Burntisland and leased a portion of the harbour from the burgh council in order to construct a dry dock. The harbour had been claimed to be the best natural harbour from London to Orkney with deeper water

1

than at Leith, the port of Edinburgh on the south coast of the Forth, and with a safe passage to it in stormy weather. So James Farnie's facilities could hardly be better; apart from constructing new ships he was able to repair very large ships, the largest recorded being a Russian frigate of 1000 tons, also the steamship the 'United Kingdom'. It was the time of the Napoleonic wars and he obtained a contract to repair and maintain British naval vessels. In due course he was elected to the burgh council and served on various civic committees. He died in 1823 aged 53.

James junior, his eldest son, Henry's father, was not quite 24 years old when he inherited the business. For some years the shipyard continued to prosper. Like his father, James became a member of the burgh council, and in 1834 he achieved what his father had not when he was elected provost to serve for a period of three years. But the business started to decline. There is no reason to suppose that this was any fault of James; the war had ended, a herring boom in the Firth of Forth, which had started in the 1790s and provided a lot of work building and repairing fishing vessels, came to an end during the 1830s, and construction of sailing ships was beginning to suffer competition from the steam driven vessels being built on the Clyde and at

James Farnie (1799-1846)
St Andrews University Library

2

Newcastle. A venture into whaling around the coast of Greenland did well for four years until the whales moved away. James was probably also suffering ill health, and in 1844 he gave up the business, leased his shipyard and dry dock to Robert Meldrum, another shipbuilder in the town, and he obtained a post as Superintendent of the Royal Infirmary in Edinburgh. He was required to live on the premises but he bought a house for his family in Duke Street. He lived only two more years and died in May 1846 aged 47. Henry was just ten years old, his elder brother who inherited the business was fourteen.

James left the family's affairs in a considerable muddle and it was fortunate that at the time of his death the Edinburgh, Perth and Dundee Railway Company was an eager purchaser of the Burntisland shipyard, which was to become the northern terminal of the world's first railway ferry, across the Firth of Forth between Granton near Edinburgh and Burntisland, but they were slow to pay and meanwhile there were creditors knocking on the door. Margaret, his widow, was obliged to sell 19 Duke Street and for the next three or four years moved into a succession of rented houses in Edinburgh. There were family nearby as several of James's siblings had previously settled in Edinburgh, and the boys were able to remain at their studies at the Edinburgh Institution. They did well there, the elder son, also named James, winning prizes at arithmetic, algebra and geometry, and Henry winning prizes in English and arithmetic. Then Margaret Farnie moved with her family to St Andrews and the census of 1851 records them living in Bell Street. Henry, now aged fourteen, had finished school and in the autumn of the previous year had entered St Andrews University where he studied Latin and Greek. It was quite normal in those days for boys to enter university at the age of fourteen or fifteen and matriculate during the first year; Henry matriculated in February 1851 and continued to the end of the session. He returned to the University the following year to study mathematics and logic, finishing in the summer of 1853, and on

12 March that year he was elected an honorary member of the University Literary Society.

He also studied music, probably with Edward Salter a music teacher and organist of the Episcopal chapel in St Andrews. Dr R. Maidstone Smith, who practised in St Andrews, wrote the words of a song, *Yon Trembling Arch*; Henry Farnie composed the tune and it was "arranged with symphonies and accompaniment" by Edward Salter, and dedicated to a prominent local, Lady Anstruther of Balcaskie, near St Monans. This would have been before 1857 when Dr Smith left the town for health reasons.

It is not known what the elder brother James was doing when the family moved to St Andrews, he was not with them at the time of the 1851 census, but in February 1854 he signed a deed with the help of trustees making a financial arrangement to sell other assets, pay off debts, pay his mother what was her due under her marriage contract, and make provision for his brothers and sisters. One clause made provision to "pay debts of brother Henry Brougham Farnie; Peter Scott draper Edinburgh about £14·1s 3d, Whitehead and Burns Bookseller Cupar about 14s, David Pattison Tailor Cupar about £1·11s 3d, Thomas Brown Boot and Shoemaker Cupar about 13s, Archibald Dowie Bootmaker Cupar about 15s, Mr Henderson Coldstream about £20, Peter Steele merchant St Andrews about £3·1s 5d, Total about £40·16s 11d." James's own similar debts amounted to £71. The deed also provided for the trustees to pay £50 to Henry for outfit and passage to Australia "whither he intends to proceed immediately", pay £150 to his sister Margaret for outfit and passage to Australia "whither she intends to proceed in the course of the ensuing summer", and to remit certain sums to me in Canada "whither I intend to proceed immediately".

James did go to Canada but returned within four years, and later joined the Royal Artillery and went to India. Henry did not go to Australia, nor did Margaret.

— — — — —

A young Henry Farnie
St Andrews University Library

There is little information on Henry Farnie's activities during the next two or three years but it seems likely that he went to London and joined the staff of King's College, probably as a junior lecturer.[1] Two things can be said with certainty, that he did a lot of writing, and that he was a keen and proficient golfer who often played on the links at St Andrews. He was reported to be present on the green at the opening of the spring tournament of the Royal and Ancient Golf Club on several years between 1859 and 1863 but contrary to a press report was never a member. The first book he wrote was 'A Golfer's Manual' by 'A Keen Hand', a pseudonym, published by Whitehead & Orr publishers of the Fife Herald, in July 1857 when he was twenty-one. He had shown his manuscript to the R & A committee before publication; it had met with their approval and the book was dedicated to them. It sold for 2s 6d with a de luxe edition bound in morocco at 7s 6d. It is highly regarded in the golfing world being acknowledged as the first ever book devoted to the technique of golf as well as being a manual of instruction.[2]

The next few years of Farnie's life were devoted to journalism though at first he seems to have worked as a freelance, rather than being a permanent member of staff on a newspaper. This would have enabled him to continue whatever he was doing at King's College, London. He worked as a feature writer for the Fife Herald but there is no record of his actually being employed by them.

The year after the publication of 'A Golfer's Manual' he achieved a journalistic coup when he discovered the existence of the journals of "Pet Marjorie". Marjory Fleming was born on 3 January 1803 in Kirkcaldy, Fife. When she was five years old she went to live in Edinburgh with her uncle and aunt, William and Marianne Keith, where her care and education were made the responsibility of their youngest daughter Isabella, Marjory's beloved cousin Isa, who was then aged about twenty. Marjory was a prodigy, a child who loved reading, was very articulate and with a lively imagination, but her spelling was that of a child of five and, in order to help her, Isa suggested that she kept a journal. Three years later Marjory succumbed to an epidemic of measles followed by meningitis and she died on 19 December 1811, a few weeks short of her ninth birthday. Her journals in three exercise books together with some loose papers, now in the National Library of Scotland, cover her comments on people who visited the house, visits to the country, comments in fact on all aspects of her daily life, together with poems and letters. Henry Farnie obtained access to these journals and published extracts from them together with his own introduction and linking passages, first serialized in the Fife Herald in October and November 1857, and the following year published, by W. P. Nimmo of Edinburgh, as a small book entitled 'Pet Marjorie : a story of child life fifty years ago'.

The publication of 'Pet Marjorie' had a curious sequel. In 1863 a Dr John Brown, best remembered as the author of a children's book 'Rab and his Friends', wrote his own version of 'Pet Marjorie' which was published in the North British Review, and then as a book. He used the whole of Farnie's title and lengthy subtitle including the name 'Pet Marjorie', which had never been used by the family who called her Maidie, and the idiosyncratic spelling of Marjorie. Brown gave as his reason for writing his version that Farnie's book had circulated only in Fife but that the story deserved a wider readership. Farnie was incensed by this use of what he regarded as his own discovery and perquisite, the more so because of the identity of title which might lead people to suppose that Brown and not he was the first to tell Marjory's story, and he immediately published a second edition of his book which incorporated almost all of Brown's additions. When Brown's book ran to a second edition he protested in his introduction about this blatant plagiarism, "this somewhat free use", but took no further action. In 1881 with reference to the death of Marjory's sister Elizabeth, The Scotsman made mention of Dr John Brown's memoir of 'Pet Marjorie' which drew a swift response from Farnie to say that he, not John Brown, had been the author. This in turn brought a reaction from a friend of Dr Brown detailing the sequence of publications, and there, for the time being, the matter rested. But in 1890, after both Dr Brown and Henry Farnie were dead, the dispute surfaced again. An article appeared in The Queen magazine briefly telling the story of Marjory and using material from both Farnie's and Brown's books, but without acknowledging either. This prompted a letter to The Scotsman from an acquaintance of Dr Brown protesting that no credit had been given to him. The dispute started again, the protagonists being an uncle of Dr Brown and Farnie's sister. It could never reach an agreed solution and became quite heated until the editor put a stop to the correspondence.

In 1904 a full edition of Marjory's journals with some account of her life was produced by Lachlan Macbean, and in 1934 a facsimile edition was produced by Arundell Esdaile.

With the very weak copyright laws at that time, 'borrowing' from another author seems not to have been uncommon. Farnie made no protest when Robert Foreman, golf club maker of St Andrews, produced a 'Golfer's Handbook' first published in 1881. Much of it is original and very readable, but the sections dealing with the technique of play are lifted straight from Farnie's 'Golfer's Manual' and the diagrams are exact copies.

In the next year, 1859, Henry Farnie produced two books, both published by John Cunningham Orr in Cupar : 'The Handy Book of St Andrews', and 'The City of St Rule'. The latter priced at one guinea, contained six "exquisitely beautiful" calotypes by Thomas Rodger, one of the pioneers of photography in Scotland, and was intended as a sampler for a book to be called 'The Kingdom of Fife Calotyped' to be published by Orr and Rodgers. The title, 'City of St Rule', refers to the tradition that a religious figure named as St Rule or St Regulus brought relics of the apostle Andrew to a site in the city; the still-standing tower of the ruined cathedral is called St Rule's tower. The production of the larger work, 'The Kingdom of Fife Calotyped', was delayed due to the expense of calotypes, and was partly accomplished using lithography, eight of the twenty parts into which it was divided being published in 1861 after which the project was abandoned.

The text was unattributed but had most probably been prepared by Farnie.

Henry Farnie was already becoming well known and The Scotsman of 28 July 1859, reporting on the opening of the St Andrew's "Grand [annual] Golf Tournament" the previous day, names prominent people among the many spectators at the starting point, and these include "Mr [Henry] Farnie". The following day, reporting the results of two days of play, it stated that "In addition to the First-Class Plate, Mr Roger, calotypist, St Andrews, has presented, as a second prize, a copy of an artwork by him, entitled 'The City of St Rule,' written by Mr H. Farnie, King's College, London."

In May 1860 he produced 'The Handy Book of the Fife Coast from Queensferry to Fife Ness', again published by J. C. Orr of Cupar but also by Nimmo in Edinburgh, and this earned national recognition. The Athenæum, a literary weekly, described it as "an amusing, instructive 'Handy Book', full of all details of interest, and so rich in social history and anecdote as to deserve a permanent place on the bookshelf as well as a position in the travelling bag." At the same time John Orr was widely advertising Farnie's forthcoming 'Handy Book of the Tay', but no copy can be traced and it is

possible that it was never published, perhaps a casualty of Orr's ever increasing financial difficulties.

Another book by Farnie known to have been published at about this time, but of which no copy has been found, was called 'Camping-Out'.[3]

His link with King's College is again recorded when on 1 December 1860 The Scotsman reported that the third of the course of lectures at the Burntisland Young Mens' Institute was delivered by Mr Henry Farnie, King's College, London, the subject being Queen Margaret and Lady Ann Barnard. "He very cleverly sketched the chief incidents in the lives of these Fife worthies – the one the Queen of Malcolm III, surnamed Canmore, having many associations with the west of Fife, Dunfermline, &c., and giving names to St Margaret's Hope and the Queensferries. Mr Farnie stated that Miss Agnes Strickland[4] was presently engaged in collecting materials for a life of this Queen, intending it as a supplemental volume to the series of which she is the author. The other lady is well known as the author of the famous ballad "Auld Robin Gray," and as being one of the Balcarres family, in the east of Fife."

In November 1861 he was elected a Fellow of the Society of Antiquaries of Scotland although he allowed his membership to lapse when he later left Fife.

Who knows what made him leave his association with King's College and publication of books in Fife, which had evidently made him quite comfortably off for a young man aged just 24 ? But early the next year, 1861, he purchased the Strathearn Herald and moved to Crieff. He informed his readers that the paper was now to be printed entirely in Crieff, and that plant for doing so had been secured – it had previously been printed in Cupar. He soon established himself in the town, in March being elected President of the Crieff Cricket Club.[5] But he did not stay there long. In August he was appointed sub-editor of the Edinburgh Courant under James Hannay, probably through the good offices of Joseph Young of Dunearn, Burntisland, owner of the Grange Distillery, who was one of the proprietors of the Courant. Young would have known Henry's father and the Farnie family well from their Burntisland days. So Henry moved to Edinburgh and sold the Strathearn Herald to Messrs Cowan & Son, paper-makers and stationers.

During his brief time in Crieff, Henry Farnie had met Elizabeth Bebb Davies who was at a girls' boarding school, St Margaret's College. The Fife Herald later described her as "a young heiress" but nothing more is known of her than that she was the daughter of Hugh William Davies, gentleman. It was a lightning summer romance and, soon after moving to Edinburgh, Henry took a few days off, followed Elizabeth to her home near Aberystwyth, and married her at the church of Llanychaiarn on 24 August 1861. He was then 25, she was two days short of her 17th birthday.

In April 1862 Joseph Young purchased the Fifeshire Journal and appointed Henry Farnie its editor. He moved with his young wife to Cupar towards the end of the month or early in May. In November he renamed the Fifeshire News, the Saturday edition of the Journal, the St Andrews Gazette, and in a letter to the University Literary Society of which he was still an honorary member, said that this paper was designed, inter alia, to be an organ of the University, and invited them to contribute to its pages whatever might be of interest to the colleges.

But he was not a good editor of a local newspaper. The Fife Herald remarked years later that "He was not quite a success as a local journalist. He had no taste for politics and devoted a good deal of his writing to poetical squibs and remarks of a personal character, which proved not at all pleasing to the people of Cupar."

What is more, his marriage was not a happy one. He was a big man, lusty in all senses, and in January 1862 while living in Edinburgh, his young wife three-months pregnant, he did (in words later used in divorce proceedings) "give himself up at different times and places to adulterous practices, fellowship and

11

correspondence with other women ... and had frequent and repeated carnal and adulterous conversation, intercourse and dealings with such women".

Farnie's wife Elizabeth gave birth to a baby daughter on 13 July 1862 whom they named Maud Magdalene Farnie, but neither this event nor their move to Cupar ended his philandering. He continued visiting Edinburgh where one of his "women" was Margaret Whittet, a milliner's assistant, daughter of James Whittet a carver and gilder. They had first met at the North Bridge on New Year's eve, 31 December 1861. He told her his name was Mr Watson, and during the following year committed adultery on several occasions at an address in Calton Hill and at the nearby Abbotsford Temperance Hotel. As a result a baby boy was born on 10 April 1863 but who died on 22 June following.

Margaret insisted upon a meeting with Farnie who went to Edinburgh on 13 May where he met her and a Mr Dawson, stationer, a friend who she had asked to accompany her. Farnie acknowledged that he was the father and agreed a payment of £10 for "lying-in charges and expenses" while the girl was pregnant. Several weeks later her father, James Whittet, together with Mr Dawson visited Cupar to ask what further terms Farnie proposed for maintenance of his mistress and baby boy. But things were getting too uncomfortable in the small county town where, the Herald later reported, his "matrimonial troubles" were a constant subject of public talk. Some time after the end of June, before any further agreement could be concluded, he fled Fife for London, abandoning his young wife Elizabeth and baby Maud in Cupar.

Elizabeth was granted a divorce in the Court of Session in December 1863. [6] In 1871 she was living at 39 London Street, Edinburgh where daughter Maud died on 24 February aged eight; but she was not at that address a month later when the census was taken. She was later reported to have remarried but nothing further is known of her.

Chapter Two

A TALE OF THREE CITIES

LONDON

Arriving in London, Henry Farnie soon found employment; he was appointed the editor of a new paper to be published by J. B. Cramer & Co., the music publishers, to be called The Orchestra, a weekly review of music and the drama. The first issue came out on 3 October 1863 and in it he published a poem of his own called *The Stirrup Cup*. At this period, before gramophone or wireless, when people had to make their own entertainment, there was an insatiable demand for new songs, for use both in the drawing room and the music halls. Cramer's lost no time in getting *The Stirrup Cup* set to music by Luigi Arditi and it was an immediate success. For this very successful song he was paid a guinea. Some time later he wrote a song to a popular French air (probably his '*Pretty Colette*) [1] and offered it to Messrs Metzler for three guineas; they refused but offered him a royalty of threepence a copy. He was not well pleased being altogether unfamiliar with the system of royalties, but in three years the royalties earned him £800 and then he sold the copyright of the words for another £600.

The success of *The Stirrup Cup* made him realize that he had the ability to write for the theatre, although he did not at once abandon journalism. But while editing The Orchestra, he set about writing more songs; his output during the following year was prodigious and it included one entitled, *Pet Marjorie*.

His connections with Cramer's brought him introductions to the most celebrated composers of the period and he was soon invited to write the libretto for a one-act operetta to be composed by Sir Julius Benedict entitled *The Bride of Song*, it received its first performance without formality when Signor Alberto Randegger formed a small company to present a new operetta of

13

his own, *The Rival Beauties*, along with *The Bride of Song* at Leeds on 2 May 1864. Three weeks later, on 23 May, it received a concert performance at "Madame Louisa Vining's Matinee" at the Hanover Square Rooms, conducted by the composer, and a week after that, on 29 May, at Mdlle Louisa Van Noorden's annual "Appeal" concert at the same venue. It was another six months before it received a fully staged performance on 3 December that year at Covent Garden. With an added chorus of soldiers, it proved to be very popular as a curtain raiser in a programme with J. L. Hutton's new opera *Rose, or Love's Ransom*. Without the chorus it was ideal for concerts, and as it was within the capabilities of amateurs and could be scaled down for drawing room performance it was thereafter in constant use.

Farnie's next piece soon followed; another one-act operetta called *The Sleeping Queen*, with music by Michael Balfe, one of the trio of renowned British composers of the period along with Benedict and Wallace. *The Sleeping Queen* was produced at the Gallery of Illustration on 31 August. The 'Royal Gallery of Illustration' was an intimate, 500-seat theatre, in the house that was the former home of John Nash the designer. It was home to the 'entertainments' provided by Thomas German-Reed and his wife Priscilla who aimed at a 'respectable' middle to upper-class audience, and avoided using words like play, extravaganza, and burlesque. It rapidly became one of the most popular and fashionable places of entertainment in London. The German-Reeds particularly favoured small scale opera which they called *opera di camera* and in this guise *The Sleeping Queen* was well received.

Farnie and Balfe set about expanding the libretto and adding five new musical numbers to turn it into a two-act piece. The papers reported that this work had been completed just before Balfe set off for a holiday in Biarritz in September 1866. It remained in frequent use throughout the provinces and lesser London venues and was revived in the West End in July 1882 at the Avenue Theatre.

The year 1864 finished with another one-act operetta, *Punchinello*, with music by William Charles Levy, which was the prelude to the Christmas show, *The Lion and the Unicorn*, at Her Majesty's Theatre opening on 28 December. But he had also found time to write a story 'Child of the Sun' which was serialized in The Musical Monthly and Drawing Room Miscellany.

With his previous record it is hard to imagine Farnie spending eighteen months in celibacy, but there is no record of any illicit associations. The following May he married again. Emma Alethea Harvey was the daughter of William Harvey, a woollen draper, and Alethea née Goodwyn, and she and Henry Farnie were married on 31 May 1865 in All Souls' Church, Langham Place, St Marylebone. He was now 29 years old, and she 20. The marriage certificate described him as a widower, and he may have said so in order to have a church wedding which would have been refused to a divorcee, but he declared later that it was a clerical error and not intended to mislead.

During 1865, while remaining editor of The Orchestra, he continued with his outpouring of songs, but his major work for the theatre was an adaptation of Gounod's opera *La Reine de Saba* (The Queen of Sheba). The commission came from J. B. Cramer & Co.; it would have been a strange choice for Farnie himself as *La Reine de Saba* had been a failure in Paris, where it was produced in February 1862, was rubbished by the critics, and had run for just fifteen performances. But following the production of his opera *Faust* in 1859, Gounod was becoming very popular in England.

All works for stage performance at this period were censored by the Lord Chamberlain and had to receive his licence before performance; amongst other strictures, he did not allow any stage representation of Biblical characters. So *La Reine de Saba* in its original form, whether sung in French or English, would have been banned. It needed to be secularized. Farnie set the scene in Istanbul; Solomon became the Turkish sultan Suliman, visited by the Greek princess Irene; but apart from the changes of place and personal names the translation was faithful to the original and The Stage later declared that "Mr Farnie has cleverly overcome all difficulties, and he cannot be too highly praised for the way in which he has worked the story so as to suit the British mind." Titled *Irene*, it received a concert performance in a slightly shortened version at the Crystal Palace, Sydenham on 12 August 1865, was repeated a week later, and again the following February. But it had to wait another fifteen years before getting a fully staged performance on 10 March 1880 at the Theatre Royal, Manchester. Quicker though than in Paris, where it was not performed again until 1900.

At about the same time as he had been introduced to Balfe and Benedict, Farnie was also introduced to the third of the trio of renowned British composers of the period, William Vincent Wallace. He began collaborating with Wallace during the winter of 1864-65 on an opera with a Spanish setting, to be called *Estrelle* (or *Estrellita*). But Wallace's health, uncertain for some years, began to fail and he returned to France early in 1865, where Farnie continued to visit him at Passy. But in mid-July he had become so ill that his doctors advised him to go to the Pyrenees for the mountain air, and he died there on 12 October. His body was returned to England and he was buried with great ceremony at Kensal Green cemetery on 23 October; Farnie was among the mourners.[2]

And there was no pause in Farnie's work with Gounod. A new carol entitled *Bethlehem*, still in use today, an anthem *By Babylon's Wave* (*Super Flumina* – "*Près du fleuve étranger*") a paraphrase of Psalm 137, and *Tobias* (*Le petit oratorie : Tobie*) were presented at a concert conducted by Sir Julius Benedict at St James's Halls on 13 February. He also set into English another large work with music by Gounod, *Ulysses*, a Drama in Four Acts from the French of François Ponsard which had first been produced at the Comédie-Française, Paris in 1852. Farnie's adaptation received a concert performance on 8 June at St

James's Halls by Miss Helen Faucit, a famous tragedienne of the period, and an ad hoc choir.

After all this music and writing of lyrics, he decided to try his hand at straight drama. Dickens's last completed novel, 'Our Mutual Friend', had been serialized between May 1864 and October 1865 but, unlike his early works, there had been no rush of stage versions. Farnie's version called *The Golden Dustman* was produced on 16 June 1866 at Sadlers Wells, and again at Astley's on 27 October following. At the same time as its first production there appeared in New York a version by George Rowe called *Found Drowned*, which made its way to London in 1870. The Penguin Companion to Dickens considers that of the eight stage versions by then circulating, Farnie's was the most successful; especially after several long speeches had been cut to reduce its four-and-a-half hours playing time.

Farnie also worked on a dramatic version or burlesque of Tennyson's poem 'The Princess' which was registered at Stationers Hall, the procedure then used to establish copyright, on 10 August 1866, but there is no record of it ever being published or performed. This was little more than three years before W. S. Gilbert's burlesque of the same name and on the same subject, which later evolved into the libretto of the Gilbert and Sullivan operetta *Princess Ida*. It would be interesting to know if there was any correspondence between them. The two men were exact contemporaries and at about the same stage in their professional development, and this would not be the only time there appears to have been shades of Farnie in Gilbert's work.

PARIS

At some point he moved from The Orchestra and succeeded Henry Hersée as editor of The Paris Times, most likely during the early part of 1866. The Paris Times was a London paper aimed at expatriates and travellers in France and beyond. The subject matter covered news from Great Britain and the world, and information on rail travel and places of interest to the visitor, while the advertisements were mainly for accommodation in and en route to France. It had no particular interest in the theatre except as one item among the tourist attractions. In one respect it seems to have been a step backwards in his career, but some time later in an interview Farnie said that when he first went to London all the musical pieces were burlesques, "there was no idea of music in them; the orchestras were small and of the most primitive description; and the chorus consisted of a handful of extra girls". He was much taken with French burlesque and opera-bouffe, and editing The Paris Times no doubt gave him the opportunity to spend a lot of time in a city which would become his home.

He was a friend of Adah Isaacs Menken,[3] and while in Paris he arranged to study under Alexandre Dumas père. He very likely knew their circle of literary friends.

Emma Alethea, Farnie's wife, recorded that they had lived at various addresses in London – Wimpole Street, Cavendish Square, Notting Hill, St John's Wood, and Maida Vale. She says little about France but they certainly spent a lot of time there; two daughters who would have been born in 1866 and 1867 both died as infants in Paris.

Though Paris would be his home and source of inspiration, London remained the principal outlet for his work and there, with composer Luigi Bordèse, he published a "Drawing-room Operetta for Ladies" entitled *The Rose of Savoy*. But Farnie had only one play produced in 1867, *Reverses*, a domestic drama presented at the Strand Theatre on 13 July by the famous Swanborough family of actor-managers, who had engaged a well-known comic actor, Samuel Emery, to play a leading role. It was very well received and after all the encores and applause for the actors there were cries of 'author' and, for the first time, Farnie had the experience of walking onto the stage in response. The play was scheduled to close on 17 August when the Swanborough company was to go on tour, but was extended for one night for a 'benefit' for Mr Emery. The practice of having 'benefit' performances was still very much in vogue, when a portion of the proceeds was part of the remuneration of the actor.

Farnie started his own theatrical paper during the year called 'Sock and Buskin'. The first issue appeared on Saturday 8 July 1867, but it was short-lived. The British Museum possessed four issues – it may be that is all there were – but they were casualties of the incendiary bombs which hit the Museum in May 1942 during the second World War, and no other copies are known.

ROMEO E GIULIETTA;

An Opera, in Five Acts,

THE MUSIC BY

G O U N O D.

THE ENGLISH LIBRETTO BY

HENRY BROUGHAM FARNIE.

AS REPRESENTED AT THE

ROYAL ITALIAN OPERA,

COVENT GARDEN.

PRINTED AND PUBLISHED FOR

The Royal Italian Opera, Covent Garden,

By J. MILES & Co. 122, WARDOUR ST. OXFORD ST.—W

TO BE HAD AT THE THEATRE;

ALSO OF

ALL THE PRINCIPAL BOOKSELLERS & MUSICSELLERS.

ONE SHILLING AND SIXPENCE.

Farnie was also commissioned by the Royal Opera House, Covent Garden to do a translation of Gounod's *Romeo and Juliet.* This was to be presented by the Royal Italian Opera Company and sung in Italian, and the opera house wanted to have a booklet with the original French libretto side-by-side with an English translation to sell in the theatre for the convenience of patrons. Farnie's English text lived on beyond this humble origin, although never used on stage during his lifetime. The Carl Rosa Opera company used it when they produced the opera in 1890 in Liverpool at the start of a tour, and then at Drury Lane, and it was used at Covent Garden from 1905, and in a BBC broadcast in April 1927.

The next year, 1868, was a turning point. Farnie and his wife separated, but Emma's later accounts of what happened are not consistent. She accused him of adultery, but she also said that her mother had discovered that he was not a widower but had been divorced in Edinburgh, and that his first wife was still living. Whatever moral view Emma or her parents may have had on divorce, this seems insufficient reason to abandon a three-year-old marriage if it was otherwise a happy one. In view of his loose behaviour when in Edinburgh and married to Elizabeth, it seems much more likely that he was up to his old tricks and playing about with other women, and that this was the immediate cause of the separation.

Emma went back to live with her parents, but Henry Farnie remained in France continuing his studies and song-writing, of which two groups deserve mention. Europe was in turmoil and although the Franco-Prussian War had not yet begun there were rumblings, and the national and war songs of France and Germany were becoming popular in England. Farnie published a volume which The Sunday Times described as "eight of the most popular songs of the war, the words being given both in the original and in the spirited translation of Mr H. B. Farnie ... the interest of which will outlive the war itself." The other group was a collection of songs, collectively called 'Songs of the Rhineland', adapted from the German and with music by Alberto Randegger. The first five songs were done by Farnie in collaboration with Louis H. F. du Terreaux, who continued the series alone. But while Farnie and du Terreaux were working together, they adapted an Offenbach operetta, *La Chanson de Fortunio* as *The Magic Melody*. This was intended for the St James's Theatre but wasn't used. It was published in 1872 by Metzler as part of their Opera Bouffe series, and was reissued two years later by Cramer as part of their 'Opera Bouffe Cabinet' for which Farnie was the general editor. There is no record of professional performance until 1890 when it was produced at the Brighton Aquarium.

He had learned a very great deal in Paris, of French opera-bouffe and the ways of the French theatre, and had made some very good friends. He wanted to try his hand at light musical works. Burlesque was very popular in America, and many British actors crossed the water for a season, some to remain permanently. Estranged from his wife, Farnie was now a free agent. He decided to try his luck in New York.

NEW YORK

Henry Farnie arrived in New York from Paris on 28 September 1868 and at once advertised himself in The Clipper, New York's weekly entertainment paper, as a writer for the stage:

> ### HENRY B. FARNIE
> Dramatist and Librettist. Collaborateur of Vincent Wallace, Balfe, Gounod, Benedict, Alexander Dumas, Victorien Sardou, Offenbach, Arditi, etc., etc. All communications from managers, artists, or composers to be directed, care Pond & Co., 547 Broadway, New York. Several New Dramas and Comedies written in conjunction with Dumas, Sardou and others, and not yet produced on any stage [4]

It was not long before he had a piece on Broadway; *The Pages' Revel* opened at Tammany, Grand Theatre on 4 January 1869 for fourteen performances "initially", meaning that it was retained in the repertoire.

The demand for songs for the drawing room and for various forms of variety entertainment was no less in America than in Britain and so he did not wait for work to come to him; he arranged with W. A. Pond & Co., the New York music publishers, to produce a series of sheet music under the general title Spirit of Burlesque, with him as series editor. The series ran to at least twenty-four songs including several of his own.

There were two other arrivals in New York at about the same time as Farnie's. In the first group were Horace Lingard, a versatile actor who had made a reputation in the music halls, and his [bigamous] wife Alice Dunning, a dancer turned actress, accompanied by Dickie Lingard, the stage name of Alice

Dunning's sister, Mrs Harriet Dalziel. Lingard had been in New York before, had become extremely popular, and was assured of a warm welcome back. They had brought with them the costumes for Henry J. Byron's burlesque *Orpheus and Eurydice*, but they wanted it given an American flavour. They would not have known Farnie but cannot have missed his Clipper advertisement, and they turned to him. With Farnie's adaptations, entirely new music by David Braham, and under the new title *Pluto, or, The Young Lady who Charmed the Rocks*, they opened at the Theatre Comique on 1 February 1869. The Lingards had taken over the management of the theatre, where *Pluto* ran for 128 performances.

This was a very good run, although the length of a run was not an accurate guide to a show's success. Many New York managements had a stock company or hired a company for a season, with a repertoire of shows which were played in rotation; a run of two or three weeks was generally only the first production of a show which would be brought back as and when required. At the time, there was a very popular song in England, *Up in a Balloon*, written by G. W. Hunt. A ladies' version had been written for Nellie Power by her mother, and taken up by other female singers including Alice Dunning. So Farnie at once wrote some American words for Miss Dunning, "One night I went up in a balloon," became, "I am, as you know, a Madison belle". Alice did use it, and it went into the Spirit of Burlesque series.[5]

The second group to arrive was Lydia Thompson and a company of artists managed by Alex Henderson, and Farnie's meeting with Henderson was the beginning of a partnership which would greatly influence their careers, and make both of them rich men.

As a young man Henderson had been guilty of some financial impropriety and had fled to Australia, and it was there that he first became involved in working in the theatre. On his return to England he leased the Clayton Hall in Liverpool, refurbished it, renamed it the Prince of Wales's Theatre, and opened on Boxing night 1861. He was a very good manager and soon earned respect, bringing to Liverpool some of the best shows and biggest names in the theatre. He soon expanded by taking on, in 1864, the very much larger Theatre Royal in Birkenhead.

Lydia Thompson had trained as a dancer. She first appeared while in her 'teens in a pantomime at the Haymarket Theatre and quickly came to public attention. Then, in 1856 she disappeared, and it was reported that she was dancing her way around the capitals of Europe, feted by students wherever she went. She returned to England in 1859, continued dancing in a variety of shows, and was enthusiastically welcomed back by audiences.

She first visited The Prince of Wales's, Liverpool in April 1863 and became a frequent visitor there. There seems to have been an immediate rapport between her and Henderson although there was no suggestion of romance. She would some years later become Mrs Henderson, but in 1863 she was newly married to John Tilbury, a horseman and riding teacher; while Henderson was a notorious womanizer – there were two women who had a reasonable claim to be Mrs Henderson,[6] and a succession of mistresses. A year later tragedy struck when John Tilbury was killed while riding in a steeplechase at Brentwood, Essex. Lydia was devastated and made no stage appearances for several months. When she did return to the stage it was for the opening of Henderson's Theatre Royal, Birkenhead, although she was at the time a member of the company of the Theatre Royal, Drury Lane. And taking what would be a profound change in her career, she appeared, not as a dancer, but in the leading role as a burlesque actress in F. C. Burnand's popular *Ixion*.

Over in New York, George Wood of the Broadway Theatre had begun building a new entertainment centre incorporating a theatre which was to be called Wood's Museum and Metropolitan Theatre. He had, for a couple of years, tried to book Lydia Thompson for a season and in 1868, Henderson and Lydia decided to go. Henderson sold most of his interests in Liverpool and Birkenhead, gathered together a core company comprising, together with Lydia, Pauline Markham, Lisa Weber, Ada Harland (who had played Lavvy Wilfer in Farnie's *The Golden*

Alexander Henderson
The Entr'acte, 3 Nov 1877, p.8

Dustman at Sadler's Wells), a comedian Harry Beckett, and musical director Michael Connelly who had been with Henderson in Liverpool. Other artists were to be engaged locally. In April, however, Lydia had joined the Strand company under Ada Swanborough for a new burlesque by William Brough entitled *The Field of the Cloth of Gold*, which had been expected to run to the end of the season. It turned out to be a surprising success; one of the greatest in the history of burlesque at the Strand and it ran for a full year; so Lydia had to negotiate her release half way through the run.

They opened at Wood's Museum under the local management of Samuel Colville on 28 September 1868 billed as "Lydia Thompson and her British Blondes", and their first show was *Ixion.* New Yorkers were not accustomed to the British style of burlesque with beautiful young ladies playing

Lydia Thompson

male roles and wearing tights, while those who played female roles wore skirts rather shorter than would be acceptable elsewhere, and New York was taken by storm. Though some elements of the press dubbed them a "girlie show" with beauty a substitute for talent, nothing could keep the public away and the theatre played to capacity night after night. Their contract with George Wood was for six weeks and Wood must have regretted having other contracts to prevent them staying longer. They moved on to Niblo's Garden, a much bigger theatre, and their six weeks stretched to forty-five before they left New York to go on tour.

Henderson realized that they would need more material than they had taken with them and he turned to Farnie. Their second show, while still at Wood's Museum, was *Ernani, or, The Horn of a Dilemma*, a burlesque by William Brough, which opened on 28 December. New music was arranged and composed by Michael Connelly and Farnie contributed one number, *The Brigand Chief,* which also went into the Spirit of Burlesque series.

Ixion and *Ernani* carried them through their engagement at Wood's Museum and they opened at Niblo's Garden on 1 February 1869 with the first show Farnie was to do for them, *The Forty Thieves, or, Striking Oil in Family Jars.* It unfortunately coincided with a reaction in the New York press against the success of the British troupe. They began praising any mediocre local talent while denigrating the Thompson troupe as "legs making up for what the head should furnish". Farnie's show was also said to be highly derivative although on what grounds it is hard to say. Ada Harland had appeared in a 'Forty Thieves' three years before at Covent Garden but Ada Harland left the troupe after the engagement at Wood's Museum and set off on her own. The alternative title suggested a play from years before which had been parodied while Farnie was still an infant.[7] Forty Thieves was his first full-length effort in a new genre, and whatever literary merits the show may have had or lacked, Farnie did write specifically for the peculiar talents of Lydia and her leading players, and did it very successfully. The show ran for 136 performances, closing on 28 May, and was followed the day after by Farnie's second show for the troupe, *Sindbad the Sailor, or, The Ungenial Geni and the Little Cabin Boy.*

When *Sindbad* opened, the anti-Blondes campaign had reached the height of vindictiveness with suggestions that they could not have achieved their popularity by their performance on-stage alone, and with a paper called The Spirit of the Times in particular making libellous accusations of immorality. Lydia Thompson felt it necessary to make a direct appeal to the public, by means of newspaper advertisements, for fair play. But the public seemed to take no notice of the press, and through the heat of June *Sindbad* played on to good houses, finally closing on 31 July after 64 performances. After which the Blondes took a short break and Farnie returned to Europe.

* * *

Chapter Three
BACK IN ENGLAND

It is not known whether Farnie took lodgings in London or Paris after his return from America. In due course he would regard Paris as his home; he liked the city, it was the source of much of the material he worked with, and a place where he spent much time and could write away from the pressures of being in London. But his shows were for the London market and he would frequently have to be in England. It is not always known when he was in one place or the other. In spite of the ferry crossing, middle class travellers and business people thought little of travelling between the two cities and the French railways allowed artists and actors a free upgrade; holders of a third class ticket could travel second class, and of a second class ticket could go first class. But he is next found in London working at the Lyceum theatre.

M. Hervé (Florimond Ronger) enjoyed a reputation in France, for opera bouffe, barely second to that of Offenbach, and what is more he acted and sang, in fact turned his hand to anything required to mount a show. The Mansell brothers were the new lessees of the Lyceum Theatre, which had been going through a bad patch, and after having it completely redecorated and fitted with a new act drop, they had arranged to have two of Hervé's recent Parisian successes to reopen the Lyceum early in 1870. The first was *Chilperic* for which Hervé had written his own libretto and in which he was to direct and play the lead as he had done in Paris, and that was to be followed by *Le Petit Faust*. The English adaptation of *Chilperic* was by Robert Reece, Frank A. Marshall and manager Richard Mansell. M. Marius (Claud Marius Duplany), who had played the role of the peasant Landry in Paris, accompanied Hervé to repeat the role at the Lyceum. *Chilperic* opened on 22 January and although Hervé's English was really rather poor (he had studied English in order to play this part in London), his acting, singing and personal charm made him a hit with his audiences and the production was a great success.

The English libretto for *Le Petit Faust* was to have been done by Dion Boucicault, an Irish actor-playwright who at 49 had already built a considerable reputation on both sides of the Atlantic, but due, it was said, to an accident he was unable to do it. It sounds a pretty poor excuse; Boucicault was having a very busy time, he had a drama *Formosa* open at Drury Lane in August 1869, another called *Lost at Sea* at the Adelphi in October, and was preparing *Paul La Farge* to open at the Princess's in March 1870 and, perhaps equally time-consuming, he had during the run of *Formosa* commenced an affair with its leading lady, Katherine Rogers. But whatever the true reason, the Mansell brothers turned instead to Farnie.

The story was based upon Goethe's drama although almost every character except Mephistopheles was the antithesis of Goethe's original, and Farnie stayed fairly true to the French librettists Hector Crémieux and Adolphe Jaime except that he transferred the action to England, the opening scene being in a fashionable ladies' school at Peckham where Marguerite is a pupil, and Dr Faust is an aged professor. Hervé's music also parodied Gounod's opera, most notably in the second act aria The King of Thule, rendered by Farnie as "There was ane Kynge in Tooley Street, whoe dranke moche bittere beere." It did, of course, contain a sprinkling of puns and topical jokes in the manner of contemporary burlesque. With the literal title *Little Faust*, it opened at the Lyceum on 18 April 1870, and as a curtain raiser added on 2 May, Farnie provided a one-acter called *Breaking the Spell* adapted from Offenbach's *Le Violoneau*.

Emily Soldene was engaged to play Marguerite. Miss Soldene had commenced her career on the concert platform singing ballads and arias and then, to gain stage experience, had doubled this with performing in music hall under the name Miss FitzHenry, her first engagement being with Charles Morton at The Oxford music hall, and as both she and Morton will feature large in this story it is worth introducing them now. Charles Morton was the originator of the purpose-built music hall [1] (he later became known as the Father of the Halls) when as 'mine host' at the Canterbury Tavern in Lambeth he started providing free entertainment, relying on the sale of food and drink to make his profit. He did not rely on amateurs, would-be comedians, and sing-alongs as was common elsewhere but engaged first class professionals and his tavern became extremely popular,

Charles Morton

particularly when he introduced ladies' nights, so much so that there was a severe shortage of accommodation. So alongside his tavern, on the site of a skittle alley, he built a large hall equipped with a platform and with tables and chairs in the auditorium – the Canterbury Music Hall, which opened in 1852. He later moved north of the river by acquiring the Boar and Castle Inn off Oxford Street and on its site built The Oxford music hall for which Soldene had been engaged. After a stint at The Oxford she abandoned the name Miss FitzHenry, and as Emily Soldene moved on to her first opera bouffe part in the *Grand Duchesse [of Geroldstein]* for a provincial tour and at Crystal Palace. There she was seen by the Mansells and engaged for *Little Faust* which would be her West End debut. In later life Emily wrote her memoirs as 'My Theatrical and Musical Recollections', one of the most entertaining and readable theatrical reminiscences ever, which caused quite a sensation when published due to her uninhibited anecdotes concerning fellow artistes and the many admiring, and often noble, beaux most of whom she named.

She records that Mr Farnie was constant in his attendance, being always found with the female chorus. "He had a very keen feeling for the beautiful ... and would call a rehearsal at any extraordinary hour ... and if the girls were very good-looking indeed, would stop with them at any length, or even give them lessons privately, one at a time." She tells that Dion Boucicault came to the theatre "pretty frequently" and adds, rather archly, that "Mr Farnie must have had a real regard for Mr Boucicault, and would not allow him to be worried by the woes of the chorus, for no sooner did the girls surround this charming author-actor than Farnie would clap his hands together and cry out, 'Now girls, to your places' ".

Emily Soldene

Whether Hervé had planned to play Faust as he had done in Paris is uncertain. Miss Soldene records that "After a long run of *Chilperic* M. Hervé got fatigued – finding the evening performance and the daily rehearsals for the production of Little Faust too much for him; so it was suggested that I should play Chilperic." For all the attractions of Emily's 'Recollections' she does like to enhance her own part in events and is prone to occasional and surprising lapses of memory. There is no evidence that she played the part of Chilperic during its run, although she did play it later; all the daily announcements in the 'small ads' list Hervé in the role.

So was he rehearsing *Little Faust*? And if so, why did he not play it? He can hardly have objected to Farnie's adaptation, for it would not be so long before they were working together again. As it happened, none of the principals in *Chilperic* stayed on for *Little Faust* except M. Marius and Mr E. J. Odell. Tom Maclagan, a well-known comedian with a broad Scots accent, took the part of Faust and there are no reports of him being a late substitute.

Also in the cast were several actors who would work with Farnie many more times – M. Marius who played Siebel, the part he had played in Paris, E. J. Odell who often played travesty parts was cast as Martha. And there were Aynsley Cook, Miss Lennox Grey, a very young actress named Jennie Lee who played a Street Arab (she would later achieve fame through her portrayal of the title role in *Jo*, the dramatized version of 'Bleak House'), Mdlle Marguerite Debreux brought over from France to play Mephisto, and then in the chorus a very attractive young lady with a lovely voice, Camille Dubois.

Little Faust was well received by press and public and ran until 2 July when the Mansell brothers' six-month lease ended and the Lyceum closed for the summer. During the last week at the Lyceum the first act of *Chilperic* was added to the programme, and this was when Emily had the chance to play Hervé's part. The Era noted that it now had considerably altered words, which can only have been done by Farnie, perhaps with an eye to future use. *Little Faust* then transferred to the Standard Theatre for a fortnight. And it soon found its way to New York where it opened at the Olympic Theatre on 22 August that same year.

Specifically written to send to the Lydia Thompson troupe in New York was a collaboration between Dumas and Farnie on a melodrama called *Mosquito*. When it was announced that there would be presented a play specially written by Dumas for Lydia

31

Thompson, the American press reacted with disbelief, but they had forgotten Farnie and his Clipper advertisement. Niblo's management responded by publishing Dumas's receipt for 10,000 francs made out to Farnie, who had presumably bought out Dumas's share in the play, to prove Dumas's part in it, while Farnie wrote to The Era, in answer to those who called it a translation, declaring that it was written "by Alexandre Dumas père and myself in the strictest collaboration. The incidents of the drama were fixed and arranged by consultation and the piece written out in English as it is now performed. It does not, and never did, exist in French at all." The Drama was full of incident and a showpiece for Lydia with the New York Mercury reporting that "whether as the imperious high-tempered Olivia, the vigilant Mosquito, the pretty barmaid, the Zingara, Miss Thompson is completely successful."

For London, at about the same time, he adapted Offenbach's *La Rose de Saint-Flour*, libretto by M. Carré, which had been first produced in Paris in June 1856. There had been an earlier English version by German-Reed called *Too Many Cooks* which played at the Gallery of Illustration in August 1863 but which was no longer heard. Farnie's version was called *The Rose of Auvergne, or, Spoiling the Broth*; it was produced at the Gaiety Theatre on 8 November 1869 and became a popular curtain-raiser with frequent revivals at the Alhambra, the Opera Comique, at Covent Garden, and throughout the provinces.

The theatre seasons in London at that time followed a pattern built around the social habits of the upper and upper-middle classes – the 'carriage trade'. Those people spent their summers in the country or at the seaside, and the winter in London. Theatres also specialized in a particular type of show and built up a regular clientele who were intensely partisan. The season started in September. Those theatres providing lighter types of entertainment would always have a pantomime or other Christmas special which opened for a short run on Boxing night. They would then go through the winter and early spring before providing an Easter novelty. In the summer they would go dark, or be let to managements to put on try-outs or inexpensive shows, and so keep ticking over until the following season. Meanwhile, the main companies would go on tour. Managements hoped to find shows which would go from September to Christmas, and from early in the New Year until Easter, hence a large number of shows which clocked up around one hundred performances. Very long runs were at this time unknown.

Although Farnie was becoming recognized with an increasing number of largely successful shows to his credit, he was trying to enter a field occupied for a decade by H. J. Byron and F. C. Burnand, and competing with Gilbert and Robert Reece who had started at about the same time as he had. The punishing amount of work which he undertook in the coming season (1870-71) suggests that he was still trying to find his niche – three burlesques, an extravaganza, and a pantomime, three operettas, a farce, and a Christmas entertainment which defies description. Extravaganzas and burlesques were the most popular forms of light entertainment. Extravaganzas had a very simple plot and a loose structure which allowed a variety of acts and styles to be introduced from circus, variety, pantomime and vaudeville. Under Madame Vestris at the Olympic Theatre they were designed more to please the eye than the ear or intellect and took elements from the French féerie, usually with a fairy story as the name implies and always lavishly dressed and costumed. Burlesques parodied something serious be it play, novel, classical myths and legends, or an historical event, so it was necessary for the audience to be familiar with the story. They were played in an exaggerated style and liberally sprinkled with puns that made the audience groan with pleasure. Both forms were decorated with songs, pretty girls and dances. Pantomimes contained most of the elements of extravaganza but generally retained the traditional Harlequinade. Theatres specialized in particular types of show and had faithful and partisan audiences. Burlesque flourished at the Strand under the Swanborough family and at the Gaiety under John Hollingshead who some years later declared his determination to "keep the sacred lamp of

Henry Farnie
Courtesy Vantage Press, New York

burlesque" burning. The phrase caught the imagination of press and public and a good many times when burlesque was declared to be dying "the sacred lamp" burned on.[2]

Farnie started with a burlesque for Mrs Swanborough at the Strand Theatre, where his *Reverses* had played three years before. It was entitled *The Idle 'Prentice, A Tyburnian Idyll of High, Low, Jack and his Little Game* and it opened on 10 September 1870. It was very loosely based on Ainsworth's novel Jack Sheppard, which in turn is based on the Newgate Calendar and its account of a real-life criminal famed for his audacious escapes from Newgate prison. Jack was played by Jennie Lee; Jonathan Wild, the detective, by Eleanor Bufton (Mrs Arthur Swanborough), Winifred, daughter of Jack's master played by Kate Santley, and Blueskin, a policeman, by the comedian Harry Paulton. Kate Santley, born in Virginia of German extraction, came to England with her parents after losing all they had during the American civil war. With a natural talent she started working in provincial theatres before switching to music hall where she made quite a name for herself. She moved back to theatre work and at the start of 1870 was engaged by the Swanboroughs for the Strand company. She would from time-to-time be closely associated with Farnie's shows. Harry Paulton began his professional career in his native Wolverhampton in 1861, and established himself in the cities of the Midlands and North of England. He was engaged for three seasons at the Theatre Royal, Glasgow where he became extremely popular, before joining the companies, first at the Theatre Royal, Birmingham and then at the Theatre Royal, Liverpool. *The Idle 'Prentice* was his first appearance in London, and he would later appear in many Farnie shows. Reviewing the burlesque, The Era thought some of the incidents confused and the show, which ran for two hours, far too long, and felt it could be much improved by some rearranging and cutting. It took the very unusual step a week later of

Kate Santley

publishing an entirely new review, commending the many improvements made and predicting a good run. A New York production rapidly followed at Miss Lena Edwin's Theatre. At the Strand it ran until it had to make room for the Christmas pantomime but was brought back again immediately after to serve as the Easter novelty. Ten years later, in May 1880, it was revived at the Surrey Theatre with the straightforward title *Little Jack Sheppard.*

Many years later the Era Almanack printed a story of this period in Farnie's life; that he was sipping his drink at the bar of the Somerset Hotel when he was handed a letter from Mark Lemon, founding editor of Punch. "They will pay for my five jokes on publication," he groaned, dropping the letter to the floor, "I wanted the money to take my Inverness out of pawn, and not for my tombstone".[3]

Come Christmas Farnie did a pantomime for Crystal Palace, an extravaganza for the Princess's and a burlesque for the Adelphi. The pantomime was *Gulliver, or, Harlequin Brobdingnag, The Fairy Enterprise, and the Demon Bow-wow.* The Crystal Palace always made a point of having splendid Christmas decorations and music, which was a very good start to a visit, and the pantomime was a colourful extra. The Era declared that "Mr Farnie has done his work with considerable credit to himself and with infinite amusement to the audience." In the cast was a young Arthur Williams who would in time become the leading comic actor in the Victorian musical theatre.

The extravaganza at The Princess's was *Little Gil Blas and How He Played the Spanish D(j)euce,* with music by Prince Poniatowski and Frank Musgrave. It was based on Lesage's novel 'The Adventures of Gil Blas of Santillane', and had in the title role Mrs Howard Paul, a very popular singer and actress who first came to notice in ballad operas like *The Beggars' Opera* and Dibdin's *The Waterman.* Born Isabelle Hill in 1833, she used the stage name Miss Featherstone until she married American entertainer Henry Howard Paul, after which she always used her married name. Miss Lennox Grey was back again, and it was felt by the critics to be entirely up to the standard of *Little Faust* and *The Idle 'Prentice.*

Another burlesque was a Christmas special at the Adelphi Theatre which opened on Boxing night and was called *The Mistletoe Bough, or Lord Lovel, Lady Nancy, and the Milk-white Steed* although some surviving scripts have another, perhaps provisional, title *The Mistletoe Bough : a merrie jest of an old oak chest.* Music was "selected, composed and arranged" by Frank Musgrave. It was a very cleverly conceived piece combining three legends about Lord Lovell and his family which are told in story or ballad, but he introduced characters from other popular songs or poems including Mary the Maid of the Inn, Simon the Cellarer, Philip the Falconer, and Young Lochinvar. The cast were mainly artistes from the Adelphi stock company but included from *Little Faust,* E. J. Odell in another travesty role as Dame Martha,

Mdlle Debreux as Philip the Falconer, and now risen from the chorus to play Mary the Maid of the Mill, Camille Dubois.

Farnie's two shows for Mrs John Wood, actor-manageress of the St James's Theatre, were not so happy. A burlesque called *Vesta* with music by Frank Musgrave opened on 9 February and was, as ever, full of incidents bright and amusing. But it was felt that it lacked a strong enough story to hold it all together and was carried by Mrs John Wood in the title role with the help of comic actor Lionel Brough as Lieut Spurius. Lionel Brough, now a member of St James's company, had for three years been a

Lionel 'Lal' Brough

member of Alex Henderson's company at the Prince of Wales's Theatre, Liverpool, and he would appear in many more Farnie shows in the future. The Era declared that "Judged as a literary production, the burlesque may not reach a very high standard; but, estimated by the applause and amusement of those who witnessed it, we must pronounce *Vesta* a very great success indeed." There was, to be sure, a clamour for encores, and the cast were recalled after every scene. At the end there were loud calls for the author, but Farnie though often brash, even overbearing, also had a shy and retiring streak, perhaps a feeling of insecurity, and declined to go before the curtain. Lionel Brough spoke for him instead.

Vesta came off after two months to be followed by a double bill commencing with Farnie's venture into farce. Entitled *Rival Romeos,* it was his first real disaster. The plot was somewhat

37

risque; it involved the efforts of rival lovers to get past an overprotective uncle in order to reach the object of their affections, which involved one being disguised as a baby in a cot, the other as a nurse, and it offended Victorian ideas of propriety. The reviews indicated that although there was much laughter, there was as much sibilation as applause; that it did nothing to enhance Mr Farnie's reputation and had best be soon forgotten.

In truth, his forte was in writing lyrics, and in writing to make the best of the skills of particular performers. A few years later he started directing and would show his skill in mounting a show – he always insisted on the best in costumes, scenery and effects, and he had an uncanny feeling for the public mood. His dialogue was his weakness and he started using "literary devils", ghost writers, penny-a-liners, call them what you will, although he exercised a firm editorial control over what was written.

He was on safe ground with operetta. A two-act comic opera *The Pet Dove* was a translation of Gounod's *La Colombes*, libretto by Jules Barber and Michel Carré, in turn taken from La Fontaine's story 'Le Falcon', and it was performed at the Crystal Palace on 20 September 1870. And a one-act operetta, Offenbach's *Les Deux Aveugles*, libretto Jules Moinaux, became in his hands *The Blind Beggars*. It opened at the Gaiety Theatre on 15 April 1871 and soon became another firm favourite as a curtain raiser, being revived at the Opera Comique the following year and the year after that, and at the Strand the next year. There were many rival English versions but Farnie's was the one that survived, being still in catalogues today.

Then came something very different for the Alhambra Music Hall. Theatres as well as the plays they put on had to be licensed by the Lord Chamberlain. Music halls, licensed by the local magistrates, were not allowed to present "stage plays", and there was a very conservative and protectionist London Association of Theatrical Managers who retained solicitors to pounce rapidly and heavily on any music hall manager who dared to try. They held that a stage play was anything that told a story whether by dialogue, song, dancing or mime. Most London music halls came within the jurisdiction of Middlesex magistrates who were hardly impartial, being much in sympathy with the theatre managers. The law was very confused being old, out-of-date, and devised before music halls had come into being, and as a result of several trials, some of which had gone to appeal, the legal definition of a stage play had become none too clear. A parliamentary committee was considering the matter, and had been for some time, but no-one held out much hope of any early clarification of the law.

The Alhambra, an imposing building in Moorish style with two towers and a dome dominating the east side of Leicester Square, was in a class of its own. It presented a variety bill, engaged the very best of acts, and it possessed an orchestra of more than a hundred players which always had a spot in each part of the programme when they played music from the classics and also, with singers engaged from the opera houses, arias and choruses from opera. Its manager was Frederick Strange who felt some sense of mission to bring the artistic best to the middle and lower classes. Strange had been summonsed and fined before for presenting "stage plays", and in the autumn of 1870 had his dancing licence withdrawn for presenting the cancan, performed very artistically by a group called "The Colonna Quadrille", who could bend lower and kick higher than most. The newspapers had been overwhelmingly supportive and sympathetic, asking why the cancan was unlawful in Leicester Square but lawful in King Street where the St James's Theatre was nightly presenting *Orphée aux enfers* complete with cancan.

The Alhambra was also famed for its ballets. Strange did not wish to challenge the law but, without a dancing licence and unable to mount a ballet, he wanted a Christmas spectacular, and he went to Farnie. Farnie, no doubt with advice from Strange's lawyers, devised a piece which he and Strange felt, based on previous cases, could not be classed as a stage play. Named *Superba*, it had minimal spoken dialogue and no recitative, the story being clear from the sequence of songs; the characters had no names and although they were in costume they did not change their costume during the piece; these things having been points of substance in earlier court hearings. Nevertheless Strange was brought before the magistrates, and although prosecuting counsel conceded that it was a spectacular piece containing the best transformation scene presented in London, they claimed that it was a stage play. The magistrates agreed, Strange was fined, and *Superba* was withdrawn on 14 January.

Strange had had enough of these arguments and after the rest of the programme, without *Superba*, had run its course, he closed the Alhambra and applied to the Lord Chamberlain for a theatre licence. He refurbished the interior, removed all the tables from the pit and replaced them with comfortable armchairs, and he resited all smoke rooms and rooms where food and drink were served to corners having no view of the stage. And despite a last ditch attempt by Middlesex Licensing Magistrates to block it, he received his theatre licence from the Lord Chamberlain, and on 24 April 1871 reopened as The Alhambra Palace Theatre of Varieties. He still presented his customary variety programmes to his faithful audience, and ballets once more, but he could now present sketches and operettas without fear of challenge. And his opening programme included another one-act operetta from Farnie, *The Crimson Scarf*, translated from *La Tartane*, with music by Isadore Edouard Legouix.

It had been a very busy season though a rewarding one, and Farnie would have been glad to return to his home in Paris.

* * *

Chapter Four

GENEVIEVE

Across the Pond the Lydia Thompson troupe managed by Alexander Henderson had enjoyed the most amazing and totally unexpected success. They had packed Broadway theatres night after night for a season which had expanded to forty-five weeks. Then they went on tour to all the major American cities. Lydia and Alex Henderson both had a flair for publicity and they were forever catching headlines; they packed houses wherever they went, and wherever they didn't go managers were clamouring for them to pay a visit. They had returned to New York for another season, gone back on the road, then back to Broadway for a third season. All the animosity of the press during their first stay in New York was gone and they were each time welcomed back as one of its own. They were too much in demand for there to be any question yet of their leaving America but they returned to England for a much needed short break. They also needed to recruit – the ladies of the company had all been very successful and Pauline Markham, Lisa Weber and Ada Harland had decided to go-it-alone. Also, they needed new material.

They still had comedian Harry Beckett and musical director Michael Connelly, and during their tours they had been joined by a comic actor named Willie Edouin, who had been born in London, gone to Australia for a spell, and then settled in America, and his American wife Alice Atherton. But the original "blondes" needed replacing. Farnie met Henderson and Lydia Thompson in London; Henderson was very good at casting – and so was Farnie, and it was no doubt on his suggestion that Henderson signed up Camille Dubois, daughter of the conductor Edward Reyloff, who had worked with Farnie in *Little Faust* and *The Mistletoe Bough* and then come to public attention in a production of Offenbach's *Les Brigands*. Henderson also managed to sign Carlotta Zerbini, a fine mezzo-soprano from a musical family, who had some good experience and a lot of promise.

Farnie had been told that they would need new material, and had ready for them his best burlesque to date – *Blue Beard*, based on Perrault's Fairy Tale. They had less than two months in England and it had been arranged that Farnie would go back to America with them. But first he had some other business to attend to.

By scouring the second-hand bookshops of Paris and asking his friends for their memories of old shows, Farnie collected the old vaudevilles and other pieces which were his raw material. But Offenbach's opera bouffe *Genevieve de Brabant*, first performed at the Théâtre des Bouffes Parisiens on 19 November 1859, had been revived in an expanded version at the Théâtre des Menus-Plaisirs on 26 December 1867 and he may well have seen it for himself. He was convinced that it would do well in London and, armed with a synopsis and pictures of the gendarmes and of Drogan the baker-boy hero, he went to see Charles Morton.

Three years before, Morton had the misfortune to see his Oxford music hall burn to the ground, all too common at a time when theatres contained much wooden construction and were lighted by gas, and this unfortunately happened at a time when he had let out his Canterbury hall. For a while he worked at Woolwich Gardens, and then he was asked by Charles Head, a successful bookmaker who had invested in a group of properties in Islington including a pub and the run-down Philharmonic music hall, to run the music hall for a few years. Morton decided that it would be better to construct a proper stage in place of the platform and to get it licensed as a theatre. He engaged Emily Soldene as principal artiste and director and they assembled a company which included Emily's sister, Clara Vesey, to present a series of potted comic operas including, of course, *Chilperic* and *The Grand Duchesse*. Following the usual custom, the season having ended, the Philharmonic had closed and the company gone on tour. And this was when Farnie called on Morton.

Morton was suspicious of Farnie; he had confided to associates that he regarded Farnie and failure as synonymous,[1] although Farnie's only real failure so far had been *Rival Romeos* that April, but he was impressed by Farnie's enthusiasm. Farnie also promised that if Morton took the show, he would cancel his trip to America and get to work on it at once. Morton agreed to take it, but upon the condition that Drogan was played, not by a tenor as in the original but by a soprano, and what is more, by his favourite soprano – Emily Soldene.

The next day Farnie travelled with Henderson's party to Liverpool where, as chance would have it, Emily Soldene was playing in *Chilperic*. They all went to see the show and afterwards Farnie went backstage to talk Miss Soldene into playing Drogan. She, too, was at first reluctant, believing that no English adaptation of a French opera bouffe had yet made money in London; but she, like Morton, was persuaded by Farnie's enthusiasm and she agreed. The next day, 26 July, Farnie saw Henderson's party off to New York on SS Queen, and then returned to London to get down to work.

Emily Soldene's tour with *Chilperic* lasted until late in September when she brought it to the Philharmonic, while *Genevieve de Brabant* went into rehearsal. Farnie's very free adaptation thoroughly anglicized the piece and he introduced several musical numbers of his own into Offenbach's score. They rehearsed for six weeks, a very long period for those days, and rehearsals were conducted in an atmosphere of absolute secrecy. West End managements had heard that the Philharmonic was planning a new French piece and though considering it rather an upstart they were curious. It served a suburban area to the north of Islington and people from central London or the more fashionable suburbs rarely went there. But neither Offenbach's music nor the French libretto by Hector Crémieux (revised from Étienne Tréfeu's earlier version) were copyright, and had another management learned what Morton and Farnie were planning it would certainly have tried to rush out another adaptation to mount before the Philharmonic's was ready. Only the principal

Emily Soldene as Drogan

artists knew the name of the piece, and most rehearsal scripts had false names of characters substituted for the real ones. It was directed by Emily Soldene but Farnie had a very big hand in it, drilling the chorus (of course) and arranging sets and lighting. To quote Emily again "there were no end of changes made in the ... small and 'it-don't-much-matter-if-the-girl's-good-looking' parts. Mr Farnie was most exigent in this department, and a new and handsome girl received with enthusiasm and declared by him to be the exact thing for the part to-day, would frequently (after a private interview) be pronounced by the same authority on the morrow totally unfitted for the proposed position." There were frequent noisy arguments between Farnie and Morton, but the show took shape. Then came the dress rehearsal, almost unheard of in those days, and Soldene credits Farnie with its introduction, "one of his foreign [French] ways which were nearly all good". Morton sat gloomily through it, convinced that it would be a total disaster. They were to open next day, Saturday 11 November, and Farnie could not be found. Morton, in a panic, sent for Emily Soldene to sort out last minute hitches.

The opening had been well planned. Saturday had been chosen so that critics could have the weekend to consider their reviews, and all the critics from major national dailies and the theatre press had been invited. The theatre was packed for the opening and it was an astounding success. Emily Soldene's *Sleep Song* was extremely popular, and the *Gendarmes' Duet* with its refrain "we'll run 'em in" was encored numerous times (some accounts say seventeen times, but that was on the last night, not the first). After the show Morton greeted the cast on stage, thanked them, and withdrew all his publicly expressed doubts. The papers on the Monday morning were unstinting in their praise, though some regretted that the name of the adapter was not known, for Farnie had not

Selina 'Dolly' Dolaro

allowed his name to appear on the programme, and suddenly Islington was on the map. On the Monday Farnie reappeared; he lost confidence on these occasions and his nervousness, almost fear, of the press, had overcome him and he had gone to Brighton for the weekend. He watched the show from a private box and declared that he had always known it would be a success. After the show he went on stage, said Emily in her 'Recollections', and all the cast gathered around expecting a little speech, but all they got was "Tomorrow morning, everybody, eleven o'clock sharp." It was not until the 26 November, a full fortnight later, that Farnie allowed his name to be printed on the programme but his identity was by then well known. The Era which published on a Sunday had guessed it the day after the opening and weeklies like Lloyd's Weekly Newspaper revealed it on the following Sunday, 19 November 1871.

Although Farnie had sold *Genevieve* to Morton, with respect to two songs of his own, *Love in Youth* and *Kiss, Kiss*, which he had introduced, he gave Morton only the exclusive rights for (with remarkable prescience) two years. After a few weeks Emily discarded *Love in Youth* and substituted another of Farnie's songs, *I Love Him So*, equally irrelevant to the story but she liked it better.

The show played to full houses and it was a dull night if the Gendarmes' duet got fewer than half-a-dozen encores. It had become part of the social scene and nightly the carriages drove through the west end on their way to Islington, with many of the young men-about-town going night after night.

Morton had been absolutely right with his choice of Emily Soldene for the lead; Drogan was a part which ideally suited her and one which she would make her own for several years to come. It was, for the most part, a strong and well-chosen cast with John Rouse, who had been in Farnie's *Punchinello* and *Mistletoe*

Bough, as the Duke of Brabant; Selina "Dolly" Dolaro who came from a musical family, had trained at the Paris Conservatoire, and whose first London appearance had been in Hervé's *Chilperic*, played Genevieve, his wife; Clara Vesey, Emily Soldene's sister as the Duke's Pet Page; comic actors Edward Marshall, who had for some years been the leading comic singer at Morton's Canterbury Music Hall, and Felix Bury were ideally paired as the gendarmes; J. B. Rae as the Burgomaster.

Clara Vesey as Pet Page

46

Marius, who had played in *Chilperic* and *Little Faust* at the Lyceum, had returned to France at the end of that season to fight for his country during the Franco-Prussian War. When fighting ceased he returned to London, penniless and with little more than the clothes he wore, which included his army shirt. Emily Soldene recounts how she asked Farnie to write in a part for him. Farnie expanded the small part of Charles Martel and added a song, and Marius joined

the cast on 21 March 1872, the night that Emily had a benefit. Selina Dolaro left the cast on 5 April in order to have her fourth child, a girl who was named Genevieve; she would return some months later, but for the moment her part was taken by Lennox Grey who had been in *Little Faust* and in *Gil Blas*.

The run of *Genevieve* was not without incident. Earlier that year Farnie had learned that M. Lindheim, formerly chef d'orchestre at Théâtre de Varietés in Paris, was living with his daughter in London to escape the fighting in France. Realising what an asset he could be, Farnie engaged him as musical director and Mr Halton, the incumbent, was given a fortnight's notice. Halton got the backing of the orchestra and on the Saturday night with a packed theatre they refused to perform unless Halton was given a new contract. One of the frequent visitors to the Philharmonic, and one of Emily's admirers, who happened to be present was Serjeant Ballantine,[2] one of London's leading barristers, and he went to Morton's rescue. He asked Halton directly if he and the orchestra would refuse to play unless he had a new contract and Halton said that was so; Ballantine declared there was no option but to give Halton a new contract and one was hastily drawn up and signed. The audience was becoming restive and the orchestra rushed in to play, while Ballantine assured Morton that the contract was worthless having been obtained with threats. An entirely new orchestra was engaged and quickly rehearsed under Lindheim's direction and a few days later they were in place, while Halton and all the musicians who had threatened to strike were refused admission. Halton sued but the outcome was exactly as Serjeant Ballantine had predicted, the court refused to recognize a contract which had been obtained under duress.[3]

There was more litigation that summer. Morton had begun early to arrange the summer tour. He advertised for managers on the No. 1 circuit to contact him and started entering into contracts. But when the entrepreneur proprietor Charles Head, who was not theatre-wise, saw what was happening he got the idea that Morton was trying to cheat him out of his share of the profits, and he applied for an injunction to stop the summer tour on the grounds that there was a clause in Morton's contract requiring him not to conduct any other business but to devote himself entirely to the affairs of the Philharmonic. Morton, who would have been personally liable to managers had the tour been cancelled, at once transferred the benefits of his contracts to a Mr King, later described as a retired wine merchant, so that when the matter went to court there was nothing on which an injunction might have been granted. Mr King was not further identified but before Marius had joined the cast the small part of Charles Martel had been played by a Mr King who may well be the same person.[4] Another cause of friction between Head and Morton related to Gaiety matinees. John Hollingshead at the Gaiety was the innovator of matinee performances, not with his own show that played in the evenings, but by visiting companies from other theatres. The Philharmonic company had played four matinees at the Gaiety and on these days Emily Soldene, who had a persistent weakness of her throat, said she could not do two performances a day and had caused her understudy to go on in the evenings at the Phil.

With the tour already underway, Head again went to court to try to stop it, but again failed. He then gave a dinner party to everyone he knew connected with the theatre at which he delivered a speech detailing all his complaints against Morton and how, he believed, Morton was trying to cheat him. It was not difficult to get a motion 'carried by acclamation' from people who had just enjoyed lavish hospitality, but he then went on to have his speech printed and widely distributed. It contained statements which were libellous and as Morton had a reputation as a good and honourable theatre manager to safeguard, he sued. The outcome was never in doubt and Morton was awarded £200 damages with costs. Relations between Head and Morton were damaged beyond repair.[5] John Hollingshead was called as a witness and when cross-examined on whether Morton should have arranged the summer tour replied, "Mr Morton could not have foreseen the success. It was not a success at first. Indeed, on the first night the author ran away to Brighton, and was not heard of for some days (Roars of laughter). He has since been seen, for I've seen him in court (Laughter)".[6]

But the matter which brought Farnie as a litigant into court concerned imitations. As there was no international agreement on copyright, Offenbach was common property in Britain, and anyone could produce another version of *Genevieve*. But what Farnie had himself created was protected by copyright. By the time the company set out on tour there were three rival versions playing; about two of these they could do nothing, but the third, at the Prince of Wales's Theatre, Liverpool, was different. At the opening of *Genevieve* the small part of Charles Martel was taken by Edward Adams who was also the prompter. The Prince of Wales's produced a version by Henry Hersée which proved not to be a success, Adams then offered them his version called

Genevieve de Brabant, or the Wonderful Pie which contained much of Farnie's material from the prompt book. As Liverpool was on Morton's tour schedule, he didn't want the waters muddied before they got there and Farnie sought an injunction to prevent the Liverpool theatre from using it. The judge took the over-simplistic view that it was Offenbach and therefore not copyright and he would not grant an injunction without a full hearing, but the defendants didn't show up for the hearing and the injunction was granted.[7]

After a very successful tour *Genevieve* reopened at the Philharmonic on 19 October. In her 'Recollections' Emily has another lovely story of how the Prince of Wales visited a cattle show at the nearby Agricultural Hall and saw, reportedly over the stall housing the prize pigs, a poster showing her in her costume as Drogan, the baker-boy hero, and he enquired who and what it was about. He was told of the show, playing at the Philharmonic "near the Angel", "a very suitable place" he remarked, eyeing the poster. He decided to see the show and Morton, equal to the occasion, had a box converted as a Royal Box complete with retiring room, and laid on the customary hospitality including the best cigars that money could buy. The cattle show opened on 9 December 1872 and the Prince's visit to Genevieve was on 18 February 1873. Emily tells a wonderful story but it is difficult to understand how Prince Edward could not have known all about the show as he was a frequent theatergoer, *Genevieve* had been all the rage for over a year, and his brother, Alfred Duke of Edinburgh, had been to see it. Perhaps it needed Emily's poster to spur him to see it for himself.

Emily records her first trip to Paris early in the New Year at the invitation of Augustus Harris, together with her husband Jack Powell and Morton and Farnie. They all knew that *Genevieve* must soon come to an end and they would need something to follow, and Harris had mentioned a show in Paris in which he had an interest which might be suitable. Emily's memory is more accurate over what they ate for dinner than concerning the show they went to see, but Kurt Gänzl has painstakingly analysed what happened.[8] They went to the Théâtre des Menus-Plaisirs to see *La Cocotte aux oeufs d'or*. Gänzl suggests that they probably bought the rights when they were there; it was never adapted by Farnie but Morton with Emily Soldene presented a version of it five years later as *La Poule Aux Oeufs d'Or* at the Alhambra.

Genevieve closed on Saturday 29 March 1873 after a record-breaking 438 performances. The following week, to allow for change-over and final rehearsals of the new show, the company played two Farnie adaptations of Offenbach operettas, *Rose of Auvergne, or, Spoiling the Broth* (*La Rose de Saint-Flour*) and *Breaking the Spell* (*Le Violoneau*) together with two other pieces. The new show which opened on 5 April was *Fleur de Lys*, Farnie's adaptation of *La Cour du roi Pétaud* by Jaime and Gille with music by Leo Delibes, Delibes's only full-length three-act comic opera. Emily was always very conscious of her position of 'prima donna' and didn't like waiting to make her first appearance. In the first act Prince Hyacinth, Emily's role, was an infant and she would not have appeared until Act II which takes place 18 years later. So some material from Act I was moved to Act II, the shortened first act was renamed a Prologue and the second and third acts were called Acts I and II; so after a short prologue Emily made her entrance in what was now Act I and her ego was satisfied. The show was an artistic success but a box-office failure, it earned rapturous reviews but did not appeal to the public; it was not opera bouffe but opera comique with a delightful story and graceful songs but without the fun in the music of Offenbach and Hervé. Farnie had added spice with three songs of his own; *That's the Way to Rule 'Em*, a topical comic song, *The Vintage of Bordeaux*, a drinking song, and *Waiting*, a ballad for Emily, but it was not enough. The young men-about-town who came to *Genevieve* night after night probably did come to *Fleur de Lys* – once. Morton's management agreement of the Philharmonic ran out on 7 July and given the state of relations between him and Charles Head there was no prospect of it being extended. *Fleur de Lys* could have run to the end of the season but it was withdrawn on 14 June so that Morton and Emily Soldene could end their stay with a flourish. *Genevieve* was brought back for a fortnight to reach its 459th performance with the final week kept for their benefit performances and a "Farewell Ball".

Emily then took the company on the customary summer tour of No.1 dates, playing both *Genevieve* and *Fleur de Lys*, which ended on 18 October. And as Morton was left without a theatre, he arranged with John Hollingshead at the Gaiety to present *Genevieve* for a six-week season before the Gaiety's Christmas show opened.

* * *

Chapter Five
THE WORLD OUTSIDE ISLINGTON

Henderson's company that Farnie had waved goodbye to at Liverpool docks duly reached New York and opened at Wallack's Theatre with his new burlesque, *Blue Beard*, on 16 August 1871; Lydia Thompson and her 'British Blondes' with manager Alex Henderson were welcomed back warmly. In striking contrast to the accusations of it being a 'girlie' show with hints of sexual impropriety The Clipper now reported that "The ladies are quiet and modest in their manner and neither in style nor manner do they appeal to sensuality. They possess shapely figures, good voices, sing well, and their acting is sprightly and vivacious." Five weeks in New York, during which three other pieces were added to join *Blue Beard* in the repertoire, were followed by a tour, and then a return to New York in the summer of 1872. Farnie had started work on a new piece for them but, being very occupied with a project at the Holborn Theatre, had to pass it to a 'friend' to complete. It opened, unattributed, as *Robin Hood; or, the Maid who was Arch and the Youth who was Archer*, at Wallack's on 22 July 1872.

In March 1873, as *Genevieve* was drawing to a close, a letter appeared in The Era from F. C. Burnand saying that he had been sent anonymously a copy of this piece with an invitation to compare it to his own *Robin Hood; or, the Forester's Fate* of ten years before, and that he had found sixty-nine lines which were a verbatim copy; he challenged Farnie to declare that he was not the author of the New York piece. Farnie explained what had happened, emphasizing that he had not claimed authorship at its production, and adding that his collaborateur, knowing that it was for the American market (there was, at that time, no copyright agreement between Britain and America) had looked at previous pieces on that theme before completing the work. He apologized for any involuntary plagiarism and offered Burnand whatever proportion of the fee he had received that Burnand thought just. Burnand asked for a half and received a cheque by return. The fact that Burnand took the course of writing to The Era rather than settling the matter privately suggests a certain antipathy between the two men, at least on the part of Burnand,[1] who did not come out of the affair unscathed. Letters followed by two authors claiming similar payment from Burnand for material taken from their works, one hinting that his *Robin Hood* itself was not original, and another from Thomas Lacy, publisher of play scripts, asking why Burnand was owed anything as he had purchased from Burnand all rights in his version of *Robin Hood*. 'The Orchestra' went on to show that Burnand's acclaimed *Ixion* was copied, scenes, characters and incidents, from Benjamin Disraeli's skit 'Ixion in Heaven'. But Burnand's complaint did not really concern copyright but the strict rules of the Dramatic Authors Society, of which he and Farnie were both members, concerning what would now be called intellectual property, or more bluntly, plagiarism.

Burnand himself wrote little that was original and boasted that he merely followed Shakespeare in taking his sources from elsewhere. At this period most writers drew from the French, something which Dickens made fun of. Nicholas Nickleby, when a member of Mr Crummles's touring company, is asked to write a play which, Crummles says, we'll do next Tuesday. Nicholas protests that his invention doesn't come that quickly. "Invention! what the devil's that got to do with it! cried Crummles . . . Do you understand French?" . . . and opening the table-drawer he handed a roll of paper from it to Nicholas. "There!" he said, "Just turn that into English, and put your name on the title page."

Farnie's commitment at the Holborn Theatre, which had caused him to hand over completion of *Robin Hood* to a 'friend', concerned a revival of Hervé's *Petit Faust*. Although Farnie's name did not appear in any advertising or on programmes it was well known and was reported in the press. He had made substantial revisions to his Lyceum version, and renamed *Doctor Faust* it opened on 20 May 1872 with Hervé himself in the title role, Selina Dolaro playing Marguerite, and Mdlle Clary as

Mephisto. Mdlle Clary (Madeleine Poirel-Tardieu) had absconded from a visiting Belgian company, and when an injunction was sought to oblige her to fulfil her contract she pleaded that she suffered so severely from sea sickness that she couldn't undertake the return Channel crossing.[2] She was at the Gaiety for a while before this engagement. Lionel Brough, familiarly known as 'Lal' Brough, and M. Loredan were also in the cast. Hervé had less scope for his singing and personal charm to cover for his poor English than he had in *Chilperic* and the reviews were not good. His part was taken over on 21 June by Mrs Howard Paul who introduced an unrelated song of Farnie's, *The First Leaf,* into the score. It closed on Saturday 13 July, the end of the season.

It was common practice for leading artistes to introduce favourite songs into a show. And as managements catered for an audience who would revisit a show many times, it was also common practice to spruce up a show which was enjoying a long run or was approaching Christmas or Easter with new costumes and scenery, new bits of business and new songs.

Farnie had also committed himself to provide the scenario for a spectacular for the opening of the new Niblo's Garden, New York, a 3,500 seat theatre replacing its earlier namesake which had been destroyed by fire. The plot of *Leo and Lotos* followed in the tradition of *The Black Crook* and was of the flimsiest, but it provided excuses for the introduction of numerous ballets and variety acts. The most extravagant of extravaganzas it had plenty of gorgeous scenery, spectacular stage effects, exquisite costumes, lots of ladies and lots of legs, singers from La Scala and from the English Opera company, and a cast of 200; it cost £50,000 to mount with running costs of £1,100 a night. It was, of course, a great publicity piece to put Niblo's back on the map and it ran for 120 performances. Farnie's contribution probably didn't require him to be there and with his heavy commitments in London it is difficult to see how he could have been. There is no indication in the press concerning his whereabouts.

His work for the Lydia Thompson troupe, for the Holborn Theatre and Niblo's were all commitments made earlier, but the unmatched success of *Genevieve* caused greater demands to be made on him. During the summer a company from Paris had performed Hervé's *L'Œil Crevé* in French at the Globe and E. P. Hingston at the Opera Comique thought to put on an English version, and he turned to Farnie. *L'Œil Crevé* opened on 21 October 1872 and closed on 22 February 1873, quite a respectable four-month run. And being, to Farnie, under a new management there appeared a number of new artistes; the highly regarded Julia Mathews had the lead, Fleur de Noblesse. Harriet Coveney, a very funny comedy actress, played The Marquise. She was the youngest of thirteen children of Henry Coveney and Sophia née Dent who were actors at Drury Lane and the Haymarket; all thirteen appeared on the stage although just four are well recorded. Pattie Laverne was not a beauty but was a very spirited performer and very popular in opera bouffe. Mdlle Clary who had been in *Doctor Faust* was back. Among the men were comedian and singer David Fisher (the elder), and Richard Temple who went on to a great career in the Savoy operas. *L'Œil Crevé* was immediately followed on 24 February by *The Bohemians*, Farnie's adaptation of *Le Roman Comique* with libretto by Hector Crémieux and Ludovic Halévy and music by Offenbach, which ran until 29 May. In deference to the management Farnie inscribed to Mrs E. P. Hingston one of his own songs, *The Old, Old Song*, which he interpolated into the show.

With all the successful work Farnie had done since the launch of *Genevieve* one critic felt able to write, if somewhat fulsomely, that Mr H. B. Farnie must, we suppose, be accepted as the best possible manipulator of a libretto in the theatrical market. Hardly – but he was one of the best lyricists and he had established himself as one of the leading writers in the field of light musical theatre. And he was beginning to develop a style of his own. He saw that he had not only to adapt dialogue and incidents in order to avoid censorship by the Lord Chamberlain, and also to suit English tastes, but that he also needed to adapt the musical content, both because in bending the plot some songs became inappropriate, and again to satisfy English tastes. The French loved musical couplets – the English loved a memorable tune that they could sing or whistle on the way home. He had never hesitated to cut sections of music or to import numbers of his own as occasion demanded. To take this to its conclusion, there seemed no reason to use music from just one composer and he began to construct pieces in his own way. John Oxenford, the benign but perceptive drama critic of The Times later wrote, "Of the art of turning an unmusical farce into a sort of opera-bouffe, with music derived from various sources, and with all the fantastical and spectacular adjuncts of burlesque, Mr Farnie may be considered the inventor."

It all began with *Nemesis; or, not Too Wisely but Too Well* which opened at the Strand Theatre on 7 April 1873. *Nemesis* was freely adapted from a French vaudeville entitled *Les Deux Noces de Boisjoli* by M. Alfred Duru, to which was added music from Offenbach, Hervé, Lindheim, Delibes, Vasseur, Lecocq, Roubilliard and Jones, selected and arranged by John Fitz-Gerald, the resident musical director at the Strand. It received excellent reviews and was an immediate hit. Although Farnie liked to retain French names, sometimes as in *Nemesis* substituting French names of his own devising for those in the original, the piece was thoroughly anglicized. The action was said to take place at a French seaside resort, but he has Mademoiselle Praline de Patoche, the heroine, singing:

"Yes, luxury I do think light on,
    Give me a small house in Park Lane,
A box on the parade at Brighton,
    And then I don't think I'll complain."

As always in a Farnie show there was the very best in scenery and costumes; and it had a strong cast with Angelina Claude, Nellie Bromley, Edward Terry, Harry Cox, and Mons. Marius

Duel scene from Nemesis

who had moved from the Philharmonic when *Genevieve* ended. *Nemesis* ran, on its first production, for 263 nights.

One very popular number from *Nemesis* was *The Language of Love* which explains how love making and the declaration "I love you" are expressed in other languages and in the animal kingdom, requiring some skill in animal mimicry. The Pall Mall Gazette ran a feature by a throat specialist explaining how it should be done. It was sung in the show by Edward Terry in his role as Calino but who later used the song in the music halls, as did Arthur Lennard. When Letty Lind, who later became famous as a skirt dancer, first appeared at the Gaiety in December 1880, it was in a try-out matinee of a new drama by Robert Buchanan; Letty had a non-speaking role. Something went wrong during the performance and the distraught author, seeing Letty standing nearby said "Couldn't Miss Lind fill in?" Without waiting to be asked, Letty ran on and recited *The Language of Love* to a most appreciative audience.[3]

Back to the affairs of the Morton-Soldene company, or Charles Morton's Opera Bouffe Company as it was officially known; Morton was without a theatre since leaving the Philharmonic and he had arranged with John Hollingshead to present *Genevieve* for a six-week season before the Gaiety's Christmas special, and he had arranged an American tour. It had not yet been decided what would be added to the repertoire and it is curious that both Morton and Farnie had missed a piece that seemed to be staring at them. During the summer a French company had appeared at the St James's Theatre and presented *La Fille de Madame Angot*. The libretto by Clairville, Siraudin and Koning was based on Alexander Dumas's novel 'Ange Pitou', the music was by Lecocq, and it had first been presented at Brussels in December 1872 before playing at the Folies Dramatique, Paris where it was immensely popular. It was brought to London by a Brussels company from the Fantaisies Parisienne (not the theatre where it had first been seen) and opened at the St James's on 17 May 1873. During the run the company was joined by the famous Mdlle Desclauzas, the original Mdlle Lange, and with her in the cast the company had played the second act as part of the programme at the Gaiety for Charles Morton's benefit on 5 July 1873. An English version would have seemed certain to be a winner.

It was left to H. J. Byron to be the first to adapt it for the English stage. After Morton's managership of the Philharmonic had ended, Charles Head put his theatre up for sale, but getting no offers decided to run it himself with Mr R. Shepherd from the Surrey Theatre as manager working under him. And displaying unexpected astuteness, he bought Byron's version which opened at the Philharmonic on Saturday 4 October 1873 with Julia Mathews as Mdlle Lange, Catherine Lewis as Clairette, and John Rouse lured from Morton's Genevieve company as Larivaudiere.

Emily Soldene's tour of *Genevieve* and *Fleur de Lys* continued to 18 October but towards the end she handed over to her understudy and took a well-earned and much needed fortnight off. During this break she went with Morton, Hollingshead and

Farnie to see what was going on at the Philharmonic. She remembered the visit for the ovation she received when she was recognized sitting in a box, but the visit had greater significance. Her party from the Gaiety decided that they could do *Angot* much better in the West End and they all looked at Farnie. He did some lightning work so that in less than three weeks they were able to announce that Charles Morton's Opera Bouffe Company would open at the Gaiety on Monday 3 November with *Genevieve de Brabant* for one week and then from 10 November they would present a new version of *La Fille de Madame Angot* for five weeks only as they were then to go to America.

Madame Angot was such an essentially French piece set in a particular period of French history and referring to historical characters, that it could not be adapted in the sense of putting it into an English setting. Farnie had one problem with it; Mdlle Lange, Emily's prima donna part, did not appear until act two and Emily's ego intervened. Clairette, the young heroine, falls in love with a no-good poet, Ange Pitou, and sings a seditious song of his, critical of Mdlle Lange and her lover Director Barras, and she is sent to prison. Mdlle Lange hears of this at the beginning of Act II. So Farnie had Mdlle Lange informed that something was afoot and go in disguise to the marketplace to see and hear for herself. This not only brought Mdlle Lange in at the beginning but handed her one of the best musical numbers (*Mère Angot was her name*) which would normally have been sung by Amaranthe.

The company did, of course, use the Gaiety chorus which could not be surpassed nor supplanted, but this led to another problem when management decided that the moustachios of the gentlemen did not go well with powdered wigs, and they were ordered to shave them off. The gentlemen of the Gaiety chorus aimed to match in elegance the celebrated beauty of the Gaiety ladies, and they were very proud of their moustachios – there was loud protest, the wardrobe mistress married to one of them was in floods of tears, there was talk of a strike – but the moustachios came off.

Madame Angot opened on 10 November. Mdlle Lange turned out to be another part which suited Emily and which she loved, and so did the public. And the cast included Annie Sinclair as Clairette Angot, Felix Bury and Edward Marshall (the Gendarmes of *Genevieve*), and Clara Vesey. It was very well received by critics and public alike, and there was much debate as to whether Farnie's or Byron's version was the better.

THE GAIETY PROGRAMME.

Sole Lessee and Manager ... ... Mr JOHN HOLLINGSHEAD

MISS EMILY SOLDENE

THIS EVENING, Friday, Nov. 21, 1873, the performances will commence at 7, with OFFENBACH'S Operetta, called

DO·RE·MI·FA

| Toccato ... | (An Italian Singing Master) | ... | Mr LUDWIG |
| Jean Matois ... | (A Breton Shepherd) | ... | Mr J. G. TAYLOR |

At 7.30, a Comic Drama, in One Act, by J. G. TAYLOR, entitled

A HAPPY FAMILY

Tom Bowles		...	... Mr J. G. TAYLOR
John Veal	... Mr E. MARSHALL	Ben Lanyard	... Mr J. B. RAE
Nancy Bowles	... Mrs LEIGH	Mary	... Miss HARRISON

After which, at 8.30, the Celebrated Comic Opera, in Three Acts,

LA FILLE DE

MADAME ANGOT

Adapted by H. B. FARNIE. Music by CHARLES LECOCQ.

NOTE.—The Version of this Celebrated Comic Opera is made with the express sanction of the French Authors and Proprietors, who have been arranged with for the Original Orchestral Score.

Mdlle. Lange (Actress of the Théâtre Feydeau, and Favourite of the Director, Barras) ... ... Miss EMILY SOLDENE
Clairette Angot (Daughter of Madame Angot, affianced to Pomponnet) Miss ANNIE SINCLAIR
Larivaudière (Creature of Barras, but plotting against the Republic) Mr. RICHARD TEMPLE
Pomponnet ... (Barber of the Market) ... M. FELIX BURY
Ange Pitou ... (A reactionary poet, in love with Clairette) Mr. E. D. BEVERLEY
Louchard (Agent of Police, in the service of Larivaudière) Mr. LEWENS
Amaranthe ... ... } Market Women { ... Mrs. LEIGH
Javotte ... ... } { ... Miss EWELL
Hersilie ... (Maid to Lange) { Miss CLARA VESEY
A Captain in Angereau's Hussars ... ... Mr. C. NORTON
Trénitz (President of the reactionary Club, " The Incredibles ") Mr. J. G. TAYLOR
Babet ... ... } (Clairette's Bridesmaid) { Miss COOK
Cadet ... ... } Market Men { Mr. LUDWIG
Buteux ... ... } { Mr. CRUTTWELL

A Group of Fashionables in 1st Act, Messrs. Ross, Daniels and Bishos.
Members of the Ladies " Ineffable Club " in 2nd Act, Mesdames Leigh, Ewell, Jolly, Leigh, Grundy, Barville, Cook, Travers.
Market Men and Women, Hussars, Soldiers of the National Guard, Conspirators of the " Incredible Club" Guests, &c., &c.

When the brief season ended it was announced that there was a "temporary but unavoidable suspension of the American engagement". The company went to Manchester for a week, during which Hollingshead and Morton arranged to rent London's vacant Opera Comique where *Madame Angot* opened on Boxing night, with the original cast except that Pattie Laverne took over from Annie Sinclair as Clairette. It ran to the end of the season, and during the run Farnie adapted another one-act operetta, with music also by Lecocq, called *My New Maid* which was added to the bill as a curtain raiser on 18 March.

At the end of the season Emily Soldene took the two shows on tour for the summer. The projected American engagement had now been confirmed for October so she had a month or two after the opening of the London season to fill. The Lyceum was vacant and she decided to rent it herself and to put on a revival of Charles L. Kenny's extravaganza *The Grand Duchess of Geroldstein* which had first played at Covent Garden in 1867. She then added *Genevieve* to the repertoire, and in preparation for her American trip, kept in rehearsal *Madame Angot* and a revival of *Chilperic*.

Under Charles Morton's management the company went to America in October. Farnie, of course, was not part of this venture and remained behind. Things did not go entirely smoothly; they opened with *Genevieve* at the Lyceum Theatre on 14th Street on 2 November 1874, only to find that a certain John F. Poole had got hold of a pirated copy of Farnie's libretto and had put on the show at the Olympic Theatre a fortnight earlier. However, due to the New York practice of playing sort runs in repertory it had closed two nights before the Morton-Soldene company opened and it seemed to have done them no harm. With a strong cast many of whom came from Morton's Philharmonic company, and a shapely chorus, they received a tremendous reception.

Back at the time of the Gaiety production, pre-Christmas 1873, Farnie had once again ventured into writing an original and non-musical comedy entitled *The Main Chance*. It was put on at the Prince of Wales's Theatre, Liverpool on 6 December 1873 unattributed. Farnie wanted to see what reception it received before acknowledging authorship, mindful, perhaps, of the drubbing he had received from the critics after *Rival Romeos* in April 1871. It was acclaimed by the local critics and loved by the Liverpool audiences and there was much speculation as to the identity of the playwright. The same company presented it at the Prince of Wales's Theatre, Manchester a fortnight later before Farnie was satisfied with its reception and had it brought to London. It was produced under his own name at the Royalty Theatre on 15 April 1874. Which was to be just the start of another busy year.

When *Nemesis* closed at the Strand it was followed by *Eldorado*, another piece in the same vein, not quite burlesque nor opera bouffe, derived from the French *La Cagnotte* and with music selected "from the best repertoires and arranged by [MD] Mr John Fitz-Gerald", and described in Farnie's own manner as a "folie musicale". It opened on 19 February 1874 with a strong cast, most of them from *Nemesis*, including Edward O. Terry, E. J. Odell, Harry Cox, Mons. Marius, Harry St Maur, Angelina Claude, and Nellie Bromley, but though very much enjoyed by the lovers of burlesque who frequented the Strand, it was not considered by the critics to be in the same class as *Nemesis* and it closed on Friday 22 May with *Nemesis* hurriedly put back until something else could be found.

After the summer he had another piece for the Strand constructed in the same manner entitled *Loo and the Party who Took Miss*, described as a "bouffonnerie musicale", which was modelled on *Le Carnaval de merle blanc* by Chivot and Duru. It opened on 28 September 1874 and was written specifically for the principals of the same Strand company that had done *Nemesis* and *Eldorado*. The Illustrated Sporting and Dramatic News felt that it "is an enormous success and promises to surpass anything previously achieved." Well it didn't quite manage to surpass *Nemesis* but it achieved 163 performances closing on Wednesday 7 April 1875 and, like *Nemesis*, repeatedly revived thereafter.

Not a great deal is known of Farnie's personal life or activities. There are a few reports of his attending dinners and other social events. He was a member of the Junior Garrick Club. He wrote pieces for some magazines and Christmas annuals. But any awkward situations seem to have driven him back to Paris. Two good friends who Farnie had made while living in Paris was the composer Robert Planquette, with whom Farnie would later be closely associated, and the theatrical costumier Charles George Alias. Charles Alias came over to London as costumier for a dance group, Les Clodoche, who had appeared in a speciality routine in *Genevieve* at the Philharmonic, where Miss Price had costumed the show. He stayed, and in due course he and Miss Sarah Ann Price were married. While courting they together costumed *Nemesis*, then as M. and Mme Alias they costumed *Eldorado*, and now *Loo*, as they would many of Farnie's later shows. Indeed, they were to become London's leading theatrical costumiers.[4]

Although Farnie had worked for the Swanboroughs at the Strand Theatre before, *Nemesis* had begun a close association which would see him provide many of its major pieces for some time to come. Donald Shaw in his book 'One of the Old Brigade; London in the Sixties' [5] says, "The Strand Theatre was a highly popular resort, run exclusively by the Swanborough family and their numerous sisters, cousins and aunts." And after reminiscing through very rose-tinted glass of the theatre and neighbouring hostelries he continues, "A few years later the family grouping that originally characterized the Strand was intruded upon by one H. B. Farnie, whose forte was the adaptation of opera-bouffe. Unquestionably an adept in this particular line, the man was a libertine of a pronounced character, with the result that the chorus at the Strand and the Opera Comique was the very daintiest conceivable. If a houri yielded to this Blue Beard's blandishments, her advancement was assured, and she was fitted to minor parts; if his overtures fell on deaf ears, nothing was too bad for her, and her lot was not a successful one. Occasionally, as a consequence, the hum-drum routine of a rehearsal was enlivened by such unrehearsed incidents as the appearance of an irate brother, and, on one occasion, an exasperated fishmonger from the Theobald's Road (the combination sounds boisterous), burst in at a critical period of a comic duet and belaboured the unhappy impresario to within an inch of his life." "Intruded" is scarcely an accurate description as Farnie's work was a minimal departure from the Swanborough's policy for the theatre, but otherwise his recollection is fair enough.

* * *

Chapter Six

THE PASTICHE PERIOD

The biggest event of the year 1874, as far as concerned the musical theatre, was the return after an absence of six years of Lydia Thompson with her troupe, and Alex Henderson. The theatre papers filled columns about Lydia, of her career from her earliest success as Little Silverhair to the present, of her years in America, and of looking forward to seeing her again on the stage in London. There had from time to time been news reports – of her personal horse-whipping of the editor of the Chicago Times after he had published an article which she considered to have maligned her by accusing her and the ladies of her company of immorality: for this she had been fined 2¢, reflecting public sympathy, but it was increased to $200 on appeal and she declared that it was worth every cent – and of her marriage to Alex Henderson which surprised everyone for it was widely believed that they were already a conjugal pair. Now the acknowledged Queen of Burlesque was back in London.

They opened at the Charing Cross Theatre on 19 September 1874 with Farnie's *Blue Beard* which had already played in America for 477 performances. He had done some very swift work updating and anglicizing all the topical allusions, and they opened to rave reviews and packed houses, and even those critics who had for some time been declaring that burlesque was dead, only just surviving at the Gaiety and the Strand, were forced to agree that with the right artistes it was still very much alive.

Willie Edouin, with his American wife Alice Atherton, had stayed with the company, come to England with them and proved very popular. Everyone was staggered at the performance of a visiting American actor, John Morris, who performed a quick-change act in full view of the audience, becoming successively eight very different characters of both sexes, guests at Blue Beard's wedding. And they had recruited comedian Lionel Brough who gave a splendid performance as Blue Beard. Farnie directed the show; costumes were designed by Lydia Thompson herself and executed by Mme Alias.

Willie Edouin

The enthusiasm of the public did not abate as the autumn progressed and nightly queues of people were turned away because the house was packed full. This was not good business, and on Christmas Eve they transferred to the larger Globe Theatre. The show was freshened with new scenery and costumes, John Morris the quick-change artist left and there were several other changes. There were new songs, new jokes, and new business, and especially for Christmas a harlequinade was added. The chorus was considerably enlarged with a lot of very pretty young girls including, from the cast of *The Black Prince*, Annie Randolph who would become Farnie's mistress; by no means his first, nor his last, but the one who had the misfortune to be sharing his bed when his wife caught up with him. But that is some years away yet.

Farnie's involvement with *Blue Beard* had not taken up the whole of his summer and he had prepared two other shows for the coming season both of which were notable in quite different ways. The *The Black Prince* was the first, with music by Charles Lecocq, which opened at the St James's Theatre on 24 October 1874. As soon as the show was announced, Lecocq had written to all the theatre papers and important dailies protesting that he had never written a piece of that name. There was an immediate riposte from Cramer's, and from Stephen Fiske the manager of the St James's, for the truth was not so clear cut; Cramer's had purchased from Lecocq's Paris agents the rights and full orchestral parts of several of his early works previously not heard in England, and the programme at the St James's contained a note stating that "This comedy has been founded on a piece by MM. Labiche and Delacour, and the music has been selected from works of Lecocq unrepresented in England, and the property of Messrs Cramer & Co." But it caused a bit of a stir as only a week before Hervé had been in dispute with the management of the Holborn Amphitheatre for producing a piece called *Melusine* based on one of his early works in which his airs had been re-orchestrated by M. Audibert; Mr M'Donogh, the manager, had approached Hervé for the orchestral parts but had been refused. Most reviewers of *The Black Prince* felt that Lecocq had been ill-advised to rush in with his protest, The Illustrated Sporting and Dramatic News declaring: "With an amount of candour which is laudable as it is rare, the piece is publicly announced as an English adaptation of *Le Voyage en Chine* [by MM. Labiche and Delacour] with music selected from the works of M. Lecocq. If, therefore, the music should be ill-adapted to the dramatic situation the entire responsibility must rest with the English adapter, and no blame can attach to him [Lecocq]. As a matter of fact Mr Farnie, the adapter, has done his work so well that there is no semblance of incongruity; and the various solos and concerted pieces are exactly suited to the music attached to them;

while the music itself appears to spring naturally from the dramatic situations. Had the libretto been furnished to Lecocq with a commission to fit new music to it, we could scarcely have had more appropriate melodies or orchestration; and it is possible that a less striking success might have been achieved." But in spite of this vindication the piece was a flop and ran for only a few weeks.

The second show Farnie had prepared was his pantomime *Whittington*. Cramer's had managed, earlier in the year, to sign Offenbach to provide the music for a Christmas show for a considerable fee – £1000 for each of three acts payable when delivered to the copyist. It was something of a scoop and the poor man little knew what he was letting himself in for! Farnie's libretto was a curious mixture; the first act followed the traditional tale of Whittington becoming apprenticed to Alderman Fitzwarren, falling in love with his daughter Alice, and going off in search of his fortune so that he might win her, except that Farnie introduced three rival suitors, the MacPibroch, the O'Shamrock, and FitzFulke. It was full of outrageous puns such as when MacPibroch is invited to stay for a meal he replies that in Scotland "we have quite enough meal", in fact, dinner might be described as "table d'oats". In the second act Whittington takes ship to the tropical island of Bambouli and somehow or other, most of the principal characters contrive to be on the same ship. Here the inhabitants of Bambouli are disgruntled by the affairs of the government and appoint some of the new arrivals to various ministries in order to introduce the 'ideal' English system. But the inhabitants are not impressed with the results and the visitors are only saved from lynching by a fortuitous invasion of rats which Whittington's cat destroys. This gave the opportunity for a lot of political satire. The third act returned to the customary story back in London where Dick Whittington, now rich, becomes Lord Mayor and wins the hand of Alice.

Offenbach cannot have been inspired and produced a score that was not his best. The reviews, generally, did like the music and liked the libretto separately but complained that the very

French music did not go well with a very English story. But it was, as always with Farnie, spectacularly produced and was the longest running show of the Christmas season, opening at the Alhambra Theatre on 26 December 1874 and achieving 112 performances finally closing on 7 May 1875. A French version by Nuitter and Tréfeu may have been prepared as soon as Offenbach had the text from Farnie[1] but it was not produced in France for another twenty years. The French librettists evidently enjoyed the English nonsense for they expanded the roles of the three suitors and introduced another odd character in the shape of a Scottish witch named Melimela. With the title *Le Chat du diable* it was produced at the Châtelet Theatre, Paris in 1893 for a three-month run.[2]

It remains a curiosity being the only music Offenbach wrote to an English text. The music, apart from vocal scores with piano part, was lost until sometime before the year 2000 when the orchestral parts were discovered in a second-hand bookshop in Paris. And as a 'Millennium' special the City of London Symphonia with soloists and a narrator put on a concert version on 28 June 2000 [3] at the Mansion House. A staged version was more recently put on by the University College, London Operatic Society with professional soloists. The libretto came in for some criticism and was extensively modified, but anyone approaching it now must accept that it was never meant to be another *La Belle Helène*, it was a Victorian pantomime that was not expected to last more than one season.

Gilbert does not seem to have been one to pass by a good idea and *Utopia Limited*, his and Sullivan's last but one opera, (Savoy, 7 October 1893) very closely resembles *Whittington's* second act, the King's daughter choosing new ministers from ordinary people who make matters worse, and even to specific jibes, as those against the Limited Companies Act of 1862.

Blue Beard ran on at the Globe until 2 July when it went on tour to the major towns and cities, the No. 1 circuit, returning to the Globe on 22 November. A second company was formed to take

Violet Cameron

it to the lesser towns. On the first company's return to the Globe they gained a notable new recruit, a pretty teenage girl who performed as Violet Cameron but whose real name was Violet Lydia Thompson. She was distantly related to Lydia Thompson but not through the Thompson name, which was sheer coincidence, but through their mothers.[4] She was looked after by Alex Henderson and Lydia, and coached and taught stage-craft by Farnie – properly! not as he did the chorus girls – and it was something which, in later life, she generously acknowledged.[5]

At the Strand, Mrs Swanborough was running a revival of *Loo* pending the opening of Farnie's new Christmas piece *The Antarctic ; or, the Pole and the Traces,* which opened on 27 December. It was, like the curate's egg 'good in parts'; one reviewer thought that "the best effect is in the scene of the Geography class where the boarding school misses are made to stand upon forms, and not upon ceremony, so that their ankles may be admired, and here there is a pretty concerted piece, in which a good accompaniment is managed by the tapping of the girls' pencils upon slates." The Illustrated Sporting and Dramatic News thought it worth a full page spread of illustrations of scenes. It struggled through the Christmas season and was taken off in early February.

Emily Soldene had returned from America in May. In July she played a couple of matinees at the Gaiety of *Genevieve* borrowing

M. Marius from the Strand company to play his original role for the occasion. At the end of October she started a season at the Park Theatre (formerly the Alexandra), newly refurbished and renamed, opening with *Genevieve* and continuing with the repertoire that she had taken to America.

Charles Morton, who had returned before Emily, was now lessee of the Opera Comique and had arranged with Farnie for a new adaptation of another Offenbach opera-bouffe, *Madame l'Archiduc*, and he had booked Emily Soldene for the lead part of Marietta, with strong support from Kate Santley as Fortunato, and with Felix Bury erstwhile Gendarme, and W. S. Penley an eccentric comedian now best remembered as Charlie's Aunt. The piece had been a failure in Paris despite some of the leading French artistes heading the cast; Farnie's adaptation was far from his best and he had failed to remove all the situations which would offend English susceptibilities. The opening night was a disaster: *Madame l'Archiduc* shared the programme with Gilbert and Sullivan's *Trial by Jury*, but it was 11 o'clock before the second act ended, and Charles Morton came before the curtain to address the audience, apologizing for the delays, and after stating that the third act would run for three-quarters of an hour he asked whether the audience would like to forgo the third act or Trial by Jury. There was a great hubbub until one voice was heard above the rest shouting, "play the lot, old man, and we'll stay if it's till two o'clock." The third act was played, and Morton again appeared before the curtain pleading with the audience, for the sake of the artistes, to let it end there, and offering them tickets for any other night. The audience was not pleased but after some more commotion, reluctantly agreed.

Even after drastic cutting the papers were not impressed, feeling that both Offenbach and Farnie were in decline, and if Morton had hoped for another *Genevieve* he must have been very disappointed. One reviewer remarked that if Farnie could not produce better dialogue than in *Whittington* or *Madame l'Archiduc* then they must conclude that he had lost the art of writing humorous dialogue and had better take a collaborateur.

Whether he took note of this remark or not, it was something he would do before very long.[6] *Madame l'Archiduc* was carried for two months by *Trial by Jury* before closing on 17 March. In spite of this, Emily Soldene liked her part and, when she returned to America in October that year, added the show to her repertoire, considerably altered by herself.

In January Henderson, at last, got a theatre of his own when he took on the lease of the Criterion, and he opened on 31 January with Lydia Thompson and company including Lionel Brough, Willie Edouin, Camille Dubois, Pauline Markham, and Violet Cameron in Farnie's new burlesque *Piff Paff*. It was adapted from the French, *Le Roi Matapa*, and the papers, having complained that *Madame l'Archiduc* had retained some objectionable indelicacies, felt that *Piff Paff* had been too well cleaned up and lost some of its point; in the words of The Era, "The young ladies of a genteel boarding school might witness *Piff Paff* without any detriment to their morals." It had a rather confused plot and was full of the most outrageous puns, but that was burlesque and, although not up to the standard of *Blue Beard*, it was what burlesque audiences wanted and was well received. It ran until Easter after which the Lydia Thompson company took it on tour along with *Blue Beard*.

In late April or early May Hollingshead at the Gaiety had bought from Farnie a burlesque called *Roulette* which contained a song, *The Two Obadiahs*, by Henry Lyste. The two Obadiahs agree to go out on the spree until each discovers that neither has any money. The tune was that of a very old march which was widely sung, whistled and played and in which there was no copyright. Hollingshead did not use the show but showed the libretto to Robert Reece who took the idea of the two Obadiahs and wrote words of his own to incorporate into his burlesque *Young Rip Van Winkle* which was playing at the Charing Cross Theatre. Farnie, too, wrote his own version and passed it to Lydia Thompson to use in *Blue Beard* on tour and later to be incorporated into *Robinson Crusoe* in the autumn. While to the chagrin of Henry Lyste who complained that he had received nothing for his idea, J. L. Toole used something close to his original version, but which was now the property of Hollingshead, in *Spelling Bee* which had played at the Gaiety and was now on tour. Farnie, for his part, would not only use the theme for a song in *Robinson Crusoe* but created two minor characters from the two Obadiahs.

And Farnie had created his own version of *Chilperic* for the Alhambra. Considerably altered, expanded, and with additional music supplied by Hervé, it was now described as a musical spectacle. Ballet being a speciality of the large 2200-seat Alhambra where everything needed to be big, it had a chorus and corps de ballet of 200 and a 'Grand Barbaric Ballet' was worked into the show, the same ballet that had been created for Whittington. It opened on 10 May 1875 for a three-month run closing on 13 August.

The summer was otherwise a quiet one for Farnie though he must have been working hard on autumn and Christmas shows. In partnership with Alfred Cellier, he created *Nell Gwynne* based on an old play, *Rochester* by W. T. Moncrieff. His name was not announced on the playbills but it was well known that he was responsible for the book. It opened at the Prince's Theatre, Manchester on 16 October 1876 for four weeks. The critics were half-hearted although the Manchester public liked it, but at the end of the run Farnie and Cellier decided not to take it to London but to dismantle it, so Farnie went off with his libretto and Cellier with his music and both would resurface some years later.

Farnie was now working closely with Henderson and would keep him supplied with shows for some time to come. Henderson had, of course, to keep the Criterion going, which he did, for most of the summer, with a comedy called *The Great Divorce Case* and a cast headed by Charles Wyndham. In September he bought the lease of the Charing Cross Theatre, had it refurbished and renamed it the Folly, and opened it with the *Blue Beard* company returned from their summer tour.

Then on 11 November he put on Farnie's latest offering, *The Very Latest Edition of Robinson Crusoe*. It had been rehearsed while the company was on tour, tried out in Manchester on 7 October, and proved Farnie's critics quite wrong for it was an immediate success. Lydia Thompson playing Robinson Crusoe was dressed in what must be the most famous costume of her career, designed by herself, it was made entirely of white

Lydia Thompson as Crusoe

goatskin with a high cap to match, set off with a bright scarlet feather, and accompanied by white satin boots and gloves and a white Chinese parasol. Willie Edouin played Friday and the other comedian, Lionel Brough, Crusoe's good friend Jim Cocks. Violet Cameron, maturing rapidly, was Crusoe's beloved, Polly Hopkins. There was one scene in which the pirates capture some of the girls in order to procure themselves wives, a hint, perhaps, of *Pirates of Penzance* (Opera Comique, 3 April 1880). *Crusoe* could have run on and on, but Henderson took it off at

Easter to make way for Farnie's next piece.

In spite of the success of *Crusoe*, Farnie had evidently decided that the time had come to work with a partner, and he teamed up with Robert Reece. It was a very good pairing; Reece was two years older than Farnie and an experienced playwright with some sixty productions to his credit. He was very good at humorous dialogue but poor on lyrics. The Era commented that "Mr Robert Reece – ever happy in titles and excellently neat in versification – happily for all

playgoers has joined hands with Mr H. B. Farnie, well known for his wedding of good tunes to funny words ..." Their method of working seems to have been that Farnie would develop the scenario of the show detailing what should happen in each scene, and would write the lyrics, while Reece would fill in the dialogue.

The first product of this new partnership, and the next piece for Henderson, was *Oxygen; or, Gas in a Burlesque Metre*, which opened at the Folly on 31 March 1877. The new partners used both Jules Verne's story 'Dr Ox' and Offenbach's operetta of the same title which was based on it, and it ran until 22 June when *Crusoe* was brought back for two weeks. The reason for this change was not clear until the American press announced that Lydia was to return to New York for another visit at the end of August under the management of Samuel Colville. Alex Henderson, with the Folly Theatre, and about to take over the Queen's Theatre, would remain behind.

Samuel Colville came to England in order to escort Lydia and her troupe back to New York, where they opened at Wallack's Theatre on 18 August with a revival of *Blue Beard*, and then added *Oxygen*, and *Robinson Crusoe* to the repertoire. Then they went on a brief tour before moving back to New York to the Eagle Theatre in November when they added *Piff Paff*. But their season ended abruptly and on an unhappy note. Henderson had not stopped having affairs after he married Lydia and she had put up with the situation, but when news drifted across the Atlantic that he had begun a relationship with a young girl, which sounded more serious than a casual affair, Lydia packed her bags; her company were given the choice of returning with her or remaining in a reorganized company under Colville's management. The long-running and successful Lydia Thompson troupe ceased to exist.

For the autumn Farnie and Reece wrote a programme of three shows, the main item being *The Creole* based on Offenbach's opera-bouffe of the same name, together with *The Sea Nymphs* from *Ondine au champagne* with music by Lecocq. The first known example of a pre-London try-out,[7] they opened in Brighton on 3 September 1877, and at the Folly on 15 September when a third piece, *Up the River* adapted from an early work of Hervé's called *Un Drame en 1779*, was added. In mid-November *Sea Nymphs* was replaced by a new and much abbreviated version by Farnie of his *L'Œil Crevé*, music by Hervé, which had been produced five years before, now under the new title, *Shooting Stars*. Despite it being intended as a supporting piece in the programme it caught the public fancy more than the main piece, but the whole programme had to end at Christmas.

Farnie and Reece also provided Mrs Swanborough at the Strand with an original piece, a "bouffonnerie musicale", called *Champagne; or, A Question of Phiz* which ran from mid-September until Christmas.

Alex Henderson had taken on the management of the Queen's Theatre which had been failing and had been closed for some time, had it done up and renamed the National Theatre, and opened it with a drama by the new partnership entitled *Russia, or, The Exiles of Angara*. It was derived from a novel by Prince Lubermirski entitled 'Tatiana, or, The Conspiracy', a strange choice as neither Farnie nor Reece had written anything like it before. The Queen's / National had gained a reputation for ill-luck and *Russia* continued the trend – it was a disaster, partly self-inflicted by a bitter dispute between Henderson and the theatre's proprietor, Henry Labouchere. Labouchere had agreed to cover any losses but he thought *Russia* hopeless from the start and had said so, and he refused to pay. Henderson covered the salaries for three weeks and then closed the show and ended the management agreement. A battle of words between them filled a whole page of The Era[8] but they must have come to some private settlement and no more was heard of the matter, which was surprising as so many lesser disputes at this period ended up in court.

In the late summer of 1877 Farnie received a commission from Miss Wallis, a well-known actress in Manchester. She had withdrawn from the stage for eighteen months following her marriage to Mr Lancaster and birth of her first child, and she wanted a vehicle to highlight her return. Farnie based his scenario on a French piece, *La Mendiante*, showed Miss Wallace the French text and his scenario, and then went to his new collaborateur, Reece, to ask him to fill in the dialogue. The result was *Hester Gray; or, Blind Love* which opened on 27 October for a week. In a review, the new-that-year weekly paper Theatre, accused Farnie and Reece of advertising their play as a "new play" whereas, they alleged, it was a copy of a play called *Ruth Oakley* which had been produced in 1857, and it placed advertisements in The Telegraph, Standard and other national dailies saying "Serious Charge against Mr Reece and Mr Farnie – see the Theatre of to-day". It also had, for several days, men with sandwich boards with large yellow posters bearing the same notice. Farnie and Reece sued for libel; Farnie later withdrew from the action and went back to France, but Reece persevered.

The Era, not waiting for what might be said in court, ran a lengthy article accepting Farnie and Reece's statement that they used only *La Mendiante* and did not know of *Ruth Oakley*, and pointed out that there were at least four other English versions deriving wholly or in part from the French piece, *The Serpent on the Hearth*, *The Old House at Home*, and *Expiation*, and in part *Queen's Evidence*. Reece's libel action reached court on 20 February 1879 at which time Farnie was in Paris. Evidence was given that *Hester Gray* had derived only from *La Mendiante* and not from *Ruth Oakley*, but also concerning the description 'new play'. It was said that by custom the term 'new play' included adaptations from the French if it was a new play to the English stage, and the term was not the same as 'new and original' which implied that it had not appeared before in any language and was the brainchild of the author. The following morning W. S. Gilbert had already entered the witness box to speak for the paper's defence when counsel said that Theatre had offered a full apology which was accepted by Mr Reece and approved by the judge.[9]

Charles Morton who had once had grave doubt about Farnie had enjoyed two of his successes, *Genevieve* and *La Fille de Madame Angot*, and despite his disappointment over *Madame L'Archiduc* still hoped Farnie would provide him with another winner. Farnie and Reece provided him with a Christmas show called *Wildfire*, from Reynolds and Lloyd's *Le Diable à quatre*, which ran to the end of February when he replaced it with a revival of *Madame Angot*. Kate Santley had taken the management of the Royalty Theatre and wanted a show which would be a vehicle for herself as well as one for the Royalty, and they provided another of those invented bouffonnerie musicales, with book from *La Chaste Susanne* and music from various sources, called *Madcap*. It had been made too 'chaste' and was full of poor puns, and the Graphic summed up "*Madcap* met with general condemnation" – it lasted just a month.

Henderson, though giving up the Queens / National, still had the Folly, and for him Farnie and Reece did an adaptation of *Les*

Cloches de Corneville with music by Robert Planquette. Planquette was one of the friends who, along with the costumier Charles Alias, Farnie had made in Paris. He was known mainly for his work in music hall, but had composed a couple of one-act operettas and then the full-length work, *Les Cloches de Corneville* with libretto by Louis Clairville and Charles Gabet, based on a play by Gabet, which opened at the Folies-Dramatiques, Paris 19 April 1877 and enjoyed a hugely successful 18-month run. *Les Cloches* was opera comique, not bouffe, and Farnie and Reece had stuck closely to the original, but adaptation done, rehearsals went badly; Farnie directed the show, he was by now directing all of Henderson's shows, and he and Henderson quarrelled, though that was nothing out of the ordinary.[10] They began to lose faith in it, consoled only by having Violet Cameron, now a mature and experienced artiste, to play the female lead, Germaine. To play the miser, Gaspard, they had engaged an Irish

Kate Munroe

actor, Shiel Barry, who clung to his brogue as part of his stock-in-trade. To cap it all Shiel Barry caught a cold just before opening night which, together with the various quack remedies he tried in an attempt to cure it, made his voice hoarse and croaky. They opened on 23 February 1878 and a printed slip was inserted into the programmes which read:

NOTICE   The indulgence of the audience is solicited for Mr Shiel Barry who is suffering from a severe cold and hoarseness.

Farnie and Henderson hung around outside the auditorium not daring to watch. When the curtain came down there was a tremendous uproar and they feared the worst, but it was ringing cheers they heard. Shiel Barry triumphed with a powerful performance and his hoarse brogue was perfect for the old miser Gaspard, and they woke next morning to find the press enthusiastic and Shiel Barry famous. Violet Cameron wonderfully captured the girlish artlessness of Germaine and reached stardom overnight. Vivacious Serpolette was played by Katherine Munroe. Kate Munroe was born in America and went to Italy to study opera in Milan and Naples. She sang in Italian opera for three years in Italy and in France, then came to England in 1874, performed in opera bouffe at the Gaiety and discovered a penchant for it. She had been in *The Creole* and *Shooting Stars* at the Folly before *Cloches* and now shared in the critical acclaim. It was full of memorable tunes and the very popular number, *The Legend of the Bells* with its catchy digue-digue-don refrain (or ding-dong-ding-dong) gave English audiences what they loved, a song they could sing, hum or whistle on the way home.

Then *Cloches* became a repeat of *Blue Beard* with queues of disappointed playgoers lining the pavement each night unable to get in. In August it transferred, as *Blue Beard* had done, to the larger Globe theatre where it continued its unprecedented first run of 705 performances; [11] there would be many, many revivals, and Shiel Barry would devote much of the rest of his career to it. It was broadcast by the BBC in 1927 and between the wars became extremely popular with amateur societies.

On this occasion Farnie and Henderson forestalled any rival productions by getting together a touring company as soon as the London production was launched; the company did one matinee performance at the Folly on 13 April, Boat Race day, before setting out on tour. Playing Germaine was a young lady, beautiful and talented, with sound experience but who had not yet got closer to the West End than Crystal Palace, named Florence St John; her star would shine brightly over the musical

The miser Gaspard as played by Shiel Barry

theatre for the next quarter of a century. Serpolette was played by Lennox Grey.

But they were not quick enough in New York where a version by Myron A. Cooney with the title *The Chimes of Normandy* opened at the Fifth Avenue Theatre on 2 October 1877, before the London production. This was followed by several productions in French, and it was three years before Farnie and Reece's version opened at the Metropolitan Casino on 26 November 1881 with Kate Munroe in her original role as Serpolette.

Farnie's next adaptation was to be Offenbach's *Madame Favart* and, according to Emily Soldene, the title role was to have

81

been taken by Fanny Josephs, but this fell through. This may well be as Fanny Josephs, after a long run in *The Pink Domino*, was keen to manage a theatre herself. She had negotiated for the St James's theatre when it reopened after extensive refurbishment and redecoration, but when the reopening was delayed she settled for the Olympic which she took over on 16 April 1879. Just before Christmas 1878 Florence St John, touring with *Les Cloches de Corneville*, had started advertising that she would be "at liberty" at Easter, but Henderson and Farnie had not forgotten her and they signed her for London. She took over the part of Germaine with the London company of *Cloches* on 10 March 1879 while rehearsing *Madame Favart*.

Favart opened at the Strand Theatre (*Cloches* was still running at the Globe) on 12 April 1879 and Florence became an overnight sensation. Critics and public loved her and from then on she moved from one lead role to the next. *Favart* had had a fair reception in Paris, but Farnie's English adaptation was considered an improvement on the original and it, too, had a remarkable run of more than 500 performances.

Florence St John

Reminiscing about this show some years later, Florence said that her great difficulty as a beginner was her inability to laugh at will. "I could act, I could dance a little, I had a voice, I could sing, but for the life of me I could not laugh." She was in despair about a laughing scene in Madame Favart and was saved on the first night by seeing, as she went on, Mr Farnie at the prompt entrance.

"To me, for the moment, he looked the very picture of ridiculous misery" – she burst out laughing, and was extolled by the critics for the excellence and naturalness of her laughter. [12]

Mons Marius played Charles Favart her husband; he would soon become her husband off stage as well as on. Violet Cameron played Suzanne and Henry Ashley the Marquis de Pont-Sablé. Once again Henderson and Farnie set up a touring company to forestall imitations, Camille Dubois was Madame Favart, and a young actor named Herbert Beerbohm Tree scored his first notable success as the Marquis.

Charles Morton now had the Alhambra Theatre and again went to Farnie for his Christmas show. *Rothomago, or, The Magic Watch* was written and directed by Farnie and was considerably better than the previous year's piece. It opened on 22 December and ran a month past Easter, which was more than was expected of it. It was followed by a version of Offenbach's *Le Pont des soupirs* adapted by Charles Searle with the title *Venice*, which Morton had Farnie arrange and direct.

1879 was the beginning of the most successful period of the Farnie-Henderson partnership and of Farnie's own work when they had a succession of big hits and for periods occupied four of London's theatres.

* * *

Chapter Seven

BIGAMY

Henry Farnie was now 43 years old. It was fifteen years since he had come to London and started writing for the theatre and after trying a number of styles had settled on light musical pieces as his chosen field. He had made French opera bouffe popular in England and then developed a style of his own in the popular *Nemesis* and *Loo*. John Oxenford of The Times had once called him "the most admirable dramatist now alive, a man of infinite taste and humour" though that was, to be sure, at a dinner when wine had flowed freely. But Farnie had earned a place among the leading dramatists of the day along with Henry J. Byron, Robert Reece, F. C. Burnand and W. S. Gilbert in the musical field and Henry Pettitt, Sydney Grundy, Paul Merritt, Tom Taylor and W. G. Wills. He was a very successful stage director with a reputation for being harsh and loud; one of his stars said of him that "he had a rough tongue but always declared in his quiet moments that he did not mean what he said in his wrath ..." His private life was not so successful by conventional standards; he had been married twice, the first marriage ending in divorce after just two years, his second ending in a separation after barely three, and he had no surviving legitimate children. He was an incorrigible womanizer with no shortage of lady friends. His large figure belied his considerable personal charm and in a feature in the Scotsman in 1925 the writer recalled that as a youth she had seen Farnie on the links at St Andrews, "the laughing centre of a gay group of angelic creatures in billowy summer gowns." He was a large man: Macqueen-Pope said of him that "He was a big burly man, who always wore a hat many sizes too small for him and coats which were many sizes too short. But he was completely satisfied with the effect, for people would turn and stare after him in the street and that was exactly what he desired." But was it? He had a curious bashful or nervous streak that made him fear first nights and fear the press on those occasions, and decline to appear before the curtain in response to calls for "author". Was his size in coats and hats, perhaps, to deny his physical size, and his brashness to hide insecurity? Paris was his home, his source of inspiration and his bolthole.

And for the moment all was well although 1879 had started with an indiscretion. Very likely many years started with an indiscretion but they were not known about. Nor was this one known about – then! On 25 March 1879 a baby girl was born in Woodbridge, Suffolk; she was named Ellen Maud Taylor and according to her birth certificate her mother was Agnes Richardson Taylor, a domestic servant aged 20. No father's name is registered. Ellen Maud must have been curious about her father, and her mother must have told all, for when she was married in 1900 she announced in the local press that the marriage had taken place between Maurice Alfred Cattermole and Ellen Maud Taylor, "daughter of the late Mr H. B. Taylor (Farnie) and step-daughter of Mr A. Harrison." On her marriage certificate her father's name is given as Henry Broughton [sic] Taylor, Author.

After that, the summer of 1879 must have seemed good to Henry Farnie, with two enormously successful shows running at the same time, *Les Cloches de Corneville* at the Globe and *Madame Favart* at the Strand, and with another Offenbach one-acter, *The Barber of Bath*, in preparation as a Christmas curtain raiser. It must have come as a shock when he was arrested for bigamy.

After a separation of more than ten years Farnie's estranged wife Emma [Harvey] sued for divorce. Perhaps she previously had no hard evidence of his adultery and had now found out about his affair with Annie Randolph, or perhaps she had found another man and wished to be free to remarry. Whatever the reason, on 18 September 1879 she filed for divorce claiming that Farnie had "cohabited with Annie Randolph at 22 Great Marlborough Street and elsewhere and with other persons unknown at various places unknown". At this period adultery by

Annie Randolph

a wife was sufficient grounds for divorce but adultery by a husband was not, it had to be accompanied by cruelty or desertion. Emma's alleged cruelty was that "In 1868 while living at Maida Vale he [Farnie] had committed adultery with person or persons unknown and contracted a venereal disease which, while cohabiting with her on a visit to her father's at 77 Boundary Road, St John's Wood, he communicated to her." Her lawyers must have felt this a weak case and difficult to prove (if, indeed, it was true) and she withdrew the suit, to be replaced by a suit for nullity of the marriage on the grounds, it was alleged, that a Scottish court had not the power to dissolve his first marriage to Elizabeth Davies, which had been contracted in Wales under English law, and that his [former] wife was still living.[1] One may wonder how she knew that, for there is now no record of Elizabeth after the death of daughter Maud in February 1871.

If the Scottish divorce was not recognized in England then Henry Farnie would be guilty of bigamy; Emma had him arrested, and on 21 November 1879 he appeared at Marlborough Street Magistrates Court. The magistrate felt that the legal issues were too complicated for him to deal with and the matter should go for trial but, by agreement, counsel for both parties suggested that, as a suit for nullity was to be heard by the President of the Divorce Division of the High Court, the matter might be held over until his decision was known, to which the magistrate agreed.

The nullity suit was lodged a fortnight later,[2] on 6 December, merely claiming that as Farnie had married his first wife in Cardiganshire under English law, that marriage could not be dissolved by a Scottish court, and citing as precedent the case of a Mr Lolly, together with numerous cases that stemmed from it. Lolly and his wife were English and had always lived in England, but Mr Lolly wanted to trade in his wife for a newer model. In 1812, when divorce was only possible in England through a bizarre procedure of raising a private bill in the House of Lords, but was possible in Scotland, Mr Lolly with his wife and his lady-friend travelled to Edinburgh where Mr Lolly committed adultery and was duly sued by his wife for divorce, which she obtained. Lolly had acted on advice given him to the effect that as a marriage in Scotland, though contrary to the laws of England, would be recognized in England, so a divorce though contrary to the laws of England would also be so recognized. When they returned to England Mr Lolly married his lady-friend and was arrested for bigamy. Herein lies the twist! His defending barrister was none other than Henry Peter Brougham, later Baron Brougham and Vaux the Lord Chancellor to whom Henry Farnie claimed to be related. The case went against Brougham, and Mr Lolly was sentenced to seven years deportation. Brougham was incensed by the verdict and what he regarded as the severity of the sentence and carried a chip on his shoulder ever after. When he became a judge, he lost no opportunity to try to discredit the Lolly judgement by a process of reductio ad absurdum, applying it in cases to which it was hardly relevant, and his "anger" at the Lolly judgement was well known throughout the legal profession.

The Farnie (or Harvey) v. Farnie case came before the court on 22 April 1880. The essential difference in Farnie's case from that of Lolly was that Farnie was domiciled in Scotland and his wife, by moving there to be with him, accepted his domicile. Lolly had been in Edinburgh only so long as it took to commit adultery and obtain the divorce before returning home to England. Because of certain unsustainable connotations Brougham had put upon words used in the Lolly judgement in his attempts to discredit it, the President felt able to disregard Brougham's judgements and to put aside arguments based upon them and he pronounced in favour of the respondent, Farnie. The case went to the Appeal Court on 22 December that year, and to the House of Lords on 30 November 1882,[3] both upheld the decision of the lower court, one of their Lordships declaring that while he had respect for Brougham in his office as Lord Chancellor, he could feel no respect for his judgements brought about by his well-known anger at the Lolly judgement. And the ruling of the House of Lords was more liberal than might have been expected when they declared that the English courts must recognize divorce granted by the tribunal of any Christian country even though granted on grounds which would not be sufficient in English law, and this ruling became an important legal precedent. It would have been a cruel irony if the man Farnie claimed to be related to, and after whom he was named, had indirectly brought about his downfall.

So although they may never have met again, Henry Farnie and Emma (Harvey) Farnie remained man and wife until death did them part.

A year after Henry Farnie's death Emma did remarry; on 25 September 1890, to Gino Lofiego aged 38, born in Naples and described as an artist, son of Joseph Lofiego (deceased) a doctor.

Henry Farnie
New York Public Library

In the census of April 1891 they were living in Lancaster Road, Kensington, both described as 'vocalists'. Thereafter they disappear from the records.

And what of Annie Randolph? She had first appeared in a Farnie show in *The Black Prince* at the St James's Theatre when she was 23 years old, and then joined the *Blue Beard* company when it transferred to the Globe Theatre in December 1874. Since then she had spent most of her time in Farnie's shows; *Piff Paff*, then the *Blue Beard* tour followed by three Christmas shows at Manchester. In the autumn of 1877 she was with Kate Santley's company in *La Marjolaine* at the Royalty, then in February 1878 joined the cast of *Les Cloches de Corneville* at the Folly. Over this period she had progressed from one of the chorus to one of the named characters given to senior members of the chorus, then to playing small roles like Gertrude in *Cloches*. She was cast as Joli-Coeur in *Madame Favart* though that is a one scene four-line part, but on 8 September 1879 she took over the part of Ruth in the curtain raiser, *Ruth's Romance*, a three-hander in which Ruth is on all the time. Would they have known what was coming ten days before the divorce was filed? Was this compensation? Or was she beginning to display real acting talent?

If she was upset at discovering that her beau already had a wife, possibly two for all that she then knew, and at her being cited as co-respondent, she did not immediately rush away. The divorce suit had, of course, been withdrawn at the end of November and she had no further part in the bigamy or nullity proceedings, but the damage had already been done. She disappeared from the cast of *Madame Favart* at the beginning of April 1880 although she continued in *Ruth's Romance* until 5 June.

Then she vanishes until the census of April 1881 which records her as an actress living in lodgings in Liverpool. Henderson still owned the Prince of Wales's Theatre, Liverpool which was being managed by his friend Frank Emery, and it is tempting to suppose that he had come to the rescue and found a job for Annie Randolph away from the limelight, but no record of her has been found in the theatre material which survives at the Liverpool Record Office, although this is incomplete. She is next heard of four months later when on 17 August 1881 she sailed from Liverpool for New York with the Hanlon-Lees Company on S.S. Helvetia, Farnie waving them off from the quay-side. The Hanlon brothers were acrobats who developed an early form of knock-about comedy; now with an entertainment based on a play, *Le Voyage en Suisse*, embellished with their gymnastics, juggling, trick scenery and other effects, they were off to stun New Yorkers with their prowess. They opened on 12 September at the Park Theatre, Annie Randolph was cast as "the village beauty" and reported to have little to do but stand around looking beautiful, which she did very well. She left the company during the run and joined the Comley-Barton Opera Company in *Olivette* at the Fifth Avenue Theatre opening on 10 October and closing 29 October. There is no further record of her until February 1882 when she was reported to have been very ill, and she left New York to return to England on S.S. Auzina on 15 February; Shiel Barry happened to be a fellow passenger.[4] For some months during 1883 she failed to collect mail which had been addressed to her at The Era mailbox, a facility provided by The Era for members of the profession, and nothing more is known of her.

- - - - -

Despite Farnie's marital problems, nothing stopped the flow of new shows and in the year between the bigamy charge and the appeal court hearing, and while *Les Cloches de Corneville* ran on at the Globe and *Madame Favart* at the Strand, Farnie provided five principal pieces and a curtain raiser. When *Cloches* did close, it was replaced by *The Naval Cadets*, an adaptation of *Der Seekadett* with music by Richard Genée which opened at the Globe on 27 March 1880. In spite of a star-studded cast led by Violet Cameron, Selina Dolaro and Harry Paulton, it was not popular with the public and came off on 14 May when *Les*

Cloches de Corneville was hastily brought back. But nor was *The Naval Cadets* a complete failure, it won critical acclaim with predictions of a long run, the Daily News opining "That the confidence shown [by the management] in its attractiveness was not misplaced was made evident upon the production of *The Naval Cadets* . . . and it would seem probable from the enthusiastic reception accorded . . . that it is destined to prove of more than curious interest, if not indeed to rival the long career of success of the far-famed *Cloches de Corneville*." It had faced serious competition with a new production of *La Fille de Madame Angot* at Drury Lane, the very successful *H.M.S. Pinafore* and then its replacement *Pirates of Penzance* at the Opera Comique, and shortly after with Farnie's *La Fille du Tambour-Major* at the Alhambra. So it went into the locker to be brought out in emergencies and Emily Soldene, who was about to set out on a tour with *Carmen* and *Les Cloches de Corneville*, added it to her repertoire. *Cloches*, gaining a second wind, ran on until the end of June at the Globe and then transferred to the Olympic theatre where it continued until mid-August. *The Naval Cadets* saw the last appearance in London of Selina Dolaro; she emmigrated to America that autumn.

Emily Soldene's and Farnie's paths would not cross again. She took to touring the provinces and another major tour abroad and kept in her repertoire what had been for her the most successful of his shows notably *Genevieve* and *Madame Angot*, but she was not again associated with him in any new production.

Farnie had also done an adaptation of Offenbach's *La Fille du tambour-major* for Charles Morton which kept its French title and opened at the Alhambra on 19 April 1880, three weeks after *The Naval Cadets* had been put on at the Globe. *La Fille du Tambour-Major* was another big success and ran through the year closing on 18 December. Morton was not again associated with Farnie on any new shows. The Alhambra was a limited company and Morton may not have been given absolute discretion in the choice of shows. When he left the Alhambra he took the Connaught for a while and then moved to the Avenue as

Acting Manager for Mons Marius where they opened with a revival of *Madame Favart*.

Morton had twice been insolvent in his lifetime; he had lost money on the Canterbury and Oxford halls and on Woolwich Gardens and had to compound with his creditors in 1867 and in 1869. The Morton-Soldene company lost £8,000 on their 1874-75 American tour[5] and Morton probably carried most of the risk. He was made bankrupt in 1875 and was not discharged until 1880 when he paid 6d in the pound to his creditors. He was then aged 61, and with an eye on the future, he adopted a more cautious attitude and preferred trusted revivals to new ventures.

Farnie's next piece, perhaps in collaboration with Robert Reece, was a surprise – a straight comedy called *The Guv'nor* which opened at the Vaudeville on 23 June 1880. Perhaps to detract from his departure from musical work he used the nom de plume E. G. Lankester. Most papers realized that it was an assumed name and speculated as to whom it might be; one or two were fooled, welcomed the new young author and offered much paternal advice. Later some 'expert' decided that it was Robert Reece and many reference books now list E. G. Lankester as his alter ego, but Farnie owned the copyright when he died and there can be little doubt that it was his or a joint effort.

Another adaptation from the French was *Olivette* from *Les Noces d'Olivette* with libretto by MM. Chivot and Duru and music by Edmond Audran. Audran had achieved recognition in the French provinces, particularly Marseilles, where *Les Noces d'Olivette* had been popular, but it had not done well in Paris. Farnie believed that he could do better with it in London and it opened at Mrs Swanborough's Strand Theatre on 18 September and proved Farnie right. Florence St John, Violet Cameron and Mons. Marius again headed the cast and it became another huge hit achieving 466 performances, excluding provincial tours, closing on 3 February 1882, and along with *Les Cloches de Corneville* and *Madame Favart* became Farnie's most enduring success having innumerable professional revivals and becoming the darlings of amateur societies through the Edwardian period and between the wars.

Marius did not do any more new Farnie shows, he went into management himself, but he did put on Farnie revivals. His marriage to Florence didn't last; although they seemed well suited and happy together, they were both temperamental and domestic squabbles turned into big bust-ups. Florence would later appear in a few more of Farnie's productions.

1880 was the year when five new adaptations appeared in different London theatres in just over seven months, and the final production of the year was for Alex Henderson at The Globe. *Les Mousquetaires [au couvent]* was adapted from the French and, again, Farnie kept the French title. Music was by Louis Varney and it had a respectable three-month run.

During August the paper 'Truth' had printed the following:

"'Albery is a rope-maker, Burnand is the editor of Punch, Byron acts, Grundy is a barrister, Taylor was a Government pensioner, W. G. Wills a painter, and H. B. Farnie, if the Autolycus of the London stage can be correctly described as a dramatist, is a stage-manager. With the exception of Robert Reece, Paul

Merritt and myself, there are very few whose sole profession is that of dramatic author.' So says Mr Henry Pettitt ..."

Autolycus was the "snapper-up of unconsidered trifles" in Shakespeare's *Winters Tale*. Farnie did, indeed, snap up unconsidered trifles and made good use of them. Some rather poor ones were turned to better account in his hands. But there was another Autolycus in classical mythology, who inherited his father Hermes's taking ways but who also possessed skill with the lyre and "melody or gracious song".

There are a number of songs for which Farnie is credited with writing the music. As a young man in Fife he had composed the melody for a song, *Yon Trembling Arch*, which had been written by the local doctor in St Andrews, R. Maidstone Smith, with harmonies added by Edward Salter. Burnand called him "composer and author" attributing to this his relations with music publishers and influence over musical artistes. A list of songs for which Farnie is credited with the music or just the melody is given in Appendix 3.

Farnie would have visited St Andrews quite frequently for although he had a singular lack of success with his own relationships, he was very fond of his family, particularly his younger unmarried sister Isabella. He paid for the education of his nephews and nieces, and one of his nephews, David J. Farnie, who later emmigrated to America, recalled that as a small boy, his uncle, "youthful in heart, loved to play and mingle with young people. A bachelor [sic] of jovial disposition, he was known for his wit and as a partner much sought after by fellow golfers."

* * *

DAYS WITH CELEBRITIES. (52).

H. B. FARNIE.

Chapter Eight

THE AVENUE

With Emily Soldene and Charles Morton gone it left, as Farnie's established outlets, Henderson, and Ada Swanborough at the Strand who, abandoning her dedication to burlesque, arranged with Henderson to present seasons of opera of whatever hue; which left Farnie and Henderson working closely together. Henderson had decided that he needed a theatre of his own; he had found a site at Panton Street near the Haymarket and building work commenced. Meanwhile their next show, *La Boulangere*, opened at the Globe on 16 April 1881. Farnie seems to have had a private joke over the advertising of some of the shows in which he retained the French title or something close to it. With the 'New and Original' controversy in mind (and Farnie had never been the worst offender) *La Boulangere* was advertised as a "New and Original opera comique by Offenbach . . . under the direction of Mr H. B. Farnie". The same pattern was followed in several other shows – new and original by either the composer or French librettists, occasionally naming himself as adaptor, more usually simply as director.

La Boulangere based on Meilhac and Halévy's *La Boulangère a des écus* was originally announced as *Margot*, the name of the heroine, but it was changed at the last moment when it was found that *Margot* had been the title of a play produced at Bradford eighteen months earlier. Once more there were good reviews predicting a long run and *La Boulangere* might indeed have run on, but Alex Henderson had a dispute with the lessees of the theatre and announced on 9 July that he was withdrawing his company. Despite newspaper predictions that it would all come out in court, and despite the Globe being left crippled so that it had to close early for the summer, nothing more was heard of the cause of the problem. When the Globe reopened in September, it was with yet another revival of *Les Cloches de Corneville*, and despite a new management and new cast, Shiel Barrie was still there playing the old miser, Gaspard.

At the Strand, when *Olivette* finally closed on 3 February 1882 after 467 performances it was replaced by Farnie's adaptation of *Manola*, from *La Jour et la nuit* with libretto by Albert Vanloo and Eugène Leterrier and music by Charles Lecocq. For New York audiences it had an additional title *Manola, or, Blond and Brunette* when it opened at the Fifth Avenue Theatre on 6 February 1882, five days before its London opening. Playing a supporting role – Tessa, a maid – was Maud Branscombe, one of the first professional beauties. Unprepossessing in person, she was incredibly photogenic and there was scarcely a photographer's either side of the Atlantic which did not display her portrait in the window. She wanted to be taken seriously as an actress and persevered, and although she never became a star, she managed to stay in the second rank for a respectable career of almost twenty years.

Henderson's new theatre was larger than those he had previously used, having 1,055 seats, and it was named the Royal Comedy. It opened in the same week as the Savoy and inevitably they became symbols of the old style opera comique and Gilbert and Sullivan's new and very English comic opera.

The Comedy opened on 15 October 1881 with *The Mascotte*, adapted from Chivot and Duru's *La Mascotte* with music by Audran.[1] It had a delightful story of Bettina, an unsophisticated country girl who possessed the magical power of bringing good luck to whoever 'owned' her. The power would, however, be lost if she married the man she loved or loved the man she married. She is in love with Pippo, a shepherd, but she is taken to the court in the hope of restoring the fortunes of the impecunious Duke Laurent XVII and they try to keep Pippo away. Bettina was played by Violet Cameron in what must have been the best role of her career, enabling her to show off her talents as the country girl in the first act, an aspiring lady of the court in the second, and as a vivandiere in the last. The low comedy part of Duke Laurent was played by Lionel Brough who kept the audience in fits of laughter all the time he was on stage. And they were supported by a strong cast including Mons. Gaillard as Pippo the Shepherd, and Henry Bracy as the visiting Prince Fritellini.

One hit number from the show was a love duet between Bettina and Pippo in which each compares the other to the most beautiful thing they know, Bettina to the sound of her turkeys which she imitates, "glou, glou", and Pippo to his sheep, "baa, baa". Popular numbers from shows were published as sheet music and Farnie had to write special words for *Glou,Glou* for drawing-room use, to make it capable of being sung as a solo, and to make the words more meaningful when taken out of context.

By-the-by, for two nights, 21 and 22 December 1881, *The Mascotte* was a party to an experiment in broadcasting through the telephone. The United Telephone Company fixed "transmitters" above the stage of the Comedy Theatre and carried their cables to the Bristol Hotel, Burlington Gardens where they set out a large number of telephones in a room for their guests of M.P.s, peers, and other notables of influence, for them to listen to the performance. But the phonograph was already a reality, the gramophone a few years away, and other developments being talked about, and the idea of using the telephone in this way never caught on.

The Mascotte was extremely popular and could have run on and on, but with excessively good planning the next show was already decided on, an adaptation by Farnie and Reece of *Boccaccio* by F. Zell and Richard Genée with music by Franz von

Suppé, and Henderson had entered into a contract with Suppé. *The Mascotte* closed on 15 April and transferred to the Strand a month later, with considerable changes of cast as Violet Cameron and Lionel Brough, together with several of the minor characters, were needed for the new show. *The Mascotte* ran until 29 July (271 performances) when the Strand had to be closed for extensive alterations to bring it up to current safety standards, but it was revived frequently in the next few years. Two touring companies had been formed under the management of Kate Santley, who played the part of Bettina with the leading company.

During the run of *The Mascotte* there was added to the bill as an after-piece a one-act comedy by Farnie called *Paradise Villa* which appeared under the name Edward Sylvester. He seems to have hidden behind a pseudonym or anonymity whenever he wrote something different from his usual output, as he had done with *The Guv'nor* under the pseudonym E. K. Lankester, and *The Main Chance* which was at first produced anonymously.

There still seems to have been time for leisure. The young lady who Henderson had taken up with, rumours of which had brought Lydia Thompson hurrying back from America, was named Elfrida Nunn, and in the census taken in April 1881 Henderson had her installed on his steam yacht, the Lively,[2] where she is listed as a stewardess! In September 1881 the Era reported that Farnie had bought Henderson's yacht and "accompanied by a distinguished number of visitors" intended taking an extended cruise around the Channel Islands. A paper remarked, in 1883, that Farnie possessed a steam yacht but there are, unfortunately, no further reports of it or its cruises.

Back in harness, Farnie and Reece stuck fairly closely to Zell and Genée's *Boccaccio*, but that in turn had borne only a passing resemblance to Giovanni Boccaccio's 'The Decameron'. The music was by Franz von Suppé and much of it had been incorporated into other London shows, but that may actually have been a help rather than as a hindrance if it made people familiar with the music. It opened on 22 April 1882, had a good six-month run, and was revived three years later.

A great deal of careful planning had gone into their next show which was to be *Rip van Winkle*. First, Farnie would arrange to collaborate with the French librettists Ludovic Meilhac and Philippe Gille with the idea of creating both an English and a French version. Why? The French had for some time complained of the English theatre's free use of 'their' scripts due to the freedom from copyright, perhaps this was a way of returning something if only goodwill and Farnie did, after all, live in Paris. The music would be by Robert Planquette. Secondly, there was really only one person to take the role of Rip and that was Fred Leslie. Leslie, real name Frederick Hobson,

Fred Leslie as Rip van Winkle

began acting as an amateur, turning professional early in 1878 when he was hired by Kate Santley, then manageress of the Royalty Theatre, to play old Colonel Hardy in *Paul Pry*, although he was just 22 years old. A month later when she put on *La Belle Helène*, Leslie was given the part of the aged Agamemnon. He was befriended by comedian Lal Brough who became his mentor and who suggested to him that he changed the name Fred Lewis, which he had first adopted, to Fred Leslie. His development as an actor earned him the respect of his peers and of managements although he was not at this time so well regarded by critics and public. It was his ability to play both young and old characters with equal facility that made Henderson and Farnie feel that he was just right for Rip van Winkle.

Macqueen-Pope tells a story of how Fred Leslie was spending a few days at an hotel at Clacton between engagements when Farnie caught up with him sitting in the sun after breakfast, and casually approaching him enquired whether he was not an actor. Leslie agreed that he was and Farnie said "what a coincidence" for he, too, was of the same profession and, continuing, told him of a wonderful new show that would make an ideal vehicle for him. Leslie was persuaded and agreed to sign a contract there and then, and as soon as it was signed, Farnie rushed off to a post office to send a telegram to Henderson which read simply "I've got him!" [3]

Rip van Winkle broadly followed the plan of Washington Irving's story, but with certain major differences notably in the character of Rip's wife, changed from the irritable woman who lost patience with the incorrigible Rip and threw him out, to a faithful and tolerant partner who no toper could complain of, a change made to suit Violet Cameron who played Gretchen, Rip's wife in Act 1 and his grown-up daughter in Act 3. W. S. Penley played Derrick, and Lionel Brough, Nick Vedder. Two other changes were in bringing a survey party of British soldiers into the first act and the introduction of an election scene into the third, both, probably, to highlight the change from monarchy and colony to a republic. It opened on 14 October 1882 at the Comedy to great acclaim. Critics were astonished at Fred Leslie's performance not believing that anyone who sang could also possess such acting skills, and he shot to stardom. The following year when his contract ran out he wanted star pay, asking £60 a week instead of the £25 he had been receiving. The management would not agree; Lal Brough tried to arbitrate telling Leslie to accept fame as part of the reward, but Leslie's riposte was that it showed Brough to be a poor businessman. The result was that Leslie left the cast on 14 July 1883. His role was taken masterfully by J. A. Arnold but audiences slumped without Leslie and the show closed on 27 October after 328 performances.

It opened on Broadway at the Standard Theatre under Richard D'Oyly Carte's management on 23 November 1882, just five weeks after its London opening. It was revived in London the year after it had closed, on 6 September 1884 when Henderson managed to get Fred Leslie back, and ran for two months closing on 13 November. The French version was late in getting produced and when it did it was not in Paris, but at the Theater an der Wein, Vienna on 22 December 1883 with the title *Rip Rip*. Planquette had, by this time, learned much of the musical tastes of audiences on both sides of the Channel and had worked with Meilhac and Gille in gallicizing it including the addition of couplets; names and locations were changed, but it was not a success. After further revisions by the French librettists and Planquette, it opened as *Rip* at the Théâtre des Folies Dramatique on 11 November 1884, this time with better, but not brilliant, results. The manager blamed its comparative failure on late delivery of the script by the librettists, sued, and was awarded a swingeing £800 damages against Philippe Gille and Farnie by a French court. *Rip* grew on French audiences becoming one of the staples of comic opera and it would enjoy as long a career in France as *Les Cloches* would enjoy in England.

The original run of *Rip van Winkle* was followed at the Comedy by one of Farnie's best. *Falka*, from *Le droit d'aînesse*, with libretto by Eugène Letterier and Albert Vanloo and music by Chassaigne, kept the theatre filled from 29 October 1883 to 26 February 1884, 158 performances. Violet Cameron played Falka, Harry Paulton was Kolbach, the Military Governor and Falka's uncle, W. S. Penley was Lay-Brother Pelican of the convent where Falka was looked after, and they were supported by Louis Kelleher and Miss (Mathilde) Wadman. Miss Wadman, who had previously been in *La Boulangere* and a revival of *Madame Favart*, headed the eight-month tour of *Falka* which followed. It became a big hit throughout the English speaking world; in England it toured extensively in the provinces and remained popular for many years to come.

The Strand Theatre, apart from measures to meet current safety standards, had undergone a complete refurbishment and The Times reported that "From being the smallest, dingiest and most uncomfortable theatre in London" it was now "one of the brightest prettiest and most commodious". With Mrs Swanborough still at the helm, it reopened on 18 November 1882 with the classic play *Paul Pry* and "a new musical comedy" by Farnie and H. J. Byron entitled *Frolique*. Farnie's only collaboration with Byron was a great disappointment, being a réchauffé of Planché's *The Follies of a Night*, the story of a gentleman who flirts outrageously at a masked ball with a lady who he discovers to be his own wife. The music was taken from various composers in the manner of Farnie's pastiche pieces but far less successfully. It did its turn as a Christmas piece but closed on 17 January.

With the sequence of successful shows showing no sign of stopping these were good times for Farnie and Henderson. A reporter taking a look around Paris came across "H. B. Farnie sitting outside his favourite café, surrounded by French composers who whistle him their new operas."

A few months after Henderson's new Comedy Theatre had opened London gained another new theatre, the Avenue on the corner of Northumberland Avenue next to Charing Cross station. A year on, the lease was acquired by George Wood who sub-let it to Henderson. Although there was no public announcement his intention seems to have been to use the Comedy for opera comique and the Avenue for opera bouffe, or burlesque opera as they began to be called.

When Henderson assembled his Avenue company his prize was in signing comedian Arthur Roberts. Roberts had lived a double life for some years working in a solicitor's office by day and in music halls by night and managing to make each believe he worked solely for them, and he kept that up for several years before devoting himself entirely to the entertainment business. He made a name for himself in music halls although gaining a reputation for rather blue material and a move to theatre was suggested to him. He did two pantomimes at Drury Lane before working in the provinces and apart from those two pantomimes the engagement for the Avenue would be his London theatre debut. He was a very funny man indeed but egocentric and totally undisciplined. He would never stick to a script and, while staying with the story, he would write his own lines or extemporize, leaving fellow actors uncertain of their cues. The next six years at the Avenue would establish Roberts as the leading low comedian in the profession but would destroy Farnie's reputation.

The first show was *La Vie* from Offenbach's *La Vie parisienne* and the reviews were generally good although some critics compared Roberts unfavourably to Lal Brough, the other low comedian, considering his style that of variety and his material rather vulgar. Henderson avoided any display of dissent from pit or gallery by having an invited audience on the first night. After a try-out in Brighton it opened at the Avenue on 3 October 1883 and with the usual sumptuous sets and costumes it had a reasonable run closing on 26 January 1884.

When *La Vie* was withdrawn from The Avenue it was replaced with *Nell Gwynne*. Farnie was ill in December, and stayed in Paris, and for this reason it had been reported that the libretto would be done by Dion Boucicault, his first attempt at opera bouffe. But perhaps as Farnie already had the libretto from the *Nell Gwynne* that he had done with Alfred Cellier and which had been produced in Manchester in 1876, he used that with some revision and new songs for Robert Planquette to set to music. It opened on 7 February 1884 and enjoyed a three-month run. Florence St John played Nell with Guilia Warwick as Jessamine, Michael Dwyer and Lyn Cadwaladr were Buckingham and Rochester with Lionel Brough and Arthur Roberts in the comedy parts. This, like *Rip van Winkle*, was supposed to have been a collaborative venture with French librettists, this time MM. Ordonneau and Emile André, and to have opened simultaneously in Paris and London, but the French version was somehow delayed. The three librettists didn't work together, perhaps because Farnie had already done the libretto, so when Farnie handed it to the Frenchmen they could, and did, do to it what he had for some years been doing to theirs! With the title *Princess Columbine*, it opened at the Nouveautés on 7 December 1886 and the Paris correspondent of The Era reported "She is an old friend of yours this *Princess Columbine*, for you have made her acquaintance three years ago at the Avenue.

Whether you should be able to recognize *Nell Gwynne* in her French toggery, however, is beyond my power to say. I am told the adaptation of Mr Farnie's version has been carried out by MM. Ordonneau and André with heathenish irreverence, but upon the justice of this infamous charge must also humbly admit my inability to judge. A brief description of the Nouveautés piece will doubtless enable you to decide." In fact it was readily recognisable, the plot and most of the incidents being the same but in her "French toggery" with new names for the characters and with the obligatory couplets added to the score.

The other half of the Manchester *Nell Gwynne* fared much better. Cellier's music wedded to an entirely different story with libretto by B. C. Stephenson and with the title *Dorothy* opened at the Gaiety on 25 September1886 and, with a transfer to the Prince of Wales's Theatre, achieved a run of 931 performances easily breaking the record for a musical show which, until then, had been held by *Les Cloches de Corneville*.

London gained yet another new theatre that spring located on the north side of Leicester Square, and the long-running guessing games as to its name, which had included the Phoenix and the Pandora, ended when it was prosaically called the Empire. Henderson took it and opened with another version of *Chilperic*. It was the only collaboration between Farnie and Henry Hersée.[4] The core play was the same as Farnie's version at the Alhambra nine years before now brought up to date, but it was even more of a spectacular with the eccentric comedian Mons. Paulus, the Freres Tacchi, that season's rage of Paris, three ballets of which the most spectacular was the "'Electric Ballet of 50 Amazons' – invented by Trouvé of Paris – the first time where three electric lamps are carried and manipulated by [each] person, with the most startling and gorgeous effect". Electricity was just a novelty in a new theatre still lighted by gas! Farnie was responsible for the staging and direction and the Era extolled, "no praise can be too great for Mr H. B. Farnie who has devoted all his skill and experience to the production of the piece ...". "Messrs Farnie and Hersée were called to the footlights and greeted with hearty applause." One of the few occasions when he did respond to a curtain call, perhaps he'd been taken in hand by Henderson, the opening of a new theatre was, after all, an important occasion. The theatre opened on 17 April 1884 and *Chilperic* ran for three months closing on 25 July.

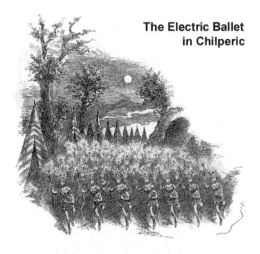

The Electric Ballet in Chilperic

At the Comedy *The Grand Mogul* opened on 17 November 1884. It was a version of Chivot and Duru's *Le Grand Mogol* with music by Audran. Florence St John and Arthur Roberts headed the cast, and as Djemma, an English girl travelling in India in the guise of a snake-charmer, Florence St John had a scene with snakes draped about her neck which took liberties she would not have allowed anyone else. Some of the critics, and audience, found this scene disgusting and the show didn't have a long run. Farnie may have got the idea from the New York production with the title *The Snake Charmer* which had opened at the Bijou Opera House on 29 October 1881 when Lilian Russell who had played D'jemma [sic] had been similarly draped.[5] After *The Grand Mogul* closed, Henderson kept the Comedy Theatre running with a series of short revivals including *The Mascotte*, *Nemesis* and *Boccaccio*.

In 1882 Henderson had had a stroke though not serious enough to stop him working. In 1885 he had another[6] and he evidently decided to cut back to one theatre and chose the more intimate and probably more profitable Avenue. In June 1885 he transferred the lease of the Comedy to Violet Melnotte.

On 1 February 1886 Alex Henderson died. He had had the strokes and had been in poor health but was not suffering from any condition that would cause concern. He set off alone for a holiday in the south of France and stepping off the gangway onto the quay at Calais he fell. He was shaken but seemingly uninjured and he continued his journey to Cannes[7]. He died in his hotel room on the morning of Monday 1 February. His wife, Lydia Thompson, was in America and there was no-one to bring his body home. There was no inquest or autopsy and no cause of death is recorded, and he was buried in an unmarked plot in a local cemetery.

By Christmas 1885 it had been three-and-a-half years since Farnie had collaborated with Reece. *Rip van Winkle* he had done with the Frenchmen and *Frolique* with H. J. Byron, while for *Nell Gwynne* he had his old libretto from Manchester. But *La Vie*, *Falka* and *The Grand Mogul* he had ostensibly done on his own. William Morton, Charles Morton's brother and biographer says that Alfred Murray, a relatively new playwright whose first piece had appeared in 1881, was known as Farnie's Ghost.[8] Farnie would later collaborate on two shows with Murray and it may well be that an informal partnership had begun. But the collaboration with Reece, who in the interim had produced some eleven pieces of his own, was resumed for the Christmas offering at the Avenue. Called *Kenilworth* it was described as a 'new fairy burlesque extravaganza' and was constructed in the manner of his pastiche pieces with music gathered from a goodly selection of composers and put together by musical director Michael Connelly. Based on Sir Walter Scott's novel the cast was headed by Violet Cameron as Dudley, Earl of Leicester, Laura Linden as Amy Robsart, Phyllis Broughton as Sir Walter Raleigh and her sister Emma Broughton as the Earl of Essex, Arthur Roberts as the villainous Sir Richard Varney, Mr J. J. Dallas as Queen Elizabeth, helped by E. J. Lonnen and Sam Wilkinson with a large supporting cast and chorus.

Lurline which followed was more of the same, a parody of the Lorelei legend of the siren of the Rhine, and of Vincent Wallace's opera *Lurline*. Reece had, surprisingly, laced the dialogue with old-fashioned puns which the audience seemed to enjoy, and the critics felt it would do well if it could be compressed – it had run for three-and-a-half hours. It had a reasonable run closing on 3 July 1886.

The next show was for Violet Cameron. Soon after *Falka* closed back in February 1884, one or two papers reported that she was leaving Henderson's company due to a disagreement with his manager, Major Lane (at the Comedy), and that she had received an offer from John Hollingshead of a place at the Gaiety. She didn't work any more that year and in September, to everyone's surprise, she married a Moroccan tea merchant named David de Bensaude. Peace restored with Alex Henderson, she was due to play Bengaline in *The Grand Mogul* but in November it was announced that she was suffering from congestion of the lungs and had been advised by her doctor to take a cruise while her place in *The Grand Mogul* would be taken by Berthe Latour. She sailed on 19 November for Gibralter and Tangier on what some papers called her honeymoon but she was back, fully recovered, in time for Christmas and was the belle of the ball which accompanied the traditional Twelfth Night Cake celebration at Drury Lane. During her time away through absence, marriage or illness, she had developed the idea of having her own light opera company but discovered that her husband, far from being a wealthy merchant, was bankrupt. Some time before, Violet had been befriended by Hugh Cecil Lowther, Earl of Lonsdale who now offered to manage and finance her company for a summer tour and an autumn trip to New York. Farnie and Reece's contribution was to write *The Commodore*, a revised version of *The Creole*, which was performed for Violet Cameron's benefit by the Avenue company at a matinee on 10 May 1886. She put on two more matinees at the Avenue and one at Crystal Palace as she began to gather her own 'Violet Cameron Light Opera Company', and then launched the summer tour presenting both *The Commodore* and *Kenilworth*.

It turned into the scandal of the decade when husband David de Bensaude dogged their footsteps, frequently getting into arguments with Lowther which, on one occasion ended in fisticuffs and with Lowther being fined by Newcastle magistrates for assault. De Bensaude followed them to New York in the autumn and the somewhat puritanical New Yorkers resented, as they saw it, the scandal being used for publicity and the idea that that sort of publicity would influence them. *The Commodore* and *Kenilworth* each played for three weeks at the Casino Theatre but were poorly attended. Violet Cameron and Lowther were turned out of hotels, vilified by the press, and secretively slunk back to England. Queen Victoria let it be known that she could do without Lowther for a while and he was persuaded to go on an exploration of the Canadian arctic, a challenge his sporting soul could not refuse.[9] Violet Cameron, after bearing him two daughters,[10] returned to the theatre to the delight of audiences, and the sorry story of the Violet Cameron Light Opera Company was never mentioned.

Meanwhile in England, Farnie's next piece entitled *Indiana* had a try-out in Manchester before opening at the Avenue on 11 October 1886. The press, which had been treating the Avenue shows as Variety, said little of the librettos and rarely mentioned Farnie at all, now generally acknowledged that this was one of his better efforts and had a good enough story to support an opera comique. But although called opera comique, that is not what the audiences wanted, and with Roberts dominating the show they inevitably became bouffe or 'burlesque opera'. Roberts could, of course, fill the theatre and bring in the money and maybe by this time Farnie was ready to settle for that. *Indiana* had been based on "an old French vaudeville" with music by Audran. This time Farnie's French counterparts discarded the libretto altogether, took Audran's music and put to it an entirely new piece.

Robinson Crusoe, Farnie's second version but this time done in collaboration with Robert Reece, was unashamedly a vehicle for Arthur Roberts. It had been suggested that it might be called Arthur Roberts-on Crusoe, but the management and authors pulled back at the last moment. Phyllis Broughton, who was fast

111

Robinson Crusoe

Phyllis Broughton as Polly Hopkins, Arthur Roberts
as Crusoe, and Charles Sutton as Friday

becoming the only leading lady in London who was prepared to play opposite Roberts, played Crusoe's beloved Polly Hopkins. It opened on 23 December and ran until 16 April, 120 performances.

Farnie's first formal collaboration with Alfred Murray was *Glamour*, a revised version of *Piff Paff*, which opened in Edinburgh on 30 August 1886 and went on a ten-week tour around the number one circuit. It was later adopted by other touring companies but never went to the West End.

The last Farnie show during Arthur Roberts stay at the Avenue, and done in partnership with Robert Planquette, was *The Old Guard*. It was a version of Planquette's *Les Voltigeurs de la 32ieme* with Planquette assisting in adapting it to English tastes. It had a try-out in Birmingham and opened at the Avenue on 26 October

Arthur Roberts in The Old Guard

1887 to fairly good reviews. It became, like its predecessors, a vehicle for Roberts with The Era commenting "Whether or not Mr Roberts's laughter-raising expedients are those of legitimate art it boots not to enquire." The Times later added that "Comic opera, as understood at the Avenue Theatre, has become little more than a medium for the humorous extravagances of Mr Arthur Roberts."

Phyllis Broughton

Fortunately some discerning folk remembered the pre-Avenue days and still had faith in Henry Farnie, and Carl Rosa commissioned him to prepare a comic opera based on Planquette's *Surcouf,* but Rosa had some particular ideas about the story. It had been revealed that Farnie's illness back in the winter of 1883-84 when he was preparing *Nell Gwynne* was due to diabetes and during 1888 he became very ill. So in early June Carl Rosa went to Paris to meet Farnie and Planquette and discuss the project. *Surcouf* awkwardly had a French hero and an English villain[11] and Carl Rosa suggested remodelling it on the lines of Fenimore Cooper's novel 'The Pilot' and its hero Paul Jones. Farnie made the hero an English Paul Jones and the villains, Spaniards. He did a good job following Carl Rosa's suggestions and had the help of Robert Planquette who had learned by now how to suit English tastes and didn't mind rewriting much of the score of *Surcouf* to please les anglais and to fit in with Farnie's story. As *Paul Jones* it was tried out at Bolton in December, then went to Liverpool where Farnie and Planquette personally superintended performances while they worked on alterations. It had a lot of new musical numbers in Bolton and a good many more by the time it reached the West End where it opened at the Prince of Wales's Theatre on 12 January 1889. The title role was taken by an American actress, Agnes Huntingdon, with a tall commanding figure and rich contralto voice. The press was by now very anti-Farnie speaking of the libretto as neither better nor worse than had been provided at the Avenue for some years. But the public formed its own opinion and *Paul Jones* ran for a year, closing on 15 January 1890 after 370 performances. It was frequently revived and was broadcast by the BBC in February 1927.

Agnes Huntingdon
as Paul Jones

In the spring of 1889, soon after the opening of *Paul Jones*, it was reported that Farnie was seriously ill in Paris. Early in the century a test for excess sugar in the urine had been developed to diagnose diabetes but no therapy was available, although during the Franco-Prussian war it had been observed that a restricted diet benefited diabetic patients.

Farnie did one more show in collaboration with Alfred Murray based on a story published in Blackwood's Magazine in 1853 called The Duke's Dilemma, and with music by Tito Mattei, his only full-length comic opera. It was originally called *The Grand Duke* but the title was claimed by the manager of Her Majesty's Theatre, Dundee, for an extravaganza produced there three years before, and it was changed at the last moment to *Prima Donna*. It was produced posthumously on 16 October but it was uninspired, most memorable for having in the cast a young Albert Chevalier who would later become famous in the music halls. *Prima Donna* ran for just two months.

Although Farnie was seriously ill, his condition had not been a cause for alarm, but he died suddenly at Rue Malakoff, Paris on Sunday 21 September 1889 aged 53. His body was taken back to his native Fife and he was buried in the kirkyard of St Andrew's Cathedral where a Celtic cross marks a family grave. He left his entire estate, valued at upwards of £23,000,[12] to his younger sister Isabella. Obituaries were generally matter-of-fact, just one or two papers writing unkindly of him. The Stage, partly quoting from Hamlet, concluded its obituary, "Most probably his like will not be seen again; the best interests of the stage compel the admission that it can advantageously be spared."

* * *

Chapter Nine

FINALE

Apart from *La Prima Donna* which was already in rehearsal at the time of Farnie's death, a few other works were produced posthumously or are worthy of note. He had begun work, in collaboration with Max Pemberton and W. Lestocq, on a comic opera called *The Brazilian*, an adaptation of Chassaigne's *La Brazilienne*. He had adapted the plot and completed the construction and detailed synopsis before his death, which was probably all he was intended to do,[1] Pemberton and Lestocq completing the dialogue and lyrics. Farnie's name appears with the others on the programme when it received a performance for copyright purposes at the Theatre Royal, Newcastle on 19 April 1890. It was intended for the American market and opened at the Casino, New York on 2 June after further revision by Edgar Smith.

An adaptation of *La Cantinière*, music by Planquette and with the title *Nectarine* was copyrighted and published by Joseph Williams; there is no record of a professional production. A collaboration between Farnie and Henry Hersée, it is curious in that the libretto is credited to Farnie but the lyrics to Hersée, the reverse of what would be expected.

S. J. Adair Fitz-Gerald, who after ten years as an actor became the leading writer for The Era, was no lover of Farnie but said of him that "of the many hundreds of operettas of Offenbach, two-thirds at least, were adapted by Farnie". Offenbach actually wrote about one hundred rather than "many" hundreds, but that still points to upwards of 60 operettas said to be adapted by Farnie of which just sixteen have been noted. A few Offenbach operettas were staged at the Gaiety and at Crystal Palace unattributed, others were published as "for drawing-room or stage" and may have stayed in the drawing-room.

Farnie wrote one piece called *V. V.* for what seems to have been a semi-professional try-out presented by Mr Parry Cole, who also wrote the music, on 27 and 28 May 1887 at Kilburn Town Hall. The name suggests a derivation from Offenbach's *Vert-Vert*, but that is guesswork! Farnie is also credited with a piece, *The Rehearsal*, which opened at Koster and Bial's Concert Hall, New York on 13 February 1893. [2]

- - - - -

After Farnie's death, the hostility of the press lasted awhile which in a perverse way was a compliment to him, for if his shows had not remained popular and been constantly revived he would scarcely have needed a mention. There were some who never liked him and who would always seek to belittle him,[3] but after a time most papers mellowed and began to look back with nostalgia. By 1899 a paper reviewing a light musical piece, *The Coquette*, said in terms of approbation that it "recalled Farnie of 20 years ago", and this was considered sufficiently appealing for the theatre to use the quotation in its advertising.

And then he was forgotten.

Farnie recalled in an interview that when he came to London "all the musical pieces were burlesques. There was no idea of music in them, the tunes were taken from the music halls, the orchestras were small and of the most primitive description, and the chorus consisted of a handful of extra girls." In fact, burlesques were becoming so degraded with inadequate stories to parody that they were barely distinguishable from the extravaganzas which were also being presented. The Morning Star, the Examiner and one or two other journals were protesting that they were nonsensical and degrading. When Farnie moved to Paris in 1866 he took a liking to the popular French opera bouffe and made light musical pieces his chosen field.

Of adaptations from the French, William Archer[4] wrote that "the English adapter's first indispensable task is to remove all the cleverness and point of a plot so that it may pass the watchful eye of the Lord Chamberlain." But Farnie had an instinct for knowing what the public wanted and knew how much of a French show to keep, to adapt or to remove, or to add to, in order to appeal to British taste and conform to Victorian ideas of propriety. He is credited with, almost single-handedly, making opera bouffe popular in Britain, a trend which he continued with his own pastiche pieces and then, with changing public taste, he turned out opera comique with equal facility. Several of his most successful shows had been failures or had an indifferent reception in France but he showed he could do better with them in London.

Although best known for his adaptations of opera bouffe, his early works cannot be ignored. His translation of *Romeo and Juliet* was especially skilled; he had been commissioned to do a translation for a booklet, with the parallel French and English texts, to be sold to patrons in the theatre. French librettists, working from a French translation of Shakespeare, had produced their text, and that having been set to music by Gounod the metre and rhythms were fixed, and not in the form of Shakespeare's blank verse. He managed to get the feel of Shakespeare, and sometimes his language so far as the scansion would allow, back into the text, well enough for to be used by Carl Rosa, Augustus Harris and the BBC, long after he was dead.

Of the very many operettas which he translated, some are still in use today. And he was a good and prolific song writer having published in excess of three hundred songs apart from those in his shows which amount to upwards of a thousand. Probably a quarter of these show songs were published singly and many were used by artistes who had sung them in the shows and by other professionals in concerts and music hall. A few are still used today. Reviewers would, from time to time, hold him up as an example of how it should be done.

He was universally acknowledged to be a very good stage director, directing most of his own shows after Genevieve and several others which Henderson put on. He always insisted on the best in scenery and costumes and while the chorus were there to look beautiful, Farnie required a modicum of acting ability to fill the minor roles and he is credited with being the first to distinguish the front row chorus from the rest.[5] And of his chosen field of work he said, "I hold that a man who makes good ginger beer and sells it as such has no right to be condemned because he doesn't sell Pommery-greno. I provide musical ginger-beer, and all I claim is that it is creditable of its kind." He kept theatres filled and audiences happy for twenty-five years and that is all he hoped for.

But most of his work died with him and he was long forgotten until the "millennium" revival of Whittington reminded the world of its librettist. As George Bernard Shaw said, "The late H. B. Farnie was for an age, but not for all time."

* * *

NOTES

Chapter 1

1 Frederick Boase, *Modern English Biography*, published in 1892 says that Farnie went from St Andrews to Cambridge, but there is no record of him at Cambridge and this seems most unlikely. Various newspaper reports, and the title page of 'The Handy Book of the Fife Coast' link him to King's College, London. There is no record of him enrolling as a student. Some reports say he was a schoolmaster but he was never at King's College School which was then a junior department of King's College. In the 1860s King's advertised junior teaching posts as "masters", which may be the origin of the reports. It is possible that he was a member of staff, probably a junior lecturer, of whom no records survive of this period.

2 'The Golfer's Manual' was reprinted in 1862 and again in 1870. It was reprinted by the Dropmore Press in 1947, the 90th anniversary of its first publication, and again by the Vantage Press, New York in 1965. Six out of the eight chapters (ch. 2-7) were reprinted in an anthology, Stewart, J. Lindsay (Ed), *Golfiana Miscellanea*, Hamilton and Adams, London; Monson, Glasgow; 1887.

3 The Musical Monthly and Repertoire of Literature, The Drama and The Arts, No 9, Sept 1864

4 Agnes Strickland (1796-1874), poet and historical author, whose best-known works include 'Lives of the Queens of England' (12 vols), 'Lives of the Queens of Scotland and English Princesses' (8 vols), and 'Lives of the Bachelor Kings of England'.

5 Porteous, Alexander, *History of Crieff*, Edinburgh and London, 1912

6. National Archives of Scotland, CS46/97/12/1863

Chapter 2

1 Interview in The Era, Sat 30 Oct 1886. Farnie said this song was *Ring on Sweet Angelus*. His memory failed him, for his *Ring on Sweet Angelus* was set to themes from Gounod's opera *Sapho*.

2 ibid. Farnie claimed to have been with Wallace when he died – perhaps, perhaps not – if he travelled to the Haute Garonne it was out of friendship, Wallace by this time would have been unable to be working.

3   When Farnie was editor of The Orchestra and Adah Isaacs Menken was coming to Britain, he wrote a piece on the morals (or lack of) in American theatre, which Menken robustly answered. Farnie became a friend of hers and after her death wrote to an unknown number of American newspapers rebutting some things said about her and speaking of her in glowing terms. vide New York 'Clipper', 29 Aug 1868, and Barclay, George Lippard, *The Life and Remarkable Career of Adah Isaacs Menken*. Barclay, Philadelphia, 1868

4   There is no record of Farnie working with Sardou or adapting anything of his. If he did so, the result never reached publication or performance. But he probably did know him; he was a friend of Adah Isaacs Menken and knew Dumas, so was very likely acquainted with their circle of literary friends.

5   Farnie's version became the basis of that used in the 1942 film *Lady for a Night*, freely adapted by Sol Meyer, in which Madison Belle becomes Memphis Belle. Also used in the 1950 film *Dakota Lil* with lyrics by Raoul Kraushaar. At some point in its evolution it seems to have been wrongly catalogued and the music credited to Farnie. The music was the sole work of G. W. Hunt and the quality of his music led Benjamin Britten to orchestrate it, with Farnie's words written in – the manuscript is in the Cambridge University Library.

6   Gänzl, Lydia Thompson, op.cit., pp. 55 & 57. Also, Steve Holland, Bear Alley website.

7   A'Becket, Gilbert Arthur, *Ali Baba and The Forty Thieves, or Harlequin and the Genii of the Arabian Nights*, Covent Garden 26 December 1866

     Lunn, Joseph, *Family Jars*, Theatre Royal, Haymarket 26 August 1822

     Unknown, *Family Jars Mended*, Surrey Theatre 26 December 1839

Chapter 3

1   Many taverns put on entertainment and had a room set aside for the purpose, and these would feature in a history of the development of music hall. Morton did it better than others and was the first to erect a purpose-designed building.

2   Hollingshead, John, *Gaiety Chronicles*, London 1898, p.400, quoting Hollingshead's open letter to his patrons, 20 December 1880.

3   Era Almanack, Jan 1899, p.73. Mark Lemon died on 23 May 1870, some months before Farnie started work at the Strand Theatre, but the columnist was writing 30 years after the event! Farnie never needed to pawn his overcoat but rags-to-riches stories seem popular in the mythology surrounding celebrities. In 1892 the Otago Witness published a tale from someone claiming to have known him when he edited the Fifeshire Journal, saying that on his editor's pay he had to support his mother and sisters and so could afford only one suit, which being observed by the Cupar community, he became known as "one-suit". In 1894 the same paper published a reminiscence of Emily Soldene's activity in Australia and New Zealand, saying that when she first knew Farnie he had his clothes patched. None of which is true.

Chapter 4

1   Soldene, op.cit. p.108
2   Serjeant or Serjeant-at-law. The highest order of counsel at the English bar who for many years enjoyed rights of audience in certain courts and monopoly of appointment as judges of certain courts. These monopolies were lost, one-by-one, during the nineteenth century and the order was dissolved in 1877.
3   The Era, Sun 30 June 1872
4   The Times, Fri 28 June 1872
5   The Times, Thur 20 Feb 1873
6   The Era, Sun 23 Feb 1873
7   The National Archives C16/788/F77; The Times, Fri 2 Aug 1872, Wed 4 Dec 1872
8   Gänzl, *Emily Soldene*, op.cit., pp. 461-2

Chapter 5

1   Burnand never liked Farnie and called him "a burly swaggerer". He was self-assured, resented intrusion into his secure world, and was capable of great jealousy. As editor of Punch, Burnand would not publish reviews of the Savoy operas. He was jealous of Gilbert and felt that he, rather than Gilbert, should have been collaborating with Sullivan. vide Furniss, Harry, *The Two Pins Club*. John Murray, London, 1925
2   The National Archives, Court of Chancery, C16/737/M194, Oct 1871

3   Cruickshank, Graeme, *The Life and Loves of Letty Lind, 1861-1923, Skirt Dancer, Soubrette and Gaiety Girl.* The Gaiety, Issue 22, Summer 2007

4   Charles George Alias and Sarah Ann Price were married in the third quarter of 1873 at Islington

5   Shaw, Donald, One of the Old Brigade; London in the Sixties. London, 1908.

Chapter 6

1   Jacques Offenbach Society Newsletters Nos. 13 (Sept 2000) and 40 (June 2007). Duployen speculates on reports that Offenbach spoke little English, and whether Nuitter and Tréfeu might have assisted him. Contemporary reports all insist that Offenbach worked with an English libretto but the two French librettists may have helped him, and if they had possession of the English text may well have started work on a French version.

2   Richard Duployen has recently prepared an English translation of the French version, *Le Chat du Diable.*

3   The last year of the second millennium was celebrated rather than the first year of the third.

4   Bampton Hunt (Ed), *The Green Room Book, or, Who's Who on the Stage.* London and New York, 1906. Footlight Families (family trees) p.384

5   The Era, Sat 26 Aug 1893

6   Farnie created a detailed scenario but was still using ghosts to help with the dialogue.

7   If *Robinson Crusoe*, Prince's, Manchester, 7 Oct 1876 tried out by the Blue Beard company when on tour, and *Nell Gwynne*, Prince's Manchester, 16 Oct 1876 which never went any further, are discounted.

8   The Era Sun 25 Nov 1877

9   The Era, Sun 23 Feb 1879 gives the longest and most detailed account of the hearing, and it reported that it was said in court that the 'Theatre' was "now defunct". This must be a legal nicety; 'Theatre' had evolved from a weekly newspaper to a monthly magazine but with the same proprietors, Messrs Wyman and Son, the defendants in the case. The British Library catalogue lists it as a continuous series.

10 Burnand, *Records and Reminiscences*, Methuen, London, 1904, says they had a serious quarrel about three times a year.

11 This was a record for a musical show, until surpassed by Cellier-Stephenson's Dorothy (1886) which reached 931 performances. But Byron's comedy Our Boys (1875) had achieved 1362.

12 Pall Mall Gazette, Wed 23 Dec 1896

Chapter 7

1 Farnie (Harvey) v. Farnie (divorce), The National Archives J77/230/6454

2 Farnie (Harvey) v. Farnie (nullity), The National Archives J77/234/6602
Law Reports 5 P.D. 153.
The case caused quite a sensation and reports of the charge of bigamy, the divorce and nullity proceedings, and the appeals to the Appeal Court and the House of Lords, were carried in most national and local newspapers.

3 Law Reports : Appeal Court 6 P.D. 35; House of Lords 8 H.L.(Sc) 43

4 The Era Sat 20 Aug 1881, Sat 8 Oct 1881, Sat 25 Feb 1882

5 Morton and Newton, Op. Cit. p.114

Chapter 8

1 Advertisements had indicated that the Comedy would open with a play called *Out of the Hunt* by Reece and Thorpe but Henderson decided that *The Mascotte* would be better in the Comedy and he hired the Royalty for *Out of the Hunt*, which was directed by Farnie.

2 The Era calls the yacht the 'Lively'. In the 1881 census return the name is obscure but looks like 'Rennie', certainly not 'Lively'. Neither name has been found in Lloyd's Registers.

3 This meeting must have been before Sept 1881 when Leslie went to America. After his return he went into *Madame Favart* at the opening of the Avenue Theatre and Farnie would have had every opportunity to see him there. When he first worked for Kate Santley in *Paul Pry* it was on a bill with Farnie and Reece's *Madcap*, but this did not, it seems, give Leslie the opportunity to meet Farnie.

4 The only collaboration between Farnie and Hersée, that is, that went into production. They also worked together on *Nectarine*, an adaptation of Planquette's *La Cantinière* which was never produced - vide Chapter 9

5   This New York production was an English language adaptation
     unattributed in programmes or reviews. Some sources say it was
     Farnie.
6   Gänzl, *Lydia Thompson*, op.cit., p.203
7   Some reports say Henderson disembarked and fell at Boulogne and
     received hospital treatment at Nice before continuing to Cannes.
8   Morton and Newton, op.cit., p.156
9   Sutherland, Douglas, *The Yellow Earl: The life of Hugh Lowther
     5th Earl of Lonsdale, 1857-1944.* Cassell, London, 1965. pp.80-84
10   Violet Cameron had a son by her husband, named Cecil Horace
     David de Bensaude, born 1885Q1, who became an actor working as
     Cecil Cameron. Her two daughters by Lowther, Earl Lonsdale were
     Nydie Lowther de Bensaude, born 1887Q3, who married a judge in
     the colonial service, and Doris Lowther de Bensaude, born 1888Q4,
     who became an actress working as Doris Cameron.
11   It was said that the librettists, MM. Chivot and Duru, set out to
     avenge a perceived slight on Gallic pluck contained in Gilbert and
     Sullivan's *Ruddigore*, "only a darned Mounseer".
12   Equivalent to some £2 million in present day value.

Chapter 9

1   Norton, op. cit. p.469 has "from a text by Farnie"
2.   Norton, op.cit. p.515
3.   Charles Head put on *Genevieve de Brabant* (Farnie version) at the
     Philharmonic in 1878. The rights belonged to Emily Soldene who
     was, at the time, in New Zealand. Neither she nor Farnie had
     anything to do with the production and the press knew it. But that
     didn't stop 'The Theatre' from slating Farnie for an updated script
     that had been done by Head's associates.
     S. J. Adair Fitz-Gerald, in writing of a new production of *La Fille
     de Madame Angot* in 1919, thirty years after Farnie's death,
     couldn't resist referring to his earlier version as a "vile concoction".
4.   Archer, William, *English Dramatists of To-day.* London, 1882
5.   Short, op.cit. p.129

PRINCIPAL REFERENCES

Campbell, A. J., *Golfing Skeletons in Family History*. Fife Family History Society, 1998

Campbell, A. J., *Bibliography of Fife Presses : The Press of John Cunningham Orr*. Dunfermline, 1992

Campbell, A. J., *Cupar the Years of Controversy : Its Newspaper Press 1822-1872*. Dunfermline, 2009

Court of Session papers, Scottish Record Office, Edinburgh

Gänzl, Kurt, *Encyclopœdia of the Musical Theatre. (3 vols)* Schirmer Books, New York, 2001

Gänzl, Kurt, *Lydia Thompson, Queen of Burlesque*. New York and London, 2002.

Gänzl, Kurt, *Emily Soldene : In Search f a Singer. (2 vols)* Wellington, New Zealand, 2007

Hughes, Gervaise, *Composers of Operetta*. Macmillan & Co., London, 1962

Irvin, Eric, *Dictionary of the Australian Theatre 1788-1914*. Hale & Iremonger, Sydney, 1985

Macqueen-Pope, W., *Nights of Gladness*. Hutchinson & Co., London, 1956

Morton, William H. and Newton (Henry Cecil), *Sixty Years Stage Service: being a record of the life of Charles Morton "the Father of the Halls"*. London, 1905

Northcott, Richard, *Jacques Offenbach*. London, 1917

Norton, Richard C., *A Chronology of American Musical Theater*. New York, 2002

Pascoe, Charles E., *The Dramatic List*. David Bogue, London, 1880

Reid, Erskine and Compton, Herbert, *The Dramatic Peerage*. London, 1891

Sharp, Keith Drummond, *The Flow and Ebb of the Tide*. Forest Row, 2001

Short, Ernest, *Fifty Years of Vaudeville*. Eyre & Spottiswoode, London, 1946

Soldene, Emily, *My Theatrical and Musical Recollections*. London, 1897.

Newspaper reports and reviews : in Britain principally, but not exclusively, The Era and The Times, in America principally the Clipper and the New York Times.

APPENDIX 1
WORKS CREATED BY H. B. FARNIE
This information is assembled from programmes, vocal scores, and other materials in the author's collection and at the Theatre Collection of the Victoria and Albert Museum, the Mander and Mitchenson collection at the Trinity College of Music, the British Library, the John Johnson collection of printed ephemera at the Bodleian Library, and from newspaper reviews.

Publication information refers to Farnie's version. The following abbreviations are used :
Dir. - Director; MD - Musical Director; ch - Choreographer; sc. - Scenery; cos. - Costumes.

THE BRIDE OF SONG
One-Act Operetta. Composed by Sir Julius Benedict.
Published : Cramer, Wood and Co., London, 1864
Concert Performances, Leeds 2 May 1864, Hanover Square Rooms 23, 29 May
Staged Performance Royal Opera House, Covent Garden 3 Dec 1864
Cast at Covent Garden ● Rénée - Miss Thirlwall ● Beatrice - Madame Fanny Huddart
● Adelbert - Mr Henry Haigh ● Hannibal - Mr Alberto Lawrence.
> Musical Numbers : 1. Overture
> 2. "Ah! do not take her from him"
> 3. 'Soldiers' Chorus' "The cattle in the clover"
> 4. 'For Her Sweet Sake' "My dream of life is fled"
> 5. Trio 'My Heart is Beating' "My heart is freely brave"
> 6. Recit & Song 'My Home in Cloudland' "Be it so; had'st thou faith .."
> 7. Trio 'News, Girls, News'
> 8. Duet: 'Night and Morning' "I love the fields all white with sheaves"
> 9. Quartette 'The Rheinland' "To all thy future years we pray"
> 10. Duet 'We Waited Late, We Waited Long'
> 11. The 'Trooper's Ditty : Boot & Saddle, Mount and Ride'

Revivals : Numerous in London and Provinces as Curtain Raiser

THE SLEEPING QUEEN
One-Act, expanded to Two-Act Operetta, composed by W. Michael Balfe. Story adapted
from 'Ne touchez pas à la Reine' (Eugène Scribe and Gustave Vaëz)
Published : J. B. Cramer & Co., London, 1865
One-Act Version - Gallery of Illustration, 1 Sept 1864
Two-Act Version completed Sept 1866, Published J. B. Cramer & Co., 1868
Cast at Gallery of Illustration ● Irene (Queen of Leon) - Miss D'Este Finlayson ● Donna
Agnes (a Maid of Honour) - Miss Poole ● Philippe d'Aguilar - Mr T. Whitten ● His
Excellency the Regent - Mr R. Wilkinson.
Sc.: Mr John O'Connor.
> Musical Numbers Two-Act Version :
> Overture
> Act 1   1. Chorus of Courtiers "On the regent so urbane"
> 2. Song 'The Prime Minister' "I'm the regent - I'm the king"
> 3. Duet 'I crave a boon' "I crave a boon which is in truth your"
> 4. Trio 'She is heartless' "She is heartless, she's ungrateful"
> 5. Ballad 'Only a Ribbon' "Twas not her face - though it was fair"
> 6. Duet 'You Love' "You love and think you love in vain"
> 7. Finale Act 1 "Live long our fair young queen, Long be her"

127

Act 2   8. Caretina with Chorus "A village maid may weave a flow'ret"
         9. Duet 'The Treaty' "Proceed my Lord, the Queen will now confer"
         10. Fandango 'Pablo the Lover' "Pablo the lover Roams here and there"
         11. Serenade 'The Noontide Dream' "She sleeps! though not a star tells"
         12. Ballad "O could I but relive the past"
         13. Trio 'Most Awful Sight' "Most awful sight for regent's eyes"
         14. Quartette & Chorus (Finale) "Fondly I dreamed my queen, my love"

Revivals : St George's Hall (Bijou Operetta Company) 1 Aug 1867, Alexandra Palace (Alice Barth Comic Opera Company) 29 June 1880, Crystal Palace (Alice Barth Co.) 27 Sept 1880, Avenue Theatre 17 July 1882. Frequently in the provinces.

PUNCHINELLO
One-Act Comic Opera. Composed by William Charles Levey.
Her Majesty's Theatre, Haymarket, 28 Dec 1864, closed 14 Jan 1865.
Published J. B. Cramer & Co., London, 1865

Cast ● Marquis de Vingtcentmillefleurs - George Hone ● Mons de Chambaudet - John Rouse ● Sous-Lieutenant Agamemnon - Mr Swift ● Chevalier de Vignolles - Mr Terrot ● Mdlle Violette de Vingtcentmillefleurs - Susan Galton ● Barbette the Auvergnate - Miss Cottrell ● A Page, Carabineers, Guests.

Musical Numbers :
1. Choral Dance "Light ending, Shade blending"
2. The 'Pedigree' Duet "Vingt-cent-mille-fleurs of noble race"
3. (Barbette) 'Sabot Song' "From Fair Auvergne I come"
4. Trio "My Lord, My Lord!"
5. Song and Chorus (Agamamnon) 'The Bombadiers'
6. Ballad (Violette) '"Coo!" says the Gentle Dove'
7. 'Highborn Beauty, Canst thou leave'
8. Song 'The Showman's Ditty' "I am but a showman I know"
9. (Vingtcentmillefleurs) 'Sixty's Serenade' "I stand beneath thy latice"
10. The 'Hidden' Quintett "He comes! My robber"
11. Finale 'To old Auvergne can you return'

Revivals : Provincial Tour with Richard Temple and Annie Sinclair Autumn 1871; Crystal Palace w/c 20 Nov 1871

IRENE
(Reine de Saba.)
Opera, composed by Charles Gounod, libretto by J. Barbier and M. Carré.
Published (English version) : J. B. Cramer & Co., London [1865]
Concert Performances, Crystal Palace 12, 19 Aug 1865, 24 Feb 1866
Staged Performance, Theatre Royal, Manchester 10 Mar 1880

Cast at Crystal Palace ● Irene (a Greek Princess) - Madame Lemmens-Sherington Lalage (her confidant) - Madame D'Este Finlayson ● Suliman (Sultan of Turkey) - Mr Lewis Thomas ● Muriel (the Master Builder) - Mr Cummings ● Pascal (a youth attached to him) – Madame Louisa Vining ● Zorast - Mr Smythson ● Raffael - Mr Montem Smith ● Phanoah - Renwick.

Cast at Theatre Royal, Manchester ● Irene Madame - Blanche Cole ● Lalage - Miss aultless ● Suliman - Mr Ludwig ● Muriel - Mr J. W. Turner ● Pascal - Miss E. Webster Zorast -Mr W. Hillier ● Raffael - Mr J. Tempest ● Phanoah - Mr Mulle.

Musical Numbers :

Act I	1.	Introduction (Instrumental)
	2.	Recit. and Air (Muriel) "Lend me your aid"
	3.	Romance (Pascal) "Hast thou seen the young day blushing"
	4.	Quartet, Recit., and Trio "Master!"
	5.	Pageant March and Finale (Irene, Suliman, Muriel, & Chorus) "Hail to thee"
Act II	6.	The Iron Sea (Irene, Muriel, Suliman, Zorast) "Master, all is done"
Act III	7.	Introduction and Chorus of Greek Maidens "Fair the rose of love is blowing"
	8	Dialogue Chorus "Oh, handmaids of Irene"
	9.	Ballet (in six movements)
	10.	Scene and Chorus "I pray you now leave me"
	11.	Cavatina (Irene) "Far greater, in his lowly state"
	12.	Duo "Oh, leave me degrading, despairing !"
	13.	Recit and Air "O Master ! Hail to thee"
	14.	Septett with Chorus (All) "O gracious power"
Act IV	15.	Chorus and Dance "Trumpet blow, music flow"
	16.	Recit. and Cavatina (Sulliman) "She alone charmeth my sadness"
	17.	Scena (Suliman, Muriel, and Chorus) "Muriel still", Cho. "Far from our land"
	18.	Duet and Cho. "Cold and proud as thou art"
Act V	19.	The Storm (Instrumental) and Scene " 'Tis the place !"
	20.	Quartett (Muriel, Zorast, Raffael, & Phanoah) "At last thou deign'st"
	21.	Finale (Irene anmd Chorus) "Weep for him" and "Welcome, no longer mortal" a.k.a. "Bear him forth through the night"

Revivals : Concert performances notably Leicester Philharmonic Choir 1899 and 1902

THE GOLDEN DUSTMAN
Dramatized version of Charles Dickens's Our Mutual Friend.
Royal Sadler's Wells, 16 June 1866

Cast ● Messrs T. Swinbourne, Barrett, H. Belmore, F. Barsby, A. Bishop, C. Warner, W. MacIntyre, W. Holland, Neilson, W. Courtley, Needham, Morris, Miss Ada Dyas, Mrs Poynter, Miss Fanny Gwynne, Miss Ada Harland, Mrs Bishop.

Revivals : Leeds Amphitheatre, Oct 1866; Astley's, 27 Oct 1866; Prince of Wales's, Liverpool, 26 Dec 1871 as 'Boffin's Legacy'; Surrey Theatre, 9 Mar 1878; Alexandra Palace 13 Apr 1878

THE PRINCESS
Drama "arranged for the stage from The Princess, A Medley by Alfred Tennyson."
Registered at Stationers Hall 10 Aug 1866   No record of publication or performance.

THE ROSE OF SAVOY
Drawing Room Operetta for Ladies
Published : J. B. Cramer & Co., London, 1866.   Oliver Ditson, Boston, USA

Musical Numbers :   Overture
1. 'Sisters Still We are Sewing'
2. 'When all the still house slumbers'
3. 'From Fair Savoy I Come'
4. 'Mariner's Daughter': cavatina "Alas! he cometh not! "
5. 'The Tear-Drops in Mine Eyes'
6. 'Ah ! Mine's a Simple Story'
7. Finale 'Heart to Heart'

129

TOBIAS
(Tobie)
'Petite oratorie' composed by Charles Gounod.
Published : Cramer, London, 1872
Concert at St James's Hall, 13 Feb 1866   With Mesdames Lemmens Sherrington and
Rudersdorff, and Miss Wytock, and Messrs Cummings, Patey, and Simms Reeves.

ULYSSES
Drama with choruses.   Translated from the French of François Ponsard;
with choruses by Charles Gounod
Published : Cramer, London, 1866
St James's Hall 8 June 1866
Read by Miss Helen Faucit.   Soloists ● Madame Rudersdorff, Miss Julia Elton,
Mr Cummings, and Mr Weiss.   Chorus assembled for the occasion.
Musical Numbers : Act I
First chorus of Naiads "Lo! buckler and morion wearing"
Second chorus of Naiads "The blood-red sun is lapping the many veined sand"
Act II
First chorus of Herdsmen "They are a mongrel crew!"
Second chorus of Herdsmen "Hail, Bacchus! thou ivy-crown'd god of good wine"
Third chorus of Herdsmen "Jav'lin in hand, Telemachus! we follow;"
Act III
First chorus of False Handmaidens "Lit by one star faintly beaming"
Chorus of Faithful Handmaidens - I "Very sad - very sad - oh widowed queen, thy story!"
Chorus of Faithful Handmaidens - II ""Grotto and stream and valley - shores and all"
Second chorus of False Handmaidens "White foam on the dark blue glancing"
Act IV
Song and Chorus (Phemius) "Would Jove a soldier's fortune send me"
Fourth chorus of Herdsmen "It is the bow Ulysses wielded"
Fifth chorus of Herdsmen "Each purple vein is higher swelling"
Chorus of Herdsmen "The sturdy vagrant's proved best bowman!"
Chorus of Servants and Retainers "Lo! the slain: In the dust their heads are lying"
Finale Chorus " Hail to Ulysses, o'er his foes victorius

REVERSES
Domestic Drama in Two Acts
Strand Theatre, 13 July 1867, closed 19 Aug 1867
Dick the Grinder - Mr S. Emery ● Mr Vaughan Tremaine - Mr W. H. Swanborough
● Charlie Jones - Mr Parselle ● Mr Plunkell - Mr H. J. Turner ● Bill Stodge - Mr F. Robson
● Kate Tremaine - Miss Ada Swanborough ● Miss Mildew - Miss E. Johnstone ● Mrs
Stodge – Mrs Manders

THE PAGES REVEL
or, The Summer Night's Bicvouac
Extravaganza
Tammany Grand, New York, 4 Jan 1869
Ernest St Pol, Captain of the Pages - Miss Alice Harrison ● Victor - Miss Lizzie Kelsey
● Tristan - Miss Sallie Madox ● Mareschal de Longueville - Bessie Sudlow

130

Musical Numbers:
A vehicle for variety acts; music particular to the performers, not written for the show.

PLUTO
Adaptation of H. J. Byron's Extravaganza 'Orpheus and Euridice'
Theatre Comique, New York, 1 Feb 1869
Orpheus - Alice Dunning ● Pluto - William Horace Lingard ● Eurydice - Lina Edwin
With ● Dickie Lingard and Ethel Norman
Farnie's role was to adapt this for the American market, musical numbers were not by him.
Revival : Grand Opera House, New York, 13 Dec 1869

FORTY THIEVES
or, Striking Oil in Family Jars
Gorgeous, Oriental, Fairy, Spectacular Burlesque Extravaganza
Niblo's Garden, New York, 1 Feb 1869
Infernal ~ Orchobrand - Emma Grattan ● Supernal ~ The Fairy Queen - Bella Land ● Exiles
from their native land ~ American Fay - Annie Byron ● German Fay - Fraulein Schroetter
● English Fay - Miss Forrest ● French Fay - Mlle. Carrie Geddes ● Mortal ~ Ali Baba - W.
J. Hill ● Ganem, his son - Lydia Thompson ● Hassim - George F. Ketchum ● Cogia - J. W.
Brutone ● Amber - Lizzie Kelsey ● Morgiana - Liza Weber ● Abdallah - Pauline Markham
● Hassarac - Harry Beckett ● The Cadi - J. W. Brutone
Musical Numbers :
I'd Like to be a Swell (Lydia Thompson)
Swinging Round the Circle (Lisa Weber)
The Bashful Girl (Pauline Markham)
Nonsense Rhymes (L. Thompson, P. Markham, H. Beckett, W. J. Hill)
Quadrille, Waltz, Gallop
Grand Finale (Act 1, Scene 3)
Grand Finale (Act 2, Scene 3)
Can Can (Act 2, Scene 6)
Revivals : Frequently used during Lydia Thompson's American tours; Niblo's Garden, New
York, 23 May 1870 (reconstructed by C. Ware); Wood's Museum, New York, 2 Jan 1871
(revised version from Farnie's original); Used as the basis for pantomimes at Glasgow and
Manchester, Dec 1879 (qv)

SINDBAD THE SAILOR
or, the Ungenial Genii and the Cabin Boy
Gorgeous Arabian Night-mare-ish Burlesque Extravaganza
Niblo's Garden, New York, 29 May 1869
The Messenger Gnome - Raphael de Solla ● Spirits of Dress, Pleasure, Wine, Cards, Turf -
Misses Strickland, Whitlock, Dutton, Crossen, Lyndwood ● The Fairy Hope – Clara
Thompson ● The Ungenial Genii - Harry Beckett ● Sindbad - Lydia Thompson The Chief
Cook and Bottle-Washer - Mr Burke ● The Sheriff of Bagdad - George F. Ketchum ● Hafiz,
Selim, Swells of the Period - Bessie Harding, Eliza Weathersby, Maggie Desmonde ● Ali
Ben Drygoods - W. B. Cahill Koh-i-noor, his daughter - Pauline Markham ● The Hadji
Blimber, a College Don - W. J. Hill
Musical Numbers :
Ask Papa
O How Delightful (music J. T. Molloy)
131

Come Down, Darling, Do! (sung by Raphael de Solla)
Cymbal Song (sung by Pauline Markham)
Go A-head! (H. Beckett)
Song (Act 1, Scene 1) (sung C. Thompson (sic), H. Beckett)
Revivals : Frequently used during Lydia Thompson's American tours; Olympic Theatre, New York, 11 Sept 1873; Used as the basis for a pantomime at Manchester, Dec 1876 (qv)

MOSQUITO
Drama in collaboration with Alexandre Dumas, père
Niblo's Garden, New York, 2 May 1870
Cast ● J W Brutone, William B Cahill, John Dunn, Lina Edwin, Harry Jackson, Pauline Markham, McKee Rankin, Lydia Thompson, Neil Warner

THE ROSE OF AUVERGNE
or, Spoiling the Broth   (La Rose de Saint-Flour)
Operetta by Jacques Offenbach, libretto by M. Carré (Bouffes Parisiens, 12 June 1856)
Published (English version): Metzler & Co., London 1872
(No.3 of Metzler Opera Bouffe series)
Gaiety Theatre, 1 Nov 1869
Fleurette (Landlady of a village cabaret) - Miss Loseby ● Alphonse (a Shoemaker) - Mr W. M. Terrott ● Pierre (a Blacksmith) - Mr E. Perriniure
Musical Numbers :
1. 'Heigh-ho! which to chose' "Two lovers claim my sole affection"
2. ' This stewpan bright and new'
3. For Her Dear Feet - Recitative and Air
4. 'Go along !' "Go along! pray don't be shy"
5. 'You blacksmith, look you here'
6. The Rustic Wedding "Ah! never was day so merry"
7. Finale 'My hand is yours!' ' and Duet "Happy now we shall be"
Revivals : frequent at the Gaiety, the Alhambra, Avenue, Cremorne, Crystal Palace, Covent Garden, Empire, Opera Comique, Philharmonic, and numerous provincial productions.
America : Robinson Hall, New York, 19 July 1875; Fifth Avenue Theatre, 14 Apr 1879
Australia : Princess's, Melbourne, 30 Aug 1871

LITTLE FAUST
(Le Petit Faust)
Opera Bouffe composed by Hervé
Lyceum Theatre, 18 Apr 1870, closed 2 July 1870 (end of season)
Marguerite - Miss Emily Soldene ● Mephisto - Mdlle Marguerite Debreux ● Faust – Mr Thomas MacLagan ● Valentine - Mr Ainsley Cook ● Siebel - Mons. Marius ● Martha - Mr J. Odell ● Karl - Miss Lennox Grey ● Fritz - Miss Ada Lucmore ● Buttons - Miss Laura Morgan ● Arab - Miss Jennie Lee ● A Cabman - Mr Wilmot ● The Little Cornet - Miss S. Lowons ● Lady Gymnasts, Pupils of Martha's Academy.
Musical Numbers :   Overture
Chorus of Schoolgirls
"I'm Marguerite, a timid young maid" (Marguerite)
Melodrame - Faust meets Marguerite
"My hot blood" (Faust)
"Mephisto's my name" (Mephisto)

132

"There was a King of Thule"
"Where shall I take my bride? " (Siebel)
Bridesmaid's Chorus
"If the Bridegroom ain't he ought to be" (Karl)
The Four Seasons of Love (Mephisto)
Parody on 'Fair' scene in Faust
The Battle of the Bards
International Valse contest
Locomotive song (Marguerite)
Mephisto is at home.
Finale

As DOCTOR FAUST

Holborn Theatre, 20 May 1872, closed Sat 13 July 1872 (end of season)
Marguerite - Miss Selina Dolaro ● Mephisto - Mdlle Clary ● Faust - Hervé (then Mrs Howard Paul) ● Valentine - Mr Lionel Brough ● Siebel - Mr Loredan ● Martha - Mdlle Prati ● Franz - Miss Venn ● Arab - Miss Adair ● Bopp (Faust's assistant) - Mr Elliott ● Cabman – Mr Arthur ● Vergiss-mein-nicht - Miss Carlyle ● Vivandiere - Miss Vokins ● Wagner – Miss Fisher ● Fritz - Miss Armour.
MD. Mr Frank Musgrave, cos. Messrs. Gask; sc. Mr. Julian Hicks.

Musical Numbers as at the Lyceum except:
Duet "I'm a timid Marguerite" (Marguerite & Faust)
The First Leaf (Farnie) introduced by Mrs Howard Paul

Revivals : Provincial tour Autumn 1872.
America : (as Little Faust) Olympic Theatre, New York, 22 Aug 1870

BREAKING THE SPELL
(Le Violoneau)
Operetta composed by Jacques Offenbach, libretto by E. Mestépès and E. Chevalet
(Bouffes Parisiens, Paris, 31 Aug 1855)
Published : Metzler & Co., London [1872]
Lyceum Theatre, 2 May 1870
Old Matthew (a Chelsea Pensioner) - Mr Aynsley Cook ● Peter Bloom (a Gardener) - Mr G. F. Neville ● Jenny Wood - Miss S. Dolaro / Emily Muir

Musical Numbers : Overture (Voices off) "Now, lads, a parting glass to the Queen!"
1. Romance (Peter) 'Jenny is False' "Goodbye! goodbye! dear happy scene"
2. Duet (Jenny and Peter) 'Oh How Happy We Shall Be' "To the war with you I'll go"
3. Song (Old Matthew) 'My Heart is Ever Gay' "The tunes I play, Blithe and gay"
4. Duet (Jenny and Old Matthew) 'Hark! 'Tis the Bugle Calls to Parade'
5. Duet (Jenny and Peter) 'Am I Awake'
6. Lament (Old Matthew) 'My Only Friend, Farewell' "Farewell, farewell, dear smile"
7. Scene (Jenny, Peter, Old Matthew) "What! It's a letter"
8. Finale (Jenny, Peter, Old Matthew) 'In My Youth'

Revivals : Philharmonic, 31 Mar 1873; Cremorne Gardens, 12 July 1875; Covent Garden, 26 Dec 1877; Royalty, 16 Mar 1878; Gaiety, 6 Apr 1891; Garrick, 26 Apr 1904; D'Oyly Carte tour alternating with Trial by Jury as curtain raiser to The Sorcerer, 9 Mar - 10 Aug 1878; numerous provincial and amateur productions.
America : Metropolitan Alcazar, New York, 25 Sept 1882
Australia : Bijou, Melbourne, 1 May 1897

THE IDLE 'PRENTICE

A 'hurly-burly-esque' based on Harrison Ainsworth's novel 'Jack Sheppard'

Royal Strand Theatre (Mrs Swanborough), 10 Sept 1870, closed 22 Apr 1871

Little Jack - Jennie Lee • Mrs Sheppard - Edward Terry • Master Wood - Mr H. J. Turner • Winifred - Kate Santley • Jonathan Wild - Eleanor Bufton • Thomas Darrell - Mr J. Burnett • Sir Roland Trenchard - Amy Sheridan • Lady Trafford - Mrs Raymond • Blueskin – Harry Paulton • Tom Tug - Bella Goodall • Mr Krackcrib - Mr Edge • The Sitting Judge - Mr C. Fenton • The Assistant Alderman - Miss E. Rose • Poll - Miss Metcalfe • Sergeant Bull's-eye - Mr E. Chamberlaine • Members of the Four-in-hand Club, The Manager of Vauxhall Gardens, a Tiger, a Shoeblack, The Watch, The Jolly Beggars, citizens, &c.

sc. Messrs Charles Fenton and Hall; cos. Mr S. May and Mrs Richardson.

Musical Numbers (incomplete) :

Stay, Johny, stay. (Winifred Wood)

The "Lar de dar" Swell (Jack Sheppard)

Oh, ain't you awful? (Jonathan Wild)

The liking for cook song (Blueskin)

True Blue (Blueskin)

We're All on the Job (Blueskin)

Revivals : Strand 23 Sept 1872 (second edition), closed 30 Oct 1872; Surrey, 15 May 1880 as 'Little Jack Sheppard'

America : Miss Lina Edwin's Theatre, New York, early Dec 1870, closed 31 Dec 1870

THE PET DOVE

(La Colombe)

Comic opera in two acts, composed Charles Gounod, libretto by Jules Barbier and Michel Carré (After 'Le Faucon' by La Fontaine)

Crystal Palace, 20 Sept 1870

Sylvia - Miss Blanche Cole • Phillis - Miss Annie Thirlwall • Hubert - Mr Haigh • Hippocras - Mr Connell • Simon (Low comedy part) - Mr Friend

Musical Numbers :   Introduction

Act I

1. Ballad (Phil) 'Pretty Pet Dove'
2. Trio (Phil, Hub, Hip) 'O let him keep his gold'
3. Arietta (Hip) 'Love on the brain'
4. Grand Air (Syl) 'If time hath lightly o'er me passed'
5. Song (Phil) 'The women, the women'
6. Trio (Syl, Phil, Hub) 'Who cometh in an angel's seeming'
7. Quartett (Syl, Phil, Hub, Hip) 'A heart-felt pleasure'

Act II

8. Duett (Phil, Hub) 'Now then bestir!'
9. Melodrame (Syl)
10. Ballad (Syl) 'Daughters of Eve!'
11. Madrigal (Hub) 'In the Spring-time'
12. Quartett (Syl, Phil, Hub, Hip) 'All doubt is o'er'
13. Duett (Syl, Hub) 'Ah! good my friend'
14. Finale (Tutti) 'Good evening to you pretty Pet-dove'

Revivals : Royal Academy of Music, Oct 1893; numerous provincial and amateur productions.

GULLIVER
or, Harlequin Brobdingnag
Pantomime
Crystal Palace, 21 Dec 1870

Gulliver - Miss Caroline Parkes ● Insolvency - Mr Henry Dudley ● The Fairy Enterprise - Miss Emeline Cole ● Snarley-yow - Mr George Yarnold ● Master Sugarplum - Mr Arthur Williams ● Saccharissa (his daughter) - Miss Annie Thirlwall ● Sir Lardy Dardy Doo – Miss Clara Shelley ● Captain Jinks - Miss Georgina Clair ● Mother Gulliver - Mr Friend ● The Sheriff - Mr Harry Marshall ● Mr McNab - Mr Joe Marshall ● H. H. M. the Emperor of Lilliput - Master Percy Roselle ● Minister of the Interior - Miss Polly Marchant ● The King of Brobdingnag - Mr H. Clements ● The Count (his Chancellor) - Mr W. Wood Transformation ~ Harlequin - W. White ● Pantaloon - Tom Lovell ● Columbine – Mlle Rosette ● Clowns - Harry Boleno & Little Rowella

Grand Ballet invented and arranged by M. Milano

Dir. E. T. Smith and T. H. Friend; sc. Mr Fenton; cos. Mr S. May & Mr and Mrs Stinchcombe.

Musical Numbers :
Chorus 'Moet and Chandon' "We don't approve at all of war!"
'Lurline' Ballet
Duet (Gul, Sac) "Yes, to foreign climes I'll go"
(Lillputian Policemen "We won't go home till morning"
"Nigger" melody and "Shoe Fly"
Hronpipe (Gulliver Topical Song)
Concerted Piece (Gul, Sugar, Sac, Lardy) 'The Parks' "Oh, here's a funny land"
Concerted Piece (Sugar, Gul, Sac, Omnes) "Then bless you both, my children dear"

LITTLE GIL BLAS AND HOW HE PLAYED THE SPANISH D(J)EUCE
Burlesque, music by Prince Poniatowski and Mr Frank Musgrave
Princess's Theatre (Webster and Chatterton), 24 Dec 1870, closed 3 Feb 1871

Dr Sangrado - Mr S. Barry ● Leonardo - Mrs Power ● Gil Blas - Mrs Howard Paul Aurora - Lydia Maitland ● Cleophas - Lennox Gray ● Don Vincent - Mr Wilmot ● Florimonde – Mary Holt ● Laura - Lizzie Russell ● Zapata - Guy Linton Rolando - Miss M. Sidney (Mrs Milano) ● Quinola (servant to Don Vincent) - Mr H. Clive ● The Bull - Jenny Elliot
Musical numbers not known

THE MISTLETOE BOUGH
or, Lord Lovell, Lady Nancy, and the Milk-White Steed
[some scripts have the alternative title 'a merry jest of an old oak chest']
Christmas Burlesque
Adelphi Theatre (Webster and Chatterton), 26 Dec 1870, closed 11 Feb 1871

Lord Lovel - Brittain Wright ● Baron de Bell - John Rouse ● Young Lochinvar - Mrs Alfred Mellon ● Lady Nancy Bell - Elise Holt ● Simon the Cellarer - H. Ashley ● Dame Margery - E. J. Odell ● Philip the Falconer - Mlle. Debreux ● The Hereditary Minstrel - Bella Moor ● The Family Herald - Miss Bellew ● Mary the Maid of the Inn - Camille Dubois ● Boniface - M. D. Byrnes ● Nip - Harwood Cooper ● The Ballon letter carrier - Jessie Powell ● Village blacksmith - Miss Jones / Miss Ada Hill ● My Pretty Page - Florence Denvil ● The Milk- white Steed - Misses Williams and Campbell ● Doll and Bet (Dame Margery's Maids) - Misses Heather and Hill ● Retainers, peasants, lords, ladies, pages, millers, &c. Dir. Mr Billington; MD. Edwin Ellis; sc. Frederick Lloyds, William Maugham; Incidental divertissements Mr J. Milano; cos. Mrs Aulph, Miss Rayner.

Musical Numbers : Music selected and arranged by Frank Musgrave
Scene 1. Exterior of Lord Lovell's Castle
Chorus "This is England in the Olden Time"
Trio (Loch, Phil, Mary) "My way I clearly now can see"
Recit. and Air (Lord) Recit "Ah me! my heart!" Air "In me you see a feudal swell"
Dance
Bridal Chorus "Ring, O merry bells, ring out"
Concerted Piece "Lady Nancy's pretty, rather!"
Balloon Music [not clear why so called - it covered a gag concerning a Postman]
Grand Finale and Procession March (Omnes) "Glory, glory, to our warlike lord!"
Scene 2. The Heron's Pool (Outside castle)
Trio (Lord, Loch, Joe) 'Indian Drum' "Hark, some one called me cad!"
Finale (Quintett - Loch, Nancy, Phil, Mary, Joe) "In thine arms, darling one"
Scene 3. The Castle Hall at Yule!
Music 'Simon the Cellerer' (Simon) "Retainers and greengrocers!"
Music on Lovell's entrance 'See the Conquering hero comes'
Song and Chorus (Minstrels) 'Oh Touch the Harp Gently'
Grand Christmas Ballet - based on Christmas games with chairs, blind man's buff, kissing
under the mistletoe, &c.
Finale (resumed) "This is a very dreadful thing / Right fol de rol de rido"
Scene 4. Dame Margery's Still Room [Housekeeper's Room]
Song (Marg) "My dream of love is over - finished up!"
Concerted Piece (Lord, Marg, Joe, &c.) "O, hear my prayer, sweet Margerie"
Finale "O woman is a sham / A champ-i-on delusion"
Scene 5. The Hamlet at the Castle Foot (in Spring)
[Strains of Bridal March under dialogue] - Repeat Finale to Scene 3

SUPERBA
Christmas Entertainment
Alhambra (Frederick Strange), 26 Dec 1870

Superba - Susannah Cole ● The Lover (Colin) - Rowland Lascelles ● Angel of Life – Fanny Huddart ● Mephistopheles. - Herr Angyalfi ● The Chorus selected from the Royal Italian Opera, under the direction of Mr G. Beale. The songs and choruses written by H. B. Farnie. The Music Selected and Arranged by Mr Frank Musgrave. The invention and production by J. Milano. The magnificent scenery, by Messrs Grieve and Son.

VESTA
Burlesque
St James's (Mrs John Wood), 9 Feb 1871

Vesta - Mrs John Wood ● Expansiva - Miss H. Everard ● Flavia - Lilian Adair ● Lalage - Alice Barrier ● Picrusto - Marian Inch ● Lieut Spurius - Lionel Brough ● Chickalearius - Harry Cox ● Titus Impecuniorus - Geo Yarnold ● Lillivickius - Mr A. W. Young ● The High Priest - Don Leeson ● Brutus - Gaston Murray ● Robertus - George Grainger ● An Augur - John Barrier ● Conscript Father - Charles Otley ● Comminius - Fred Mervin ● Caesar - Julian Crosse ● Gladiators, Vestals, Soldiers, Leaguers, Captives, &c., &c.
The music selected and arranged by Frank Musgrave; the Groupings by Milano; Scenery by Hann; Costumes by May.
Musical numbers not known

136

RIVAL ROMEOS
Farce
St James's Theatre (Mrs John Wood), 8 Apr 1871
Gloriana - Miss Marian Inch • Mrs Snooks - Miss Sallie Turner • Plantaganet Snooks – Mr Harry Cox • Charles Smudge - Mr Gaston Murray • Peter Peppercorn - Mr George Grainger

THE CRIMSON SCARF
(La Tartane)
Operetta, composed by Legouix
Published : Metzler & Co., London, 1872; Cramer & Co.
(Cramer's Opera Bouffe Cabinet No.4)
Alhambra Theatre of Varieties (Frederick Strange), 24 Apr 1871
Cornerino - Signor Bordogni • Sassafrasso - Mr E. J. Odell • Ernesto (Cornerino's Son) - Roland Lascelles • Marco (Cornerino's Steward) - Mr Everard • Bianca (Sassafrasso's Daughter) - Miss Th. St. Ange • Tessa (Her Maid) - Minnie Sidney (Mrs Milano)
 Musical Numbers :
 Overture
 Duet (Bian, Tess) "Should my father come"
 Barcarolle (Ern) 'My Love She is Youthful'
 Air (Corn) 'Venice for the Offender'
 Trio (Tes, Bian, Sass) 'Signor Since You Wish Me'
 Trio (cont) "I'm puzzled and confounded"
 Romance (Bia) 'One April Night'
 Venetian Air (Tess) 'Beppo is Young and Gay'
 Duet (Corn, Sass) "When the midnight hour is striking"
 Ariella (Ern) 'Bless you, Bless you'
 Concerted Piece (Tutti & Choro) 'Friendly Night'
 Finale (Tutti & Choro) 'Truly the Poets Tell'
Revivals : Haymarket, 24 Nov 1873; Brighton Aquarium, 30 June 1889; numerous provincial and amateus productions.

THE BATTLEFIELD
Alhambra Theatre of Varieties (Frederick Strange), 24 Apr 1871
Music by F. Van Herzeele
Drama with orchestra and chorus in 8 movements

BLUE BEARD
Wallack's Theatre, New York, 16 Aug 1871
Blue Beard, the Great P'shaw! - Harry Beckett • Ibrahim - John Bryer • Fatima, his Daughter - Camille Dubois • Sorosister Anne - Carlotta Zerbini • Selim - Lydia Thompson • Corporal Zoug-Zoug - Willie Edouin • Hassan, the First Page - Hetty Tracey • The O'Shacabac, Bluebeard's Buttons - Henry W. Montgomery • Fez, an officer of "Curs" - Tilly Earl • Said, a wild young dog - Kate Egerton • Beda - Nellie Cook • Pages, the "Spiritual Wives" of Bluebeard, the Body Guard (Marmelukes) of the Great P'shaw, Turkish Girls and Wedding Guests, &c., &c.
 Musical Numbers :
 Chorus of Peasants "Water cold and melons rare"

137

Song "When I was three, my sainted mother"
Solo and Corus "Come and have some luncheon"
Song and Chorus Yes, of an evening, when gas is lighted"
Duet "My Fatima My Selim"
Song and Chorus "O, Fortune, wherefore on me frown"
Song "Some folks there be whose custom is"
Pages Chorus "Dreaming by night, Dreaming by day"
Solo and Chorus "The silvery moon is winking"
The "Pool" Song A young man's brain, if brain he has"
The "Oyster" Song "Dearest, I see, that you have got the key"
Trio "Who is not fond of dancing?"
Duet "Guide me, guide me, guide me"
Song "Oh my ! just see, this stupid old key"
Solo "Boys, give it another rub"
Finale "Now old friend, just pull yourself together"
   Added later :
'He's a Fraud' "The world as we all know is hollow ..."
That's the Sort of Man I Am "My pet name is Bluebeard"
Chic "No more for me"
Nothing a Year
Dreaming ("pretty serenade")
The Two Obadiahs

Revivals (America) : Wallack's, 12 Aug 1872; Olympic Theatre, 6 Dec 1872; Academy of Music, 5 May 1873; National Tour; Wallack's, 18 Sept 1877; Bijou Opera House, 6 May 1884.
Britain : Charing Cross Theatre, 19 Sept 1874, trans. Globe Theatre 24 Dec 1874
Revivals (Britain) : Folly (formerly Charing Cross) Theatre, 6 July 1877

MARIAGE AUX LANTERNES
As Le Tresor à Mathurin, Opéra-Comique, 1 act, composed by Jacques Offenbach, libretto
by Michel Carré and Léon Battu (Salle Hertz, Paris,
May 1853); Later re-written as Le Marriage aux lanternes, Operetta,
1 act, libretto by Jules Dubois (from Michel Carré and Léon Battu)
(Bouffes-Parisiens, Paris, 10 Oct 1857)
Published (as Paquerette) : Boosey & Co., London, 1884 (Boosey & Co.'s Operettas for
Drawing-room or Stage)
Gaiety Theatre (John Hollingshead), 11 Oct 1871
Guillet (a Young Farmer) - Mr F. Wood ● Denise (his cousin) - Miss K. Love ● Fanchette,
Catherine (Young widows of the village) - Constance Loseby and Annie Tremaine ● Rural
Policeman - Mr Ledwidge.
   Musical Numbers (from published Paquerette) :
   1. Complets À Due 'Upon my Word'
   2. Trio 'Uncle Zach's Letter'
   3. Song & Burden ' 'Tis a poor heart is never merry'
   4. Quarelling Duett 'Every Eve must have her Adam'
   5. Angelus Quartette 'Hark ! the Angelus is ringing'
   6. Melodrame Seeking the Treasure
   7. Recit and Reprise of Quartette 'Strange! It Cannot Be'
   8. Finale 'One Other Cup'
NB: Northcott, op.cit., p.48 is the authority for saying that the Gaiety production was
Farnie's version later published as Paquerette. If so, the names were altered before

138

publication. In Paquerette the characters are Babolet, Paquerette, Navette, and Bluette. And the 13 year delay in publication is surprising. The Gaiety version could be by Hollingshead himself.

GENEVIÈVE DE BRABANT
Opera Bouffe, composed by Jacques Offenbach, revised by Hector Crémieux from libretto by Etienne Tréfeu (Bouffes Parisiens, 19 Nov 1859)
Published (Farnie's adaptation) : London, 1872
Philharmonic Theatre, Islington (Charles Morton), 11 Nov 1871

Corcoriko, Duke of Brabant - John Rouse ● Geneviève, his wife - Selina Dolaro / Miss Lennox Grey ● Golo, his favourite - Henry Lewens ● Drogan, a pastrycook - Emily Soldene ● Oswald, the Duke's peculiar page - Miss Clara Vesey ● Brigitte, confidante of Geneviève - Miss E. Cooke / Miss Vaughan / Marie Clifton ● Charles Martel - Mr Adams / Mr King / Mons Marius ● Philibert (page to Charles Martel) - Miss Ada Lee ● Graburge, a police sergeant - Edward Marshall ● Pitou, a low ranking police officer - Felix Bury ● Vanderprout, the burgomaster - Mr J. B. Rae ● The Hermit of the Ravine - Mr Charley W. Norton ● In the last scene a Quadrille called 'Le Drogan' danced by Mdlles Sara, Wilford, White, and Gerish.
Dir. Emily Soldene (& de facto Farnie); MD. Halton / Lindheim; sc.Calcott and Hann; cos Auguste & Co.

Musical Numbers :
Act I
1. Chorus of Sightseers (with Christine) "We fear that something's going wrong"
2. The Burgomaster's Song "Thanks to our sage consultation"
3. Song of the Pie (Drogan & Citizens) "This plât, O gentlemen and ladies"
4. The Balcony Duet (Drog, Genev) "My devotion she's approving"
5. Crowing Chorus (+ Genev, Duke, Drog) "Chanticleer upon the wall"
6. Sewing Stanzas (Tutti, Christine, Gudule, Isoline, Gretchen)
7. The Toilette Song (Christine, Gretchen, Tutti) "This rig, my dears"
8. Ballad (Drogan) 'Love in Youth' "Youth has a wisdom of its own"
9. Trio of the Pulse (Drog, Brig, Genev) "A gratuity; ... a gratuity! "
10. Trio (Duke, Genev, Drog) 'The Fact Is, Duke'
11. Song & Chorus (Duke) 'A Cup of Tea ● A Temperance Stave'
12. The Armourer's Ditty (Martel) "Tap him gently, look intently"
13. Grand Finale to First Act (Tutti & Chorus) "Off the Duke is going!
Act II
14. Bugle Chorus "The hunt is up! Hark to the echoing horn! "
15. The Bigotted Crusader. Ronde d'Escrime (Martel)
16. Hermit's Song ("an automated prophet") "I'm the Hermit of the Valley"
17. Storm Trio (Genev, Drog, Brig) "Thunder, wind, rain all come together"
18. Sleep Song (Drog) "Sleep on, sleep on, my Queen! "
19. The Gend'armes Duett (Grab, Pit) "We're public guardians, bold, yet wary"
20. Quartette (Grab, Pit, Genev, Drog) "A lady can but die at most"
21. Tyrolienne (Ensemble) "How bright hath grown the day! "
22. Ballad 'Kiss, Kiss' "Who hath not felt, when sad and lone"
23. Farandole and Anacreontic "Dance we now a joyous measure"
24. Romance of the Ringlet " 'Tis true her hair was raven black, and now 'tis grey"
25. Song of the Witnesses (Drog, Brig, Genev, & Chorus) "Fate to shield you"
26. Hope and Love (Tutti & Chorus) "Hope! unto thee we sing a strain"
27. Final Chorus "Long live Genevieve de Brabant"

139

Revivals : Gaiety, 6 Nov 1873; Opera Comique, 18 Apr 1874; Park Theatre, 31 Oct 1875; Opera Comique, 18 Mar 1876; Philharmonic, 23 Jan 1878; Alhambra, 16 Sept 1878; Alexandra Palace, 6 June 1881; Crystal Palace, 13 Sept 1881; Royalty, 21 Nov 1881; numerous provincial and amateur productions.
America : Olympic Theatre, New York, 19 Oct 1874 (pirated version); Lyceum Theatre, New York, 2 Nov 1874 (authorized version)

ROBIN HOOD
Wallack's Theatre, New York, 22 July 1872
Robin Hood - Lydia Thompson • Cœur de Lion - Amy Sheridan • Sir Gilbert Montfalcon - Camille Dubois • Will Scarlet - Marie Parselle • Alice - Eliza Weathersby • Blondel - Louise Beverley • Little John - Tully Earle • Much - Pauline Leslie • Will-o'-the-Wisp - Fanny Leslie • Baron Front de Bœuf - Willie Edouin • Friar Tick - Mr. Brier • Maid Marian - Harry Beckett

L'ŒIL CREVÉ
or, The Merry Toxophilites
Opera Bouffe, composed and written by Hervé (Florimond Ronger)
(Folies-Dramatique, 12 Oct 1867
Published (English version) : Boosey & Co., London [1875]
Opera Comique (E. P. Hingston), Mon 21 Oct 1872
Fleur de Noblesse (the demoiselle of the Château) - Julia Mathews • The Marquise – Harriet Coveney • Eclosine (Hostess of the "Bull's Eye Inn") - Blanche de Londre • Mariette, Mimi, her Gossips - Kate Phillips, Miss G. Corinne • Françoise - Miss Verrini • Bouton de Rose, Patte de Velours, Pages to the Marquis - Blanche Beverley, Abbie France • Dindonette (a foundling and Local Soprano) - Pattie Laverne • The Marquis (Feudal Superior of the village) - David Fisher • The Duke - Mr Odell • Alexandrivore (Champion Crossbowman) – Mdlle Clary • Géromé (the Local Posse Comitatus) - Mr R. Temple • The Préfet (an Arcadian Pluralist) - Mr Perrini • Totole (a Journeyman Cabinet Maker) - George Beckett • Chavassus, Copeau, Dufour (Shooting Stars) - Thurley Beale, Knight Aston, Mlle E. Viner • The Sentry - Mr R. Barker • Village Chatterboxes, Members of the Toxophilite Corps.

Musical Numbers :
1. Eloge and Refrain (Fran, Mari, Eclo) "Like Cupid in the myths of old"
2. Dindonette's Lament "But if, perchance, my lover"
3. Archers Chorus "Rouse! each gay toxophilite, off to the butts be wending"
4a Duo (Alex, Dind) 'Love and Pride' "I long for this archery meeting"
4b Ensemble "From thy ream of ambition awaking"
5. Song (Marq) 'The Marquis and the Shepherdess'
6. Finale Sc. 1 (Alex, Eclo, Dind, Chor) "Now then! en route, "
7. Valse Rondo (Fleur) "A joiner's calling To me's enthralling"
8. Trio (Tot, Fleur, Pref) 'Tho' Nature Smiles' "Tho' nature smiles and all is gay"
9. Song (Ger) 'Love and a Kettle-Drum' "To the great my thoughts incline"
10. Competitors' Chorus "Pleasant the duty Of shooting for beauty"
11. Septuor and Chorus 'The Dark Horse' "Who's this archer so grim"
12. Rustic Ballad (Alex, Fleur) 'The Path by the Wood'
12. Chorus of On-lookers "Oh! this day of woe"
13. Finale Act I. (Chorus) "Run him in! run him in!"
14. Song (Alex) 'From Prison Bars' "Here through my prison bars"

140

15. Duo (Alex, Dind) 'O What Joy Once Again'
16. Solo & Chorus (Cope, Chav) 'Cure or Kill' "Now then! anybody ill?"
17. Bolero (Fleur) 'The Alcalde's Daughter'
Recit. "Would'st know what is above the healing art?"
Air "Young Pedro loved the Alcalde's child"
Rustic Divertissement, Les Roses et Les Marguerites, Final Chorus.
Dir. Mr R. Barker; MD. Mr Mallandaine; Dance arranged J. Milano; cos. by Cheret

FORTY WINKS
(Une Nuit blanche)
Operetta, composed by Jacques Offenbach, libretto by Edouard Plouvier (Bouffes
Parisienes, 5 July 1855)
Published : Metzler & Co., London 1872
(No.5 in Metzler's Opera Bouffe series)
Theatre Royal, Haymarket (John Baldwin Buckstone), 2 Nov 1872
NB: The opening night programme has "First time in London" suggesting that it had
previously been performed elsewhere.
John Samson (a Pilot and Smuggler) - Edward Osborne ● Sam (a Coastguardsman) – Mr
Weathersby ● Annette (a Bride) - Fanny Wright
> Musical Numbers :
> Romance " 'Tis my wedding night" (Annette)
> Song "Come, be consoled," (Sam)
> Duet "At last my longing eyes behold" (John, Annette)
> Rondo "A Smuggler am I" (John)
> Trio "Pour out the wine" (John, Sam, Annette)
> Finale "Ah, cheerless and cold" (John, Sam, Annette)

Revivals : Haymarket and elsewhere as curtain raiser, too numerous to detail; numerous
provincial and amateur productions
America : Grand Opera House, Baltimore, 12 Nov 1874; Opera House, Albany, 31 Jan
1876; and many more.

THE BLIND BEGGARS
(Les Deux Aveugles)
One-act comic opera, composed by Jacques Offenbach, libretto by Jules Moinaux (Bouffe
Parisiens, 5 July 1855)
Published (Farnie version) : Metzler & Co., 1872
(No.7 in Metzler's Opera Bouffe series)
Opera Comique (E. P. Hingston), 30 Nov 1872
Mr Zachariah Morgan - Mr K. Barker ● Mr Baffles - Mr E. Perrini
> Musical Numbers :
> 1. (Zach) 'The Soft Trombone' "I am called Zachariah Morgan"
> 2. Duo (Buff, Zach) 'Off to Battersea' "Ladies, gentlemen, women and men"
> 3. Serenade (Buff, Zach) 'Scrumptious Mary'
> 4. Melodrame 'O Fortune À Ton Caprice'
> 5. Finale - Serenade (Zach, Buff) "Lum tiddle um / Scrumptious Mary"

Revivals : Strand Theatre 1 Apr 1874; Royal Amphitheatre, Holborn 17 Oct 1874; St
George's Hall (German-Reed) 4 Nov 1895; numerous provincial and amateur productions.
BBC Broadcast 30 Mar 1928

LEO AND LOTOS
Niblo's Garden, New York, 30 Nov 1872
Prince Leo - Mlle Ermesilda Diani ● Princess Lotos - Mlle Marie Rosetti ● and with Laura Joyce, Millie Cook, E. D. Davies (ventroliquist), Herr Wieflenbach (drummer), Master Henry Collard (vocalist - imitated Mr Sims Reeves), Henry Collard (dwarf famous for his imitations of great tenors), "Young America" (violinist), Miss Josephine Wells (skipping-rope act), Acrobats, &c., &c.

MAGIC MELODY
(La Chanson de Fortunio)
One-act operetta, music Jacques Offenbach, libretto Hector Cremieux and Jules Servieres
(Ludovic Halevy)
Published : Metzler & Co., London, 1872
(No.6 in Metzler's Opera Bouffe series)
Brighton Aquarium 30 June 1890
Arnold - Madge Rockingham ● Dorick, Grace, Betty, Toby, and clerks - not known
Musical Numbers : Act I   Dorick's Office
1. Chorus & Drinking Song (Arn, Wil, Ral, Ned, Bas) 'He is gone'
    Drinking Song 'Adam's Ale' "Adam's pale ale, brewage of Eden"
2. Rondo (Wil, Ral, Ned, Bas, Tob) 'Long ago, Now-a-days'
3. Bolero (Grace) 'Best not go Too Far' "My worthy guardian"
4. Duett and Ensemble (Tob & Arn) 'The Finding of the Song'
            Act II   Dorick's Orchard
5. Song (Tob) 'The Office Boy' "I am an active office boy"
6. Song (Arn) 'I Love Her'
7. Duett (Grace & Arn) 'Did Ever Eyes'
    Fortunio's Song 'Hidden Love'
8. Finale (Tutti) 'If You Demand' "If you demand what maiden solely"
Revivals : Brighton Aquarium, 4 July 1892; Royal Academy of Music, 11 Dec 1907

THE BOHEMIANS
(Le Roman Comique)
Opera Bouffe, composed by Jacques Offenbach, libretto by Hector Cremieux and Ludovic Halévy (Bouffes Parisiens, 10 Dec 1866)
Published : Metzler & Co., London, 1873
Opera Comique (E. P. Hingston), 24 Feb 1873
Baron de Trente-Sept Tourelles - George Honey ● Mesire Trinquedondaine - David Fisher ● Enguerrand de Moranges - Mdlle Rose Bell ● La Belle Adriennes - Mdlle Clary ● Trompe la-Balle (Sergeant of the Watch) - Mr T. Paulton ● Bouton d'or - Rose Berrend ● Grand Goblet Bearer of Burgundy - George Beckett

The Bohemians ● Guillerette (Singing lady) - Pattie Laverne ● Belle au-soir (Tragedienne) - Louisa Carlyle ● Graine-de-Beaute (General Utility) - Mr R. Barker ● L'Abime (Heavy Man) - Mr Hogan

Members of the Company ● Galaor - Mr Knight Ashton ● Cunegonde – Miss Heath ● Beauguillard - Miss E. Viner ● Aventurine - Miss Mabel Stuart ● Florette - Miss Smith ● Gaston - Miss Cressy ● Blaise - Miss Banks ● Mange- Tout - Mr White ● Boire-Sec – Mr Clifford ● Croquinole (Manager of the Troupe) - Mr E. J. Odell ● Leonard (Page to the Baron) - Miss L. Moore ● Other Pages, shopkeepers, burgesses, Halbadiers, waiters, Ladies and Nobles of the Court, &c., &c.

Characters of the Incidental Tragedy 'The Bravo of Brindisi' ● Il Conte Spiflicato (a Feudal Ruffian) - Mr R. Barker ● Rococo (Grand Duke of the Adriatic) - Mr Hogan ● Tomato (a Young Nobleman) - Mr G. Beckett ● L'Ingognito (a masked stranger) – Mdlle Clary ● Misterioso (retainer of the Court) - Mr Clifford ● Sforzanda (eldest daughter of the Duke) - Mlle Rose Bell ● Her five sisters - Misses Sheriff, Osborne, Clifford, Brewster and Lennard

Ballet-Divertissement of French Vintagers entitled 'Les Vendangeurs'. Invented by Mr Milano. Music by Mr Malladaine. Supported by The Sisters J. & L. Elliott, assisted by Mesdames Bruce, Seymour, Walton and C. Palmer.
Dir. Mr R. Barker; MD. Mr Mallandaine; sc. Messrs Grieve & Sons; cos. Mr S. May, Miss Price and Assistants; Divertissements by Mr J. Milano.

Musical Numbers :

Act I

1. (Grand Provost & Chorus) 'Trouseau Chorus' "Silk, satin and flower,"
2. (L'Abime, Galan, Cunegonde, Guill, & Bohemians) 'The Bohemians'
3. (Enguerrand) 'Daughters of Eve' (Drinking Song)
4. (Sergeant, Halbadiers) 'Sleep, Ratepayers, Sleep' (Round of the City Watch)
5. (Eng. & Grain de Beaute, and Serg) 'Oh He's a Downy Bird' (Trio Buffe)
6. (Eng, Adr) 'Star of Love' (Duet - Serenade) "No bow'r sweetheart, can I offer"
7. (Baron) 'Love's Grammar' (Didactic Ballad) "I'll teach my lady love her grammar"
8. (Bar, Prov) 'Modern Accomplishments' (Duo Buffo) "You're aware ? I am aware !"
9. (Coro, Serg, Bar, Prov, Eng, Adr, Bohemians) Finale to the First Act
   a. "Rataplan! Rataplan! / We, of course, have missed our man"
   b. (Bohemians) "Come along ! each mime and mummer"
   c. (Ensemble) "He little knows his gentle bride / Is not so far away"

Act II

10. 'Bohemian's Song' (from 1st Act Finale) "Come along ! each mime and mummer"
11. (L'Abime, Cune, Host, Galaor, Guil, Coro) 'Pancake Rondo'
12. (Baron, Guil, and Bohemians) 'An Actor's Life' (Rondo)
13. (Guil, and Chorus) Pastoral and Ballad
   a. (Vintage chorus in the distance) "Round and round the winepress turn"
   b. (Ballad) [The Old, Old Song] "How sweetly falls on heart and ear"
13 (sic) (Adr, Eng, Baron) Terzetto "Tis he ! / Baron - / Trente-sept Tourelles !
14. (Eng, Adr) Duettino "When they ask me If I love thee, / Fain I'd answer"
15. (Prov, Coro, Host, Serg, Eng, Adr, Tutti) Finale to Second Act "Now at last"

Act III

16. (Adr) 'Mine Alone !' (Romance) "I dreampt of a lover - what maiden does not ?"
17. (Guil, Coro) Vocal Minuet "Move we in fastidious measure"
18. (Baron, Prov, Guil, Chorus) 'Epithalamium' "In charming confusion"
19. (Adr, Eng, Guil, Baron, and Chorus) Finale 'Daughters of Eve'

FLEUR DE LYS

(La Cour du roi Pétaud)
Opera Comique, composed by Leo Delibes
Published : Metzler & Co., London, 1873
Royal Philharmonic Theatre, 5 Apr 1873
Prince Hyacinth (Son and Heir of Toc-e-Toc) - Emily Soldene ● King Toc-e-Toc – Mr Chessman ● Grand Duke of Madapolam - Mr Marshall ● Fleur-de-Lys (Daughter and

Heiress of the Duke) - Selina Dolaro ● La Gironette (Prime Minister of Madalopam) - John Rouse ● Bouts-rimés (Court Laureate) - Mr Rae ● Tate-pouls (The Duke's Leech) - Mr Drew ● Valerien (Captain of the Duke's Own Musketeers) - Miss Clara Vesey ● Cupbearer – Miss Ada Lee ● Floranthe (Maid of Honour) - Miss Clifton ● The Professor (Tutor to Prince Hyacinth) - Mr H. Lewens ● Pages to the Duke, Gloria - Miss Blanche Roe, Mazagran – Miss Eugenie Vincent, Vermith - Miss Lucy Clifton, Cassis - Miss St Clare ● Pages of the King ● Pen-de-choses - Miss Annie Richardson, Rien-de-tout - Miss Kate Lee ● Cup Bearer of the Duke - Miss Ada Lee ● Equeries, Pages, and Maids of Honour, &c. Dir. Emily Soldene (& de facto Farnie); MD. Mons Lindheim

Musical Numbers :

1.	Patrol Chorus "Soldiers a dozen deep"
2.	Birthday Chorus "Princess! Smiling in beauty, sleep"
3.	Chorus resumed
4.	Song and Chorus 'Nod, Nod!' "I've taken it into my head"
5.	Serenade "Thy name, O lady, I know not"
6.	Arrest of the Serenader "Not yet! A pretty serenade"
7.	Topical Rondo
8.	Concerted Piece and Air 'Eighteen Today'
●	Song and Chorus 'Good Bordeaux' "Pour out for me the good Bordeaux"
9.	Duet 'Sometimes a Lonely Bird'
10.	Finale "O horror! What an awful blow"
	Act II
11.	Scene, Recitative, and Cracker Chorus "Forget not, when the world"
●	Song 'Waiting' "Here my darling with song hath charmed the hour"
12.	Recitative, Pastoral, and Duo "O love who then art thou"
13.	Quartett and Chorus "Let us mysteriously dodge about the guard"
15 (sic)	Song and Refrain (Duet) "O thou whom my playmates call Cupid"
	Ensemble
	Finale "Ah! Who can hear her, who can hear her".

NEMESIS
or, Not Wisely But Too Well
Musical Extravaganza in Five Tableaux. Music from Offenbach, Hervé, Lindheim, Delibes, Vasseur, Lecocq, Roubilliard and Jones; selected and arranged by John Fitzgerald.
Royal Strand Theatre, 17 Apr 1873, closed Tue 17 Feb 1874 (263 performances)
Re-opened Sat 23 May, closed Wed 1 July 1874

Calino (an expectant Benedict) - Edward Terry ● Zidore de Filoselle (a Bachelor Friend) - Topsy Venn ● Roland-de-Roncevaux-Ramponneau (Retired Major of the Chasseurs d'Afrique) - Mons. Marius ● Rosalie Ramponneau (his daughter) - Angelina Claude ● M. Potiphar de Patoche (of the Legion of Honour - Retired Button Maker) - Harry Cox ● Praline de Patoche (his daughter) - Nellie Bromley ● Aunt Turlurette (sister of M. de Patoche) – Mrs Raymond ● 'Cre-nom (Gendarme) - Mr H. J. Turner ● Balivernes (Beadle) - John Wallace ● Perdrichon (Innkeeper) - Mr H. Carter ● Toinette and Justine (Domestics) - Misses La Feuillade and Burville ● Touch-a-tout (Flaneur and Friend of Zidore) - Maria Jones ● Loungers by the Sea-Side, Belles of the Beach, Waiters at the "Naiad's Arms", Friends of MM. Ramponneau and Petoche.
Dir. H. B. Farnie, Mr Vernon, Mrs Swanborough; MD - John Fitzgerald; sc. H. P. Hall.

Musical Numbers :

1	Song and Chorus 'The Bachelor's Legacy' "Poor old man"
2	Chorus 'Porters we be' "Porters we be, ready for fee"

3 Duettino (Ros & Ramp) 'Now to Bed and Dream'
4 Barcarolle (Ros & Calino) 'O Catarina Bella'
5 Finale (Ros, Ramp, Calino & Chorus) 'Now All is Said'
6 Chorus 'The Briny' "The briny to my fancy is so dear"
7 Canzonette (Praline) 'What Are a Lady's Wants'
8 Tiffin Rondo (Patoche, Pral, Touch, Calino & Chorus) 'Will You Take My Arm?'
9 Song (Calino) 'The Language of Love' "For 'love' each country has its own name"
10 Luncheon Sestett (Ros, Pral, Ramp, Toin, Pat, & Jus) 'I Expect My Love'
11 Chorus of Mystery (music from Madame Angot) "Something mysterious"
12 Duet (Pat and Ramp) 'A Warrior Bold' "A warrior bold is an awkward cuss"
13 Finale 'That Little Difficulty Over'
14 Song (Zid) 'My Rosalie' "I've come from Paris bright and gay"
15 Duet and Chorus (music from Madame Angot) 'Let's Go and Hear the Service'
16 Marriage Bell Chorus "Oh radiant and happy the beautiful bride"
17 Tickling Song (Ros) 'Don't Make Me Laugh' "I'm ticklish by birth"
18 Finale 'Come To Breakfast' "There's my hand"

Revivals : Strand, 3 July 1875; Strand, 7 Oct 1878; Comedy, 26 Feb 1885; Provincial Tours.
America : No record of production on Broadway but songs used there - The American name for 'Language of Love' was 'I Love You'
Australia : Opera House, Melboourne, 2 Feb 1874

LA FILLE DE MADAME ANGOT
Opera Comique, composed by Charles Lecocq, libretto by Clairville, Paul Siraudin and Victor Koning, from a novel by Alexander Dumas, 'Ange Pitou' (Fantaisies-Parisiennes, Brussels, 4 Dec 1872)
Published : Libretto printed W. Gee, Loondon, 1873
Gaiety Theatre (John Hollingshead and Charles Morton), 10 Nov 1873
Clairette Angot - Miss Annie Sinclair • Pomponnet - M. Felix Bury • Mlle Lange – Miss Emily Soldene • Larivaudière - Mr Richard Temple • Javotte - Miss Ewell Amarante – Mrs Leigh • Buteux - Mr Cruttwell • Louchard - Mr Lewens Hersilie - Miss Clara Vesey • Babet - Miss Cook • Trenitz - Mr J. G. Taylor • Ange Pitou - Mr E. D. Beverley • Cadet – Mr Ludwig • A Captain in the Hussars - Mr C. Norton

Musical Numbers :

Act I 1. Chorus and Solo "Arm in arm, here we come, altogether"
2. Song and Chorus (Lange) 'Madame Angot' "To sell fish was her calling"
3. Song (Pitou) "Of course, Clairette I will love for ever"
4. Duett (Pitou, Clair) "When seeking out the 'why' and 'whether' "
5. Duo (Pitou, Lariv) "So you are Larivaudiere?"
6. Finale to Act I (Tutti and Chorus) "Come, come, poltroon"
    The Sedition Rondo (Clair) "Time was that monarchy meant plunder"

Act II 7. Scandal Chorus (Ineffables) "Since you say so, we will receive it"
8. The Hussar Song (Lange) "Augerean's soldiers are fine fellows!"
9. Duet (Lange, Clair) "Dear days of childhood, time of gladness"
10. The Fascination Duet (Lange, Pitou) "How find you politics?"
11. Quintette (Lariv, Louch, Lange, Clair, Pitou) "What! 'Tis the truth I tell!"
    Ensemble "O joy, I am a happy woman"
12. Finale to Act II Chorus "When folk conspire to intrigue and plot"
    Soldiers Chant "Down with plots and down with plotters"
    Valse de Seduction "Whirling - whirling, In perpetual motion of pleasure"

Act III 13. Chorus and Song "Spite of bearing, spite of dressing"
    Air (Clair) "You sent me, at much cost, to school"

145

14. The "Roughs" Duett (Pomp, Lariv) "What do you want? You ass! a cuff?" Ensemble "It was the barber!"
15. Finale (Tutti) "Oh dearest enemy! It is my fate"
    The Quarrel Duo (Clair, Lange) "Ah, now I've trapped you, madame, fine"

Revivals : Opera Comique, 26 Dec 1873; Gaiety, 14 Mar 1874; Lyceum, 1 Aug 1874; Park Theatre, 1 Dec 1875; Opera Comique, 3 Apr 1876; Alhambra, 12 Nov 1877; Alhambra, 25 Feb 1878; Connaught, 17 Nov 1879; Numerous provincial and amateur productions.
America : Lyceum Theatre, New York, 16 Nov 1874

THE MAIN CHANCE
"An Entirely New Farcical Comedy in Two Acts"
Prince of Wales, Liverpool, 6 Dec 1873

Mr Egomet (a retired member of the Stock Exchange) - Mr John L. Hall ● Mr Keenie Pyke (a Companies Promoter) - Mr F. Marshall ● Dr Lamb (a fashionable Physician) - ... ● Mr Owngood Dart (of a Private Bill Office) - ... ● Walter Mansfield (Nephew to Egomet) – Mr Ashley ● Norman Dart (his friend - son of Old Dart) - Mr Vere ● Joshua (Egomet's servant) - ... ● Florence Lethbridge (a Young Widow - daughter of Dart) - Miss F. Cowell ● Mrs Tubbs (Egonet's Housekeeper) - Mrs C. Elton ● Cissy Vane (Egonet's Ward) - Miss Nellie Claremont ● Other parts Messrs Roberts and Constantine and Miss Corsell (sic)
Royalty Theatre 15 Apr 1874

Mr Egomet - Mr E. Righton ● Mr Keenie Pyke - Mr T. B. Bannister ● Dr Lamb – Mr Fosbrooke ● Mr Owngood Dart - Mr Charles Steyne ● Walter Mansfield - Mr G. F. Neville ● Norman Dart - Mr W. Holman ● Joshua - Mr Russell ● Florence Lethbridge - Miss Maggie Brennan ● Mrs Tubbs - Miss Emily Thorne ● Cissy Vane - Miss Henrietta Hodson

ELDORADO
Folie Musicale, music selected and re-arranged by Mr John Fitz-Gerald.
Strand Theatre (Mrs Swanborough), 19 Feb 1874, closed 22 May 1874

Mossieu Pignouf (Maire of the Hamlet of Fouilly-les-Oies) - Edward O. Terry ● Mossieu Blagados (Wind-Miller of the Hamlet) - E. J. Odell ● Mossieu Boule-de-Suif (Village Innkeeper and Grocer) - Harry Cox ● M. Patatras (Officer de Paix) - Mons Marius ● Verpillon (Sergeant of Police) - Harry St Maur ● Narcisse Pignouf (Son and heir of Pignouf) - Mr H. Carter ● M. Seraphin (A Matrimonial Agent) - Angelina Claude ● Le Petit Vicomte Vas-y-Voir (A young Aristocrat) - Maria Jones ● Vian (Head Waiter at the "Trois Frères Provençaux", Paris) - Topsy Venn ● Widow Cri-du-Cœur Vertuchoux (Cousin of Mossieu Pignouf) - Sally Turner ● Marjolaine (Daughter of Boule-de-Suif, and waitress at her Pa's Cabaret) - Miss Prescott ● Gustave and Adolph (Two garçons at The Trois Frères) - Misses Lillie Moore and Miss Sarah E. La Feuillade ● Fifine, Titine, Epaminonde, Erostrate (Hired aristocrats at M. Seraphin's matrimonial meetings) - Misses Kate Lee, Julia Courtenay, Gertrude Winter and Minnie Venn ● Captain of Zouaves - Miss Hastings ● Verdurette (Beloved of the little Vicomte) - Nellie Bromley ● Groups of Peasants, Garçons, Zouaves, Hired Guests, &c., &c.
Dir. Mrs Swanborough, C. H. Stephenson, H. B. Farnie; sc. Mr H. P. Hall; cos. MM. Constant (Gaiété Theatre, Paris), Compton, O'Neill, and Mrs Richardson.

Musical Numbers :
1. Card Chorus (Tutti) "Labour done, Cards and fun"
2. Quintett (Maire, Miller, Grocer, Widow, & Verd) 'Reading the Letters'

3. Song (Maire & Coro) 'The Local Swell' "I am the most tremendous local swell"
4. Duett (Verd & Vicomte) 'Toujours' "Forget not to remember"
5. Finale Sc.1 (Tutti) "Paris! what rapture! shall I see that wonderland?"
6. Song (Vlan & Coro) 'The Menu' "Purée de Gibier, Tortue claire"
7. Concerted Piece (The Breakfast Party) 'A Round of Toasts' "Vive, vive, vive la reine!"
8. Finale (Maire, Miller, Grocer, Widow, Verd, Vlan, Sergeant & Coro) "Fetter'd go? No, no!'
9. Song (Patat) 'The Modern Soldiers Dream' "Happy and bright unto civilian's eye"
10. Duett (Seraph & Patat) 'At Nine Tonight' "At nine tonight, your hearts delight"
11. Concerted Piece (Maire, Miller, Grocer, Verd, & Widow) 'The Escape'
12. Song (Pignouf) 'The Maire's Lament' "Tum-ti-tum, ... In the land of the olive and fig"
13. Finale Sc.3 (Tutti) "Now is my heart all wildly beating!"
14. Song (Seraph) 'For Better or Worse' "There is no passion flower I love"
15. Duett (Verd & Seraph) 'Palpitation' "Oh, she indeed is very pretty"
16. Vocal Mazurka (Tutti) 'Round and About'
17. Sestett (Patat, Seraph, Verd, Pignouf, Boule, & Blagados) 'The Avowal' "My love, my own"
18. Finale - part of No. 5 "Cric! I will be your guide, philosopher and friend"

MY NEW MAID
Operetta, Music by Ch. Lecocq
Published : Cramer's Opera Bouffe Cabinet No.3, London, 1874
Opera Comique (Charles Morton), 18 Apr 1874 (Curtain Raiser to Genevieve)
Lady Lucy L'Estrange, A Young Widow - Miss Albertazzi • Countess Grasmere, Disguised as a Lady's Maid - Miss Violet Granville
Musical Numbers :
Overture
1. Song (Lucy) 'Yes! Love has turned quite moodish'
2. Aria (Gras) 'The Model Maid'
3. Duett 'You are awkward and rude'
4. Duett Finale 'Tonight I give a dance'

LOO, OR THE PARTY WHO TOOK MISS
Bouffonnerie Musicale, derived from Le Carnaval d'un merle blanc, by Henri Chivot and Alfred Duru, music by John Fitz-Gerald.
Royal Strand Theatre (Mrs Swanborough), 28 Sept 1874, closed 7 Apr 1875
(163 performances)
Tabardon (retired notary) - Harry Cox • Louisa (his only daughter) - Lottie Venne • Emilion, aspirant to the hand of Louisa - Mr E. Terry • Rimbombo (Last Prince of the Abruzz - a mysterious Italian) - Mons. Marius • Bagatelle (Prima Donna of a travelling Opera Bouffe company) - Angelina Claude • Fiasco di Gamut (Tenor of the said Company, in love with Louisa) - Mr H. St Maur • Clicquot (Garçon of the café "Aux intrigues pures") – Mr H. Carter • Postiche (Coiffeur and Fancy Ball Costumier) - Kate Phillips • Gaston (A rejected suitor of Louisa) - Miss La Feuillade • Basquise (Confidante of La Bagatelle) – Ethel Prescott • Suitors of Louisa and bond slaves to Tabardon, Ladies of the travelling opera bouffe company, Masqueraders, Hairdressers, &c., &c.
Dir. Mrs Swanborough, Mr C. H. Stephenson and H. B. Farnie; sc. Mr H. P. Hall; cos. Mme Alias.

Musical Numbers :   Scene 1
1. Duettino (Loo & Fiasco) "Neath the left breast of this coat of mine"
2. Trio (Loo, Tab & Fiasco) "Pray be cool, sir, do not splutter"

147

3. Song & Chorus (Tab) "Have you the vats where grape"
4. Song & Chorus (Emil) "They call me the Lachrymose man,"
5. Concerted Piece (Tab, Loo, Fiasco & Coro) "Pack up your traps and quickly go"
6. Song & Chorus (Bagatelle) "After town life oh what fun"
7. Song & Chorus (Bagatelle & Coro) "Let us swear! In pursuit of this lark"
8. Scena (Rimbombo) "When the lightning is flashing red"
9. Finale (Bagatelle, Fiasco & Coro) "Take good care that your boots don't creak"
   Serenade "Day is fading from the lea"
   Rataplan Chorus "Lead him astray, girls, lead him astray"
                    Scene 2
10. Song (Postiche) "Tho' hustled, bustled, all the day"
11. Duet (Bagatelle & Emilion) "You're the ladies' man"
12. Duet (Rimbombo & Fiasco) "I'm crème de la crème, sir"
13. Trio (Bagatelle, Fiasco & Emil) "Take me, take me, into the dance sirs,"
                    Scene 3
14. Chorus "Come, have you your hair done, each belle and dandy"
15. Song (Loo) "If man, weak man try woman to deceive"
16. Sestett (sic) (Rimb, Fiasco, Emil, Tab, Bag & Loo) "The Vivandière!"
                    Scene 4
   Masquerade, Galop, and Rataplan Chorus

Revivals : Strand, 13 Nov 1875; numerous provincial productions and tours.

THE BLACK PRINCE

Comedy Bouffe in three acts; music selected from works of Charles Lecocq; founded on Le
Voyage en Chine by MM. Labiche and Delacour.

St James's Theatre (Stephan Fiske), 24 Oct 1874, closed 16 Dec 1874

Sybil (younger daughter of Old Cobb) - Selina Delaro ● Flossie (elder daughter of Old
Cobb) - Nellie Bromley ● Gab, Bab, and Mary (their Maids) - Misses Inez D'Aquilar,
Linda Verner, and Belle Britain ● Dr Maresnest (of the Society of Antiquaries) - John Hall
● Old Cobb (retired Tradesman) - John Rouse ● Hon Mr Fluensee - Mr C. W. Norton
● Lord Skyraker (of the Royal Yacht Squadron) - Emily Duncan ● Admiral Freeboard (of
the Ironclad "Flat Iron") - Mr P. Lawson ● Mash (County Vet) - Mr Belleville ● Ringtail
(Bo'sun of the Steam Yacht "Firefly") - Mr H. Clifford ● Tom (a Cowes Boatman) - Chas.
Campbell ● Sir Roland Scate (President of the Summer Ice Club) - Mr E. W. Latham (the
Champion Skater) ● Cactus (Factotum to Old Cobb) - Mr W. Vernon ● Mr Lardy, Mr
Dardy (of the R.Y.S.) - Kate Lee and Miss Grahame ● Cumin (Waiter of the R. Y.
Clubhouse) - Mr Whitney ● Forestay, Backstay, Bobstay (of the "Firefly" yacht) - Eugene
Vernie, Julia Beverley, Elise Vernie ● Nivian Gale R.N. - Mr Chatterson ● Gardeners,
Housemaids, Villagers, Members of the R.Y.S., Boatmen, Visitors at Cowes, Sailors,
Stokers, &c., &c.

sc. Grieve & Son; cos. Mme Neveux, Gask & Gask, Sam May, Poole & Skinner (of Jermyn
Street)

                    Musical Numbers :
                    Act I
1. Smash Chorus and Soli (Cactus, Gab, Bab, Housemaids & Gardeners) "Oh dear! oh dear!
   A dreadful smash!"
2. The Antiquarian Song (Maresnest & Chorus)
3. Romance (Viv) 'The Rose and the Glove' "Dainty little glove, Of my dainty love"
4. The Chaff Duet (Syb & Viv)
5. Quartette (Syb, Floss, Viv, Cobb) 'Get Out' "Hush! - he comes - do not meet my father"

6.   Song (Floss) 'My Ideal' "Other damsels may pray to Cupid"
7.
8.   Finale to Act I (Tutti e coro) "A deputation in education"
      Quintette (Syb, Floss, Gab, Bab, Viv) "You, 'tis you? That is true."
            Act II Scene - At Cowes in the Isle of Wight
9.   Morceau D'Ensemble and Chorus (Syb, Floss, Cobb, Mares, & Chorus) "With the Greeks"
      Boatmens Chorus "We see as how your honour wants a boat"
10.   Song (Flossie) 'Eve's Apple' "In the grape men find elation" (Metra)
11.   Duettino (Viv, Cobb) 'Will You Go?' "Your presence, sir, is hateful, I wonder that you stay"
12.   Couplets (Syb) 'Two Loves' "A lover sought my hand and me"
13.   Valse Chorus 'Summer Skating' "Sing we cheerily, Dance we merrily"
14.   Finale to Act II (Tutti e coro) "Lo! the yachts - we will toast the winner"
            Act III Scene - Deck of the S. Yacht "Firefly"
15.   Daybreak Chorus "The light of stars is gone, The ruddy day comes on"
      Capstan Song and Solo (Solo - Ringtail) "Were you ever in Quebec?"
16.   Song and Chorus (Viv & Chorus) 'Sailors' Larks' "I love a lass, but then her father"
16 (sic) The Hammock Duet (Syb, Viv) "Where art thou, my own love?" (Roques)
17.   Castagnette Song (Syb, Viv, Flos & Chorus) 'Cigars and Guitars'
18.   Mutiny Chorus and Soli (Syb, Flos, Mares, Ring, Cobb & Chorus) "Our Captain's ways"
19.   Hornpipe (Maresnest)
20.   Finale (Syb & Chorus) 'Rule, Britannia'

WHITTINGTON
Opera bouffe, composed by Jacques Offenbach
Alhambra Theatre, 26 Dec 1874, closed 7 May 1875, (112 performances)
Dick Whittington ('Prentice to Fitzwarren) - Kate Santley ● Alice Fitzwarren (Daughter of Fitzwarren) - Julia Matthews ● Dorothy, the cook to Fitzwarren - Lennox Grey ● Alderman Fitzwarren - Charles Heywood ● The Bell-ringer of Bow - W. M. Terrott ● The Sergeant of the Patrol - Harry Paulton ● Captain Bobstay of the Galleon Z.10 - John Rouse ● Hirvaia, Princess of Bambouli - Grace Armytage ● The MacPibroch, a Scottish Chieftain – Mr Swarbreck ● The O'Shamrock, an Irish Chieftain - Alice Hilton ● FitzFulke, an English Fop - Jennie Howard / Inez Harland ● King Bambouli XIX - Fred Clifton ● The Chief Moonshi - W. Worboys ● Colza, Captain of the Amazon Guard - Miss Wright ● Naphtha - H. Parry ● Omawa, Taia, Lalaza, Wyme (Maids of Honour to Hirvaia) - Misses Marie Barrie, Inez Harland / Miss Cecil, Clara Risson, Christopher ● Thomas, a cat - Master Abrahams ● Edward III, King of England - Mr Hutton ● Piers, a Countryman - Mr T. H. Paul ~ Ballet ● Mdlles Jacobi, Pertoldi, Sidonie; M. Dewinne / Betty Rigl
MD. Georges Jacobi; ch. M. Dewinne; sc. A. Callcott; cos. Alfred Thompson
    Musical Numbers : Overture
    1. (Fitzwarren, MacP, & Coro) 'Shop Chorus' "Come Shop, There Shop"
    2. (Bellringer) 'The Bell Ringer' "From sand glass and sundial"
    3. (Whitt) Rondo "A prentice linen draper my youth I gaily pass"
    4. (Alice, Dorothy, MacP, Fitzwarren) Finale Act 1, Sc. 1 "So long as there's good beer"
    4 (bis) Marche de la Patrouille
    5. (Alice) Ballad 'Slumber and Dream' "O slumber and dream for dark the way"
    6. (Alice, Whitt, Dorothy, Serg & Coro) Finale Act 1, Sc. 2 ""Lock him up, lock him up"
    ? (bis) Hornpipe
    7. Serg & Coro 'The Haunted Kickaboo!' "Ah! well I remember Tom Bellows"
    8. (Alice, Whitt, Fitz, Bobstay) Finale Act 1, Sc. 1 (sic) "Sweet heart here I am"
            Act 2 Entr'acte
    1. 'Hammock Chorus' "Here in dreamy leisure"

2. (Hirvaia) Couplets 'Woman's Will' "A Princess I but still a woman"
3. (Whitt, Dorothy, Bellringer, Bobstay, Serg) Quintette "The ship was old"
4. (Princess, Whitt) Duett "O tell me pray what's a cat?"
5. (Ensemble) Rondo & Chorus "Great at colonizing, Is England understand"
5 (bis) Reprise
6 - 13. Cortège - Ballet - Ballet - Corps de Ballet - Variation - Variation - Variation - Galop
Finale
14. (Dorothy) Ballad 'Oh! Wind that Blows Across the Sea' "I wander where fair
flowers"
15. Chorus of Moonshi's "We are very wise men"
16. (Hirvaia & Coro) 'The Rat Song' "The song of the bird and the maiden"
17. Finale a. Chorus "The Banquet's prepar'd, banish sorrow"
b. (Ensemble) Dinner Rondo & Chorus "English meats we've brought together"
Act 3
19. (sic) Chorus and Ballet "While yet earth is sleeping"
20. Valse
21. (Alice) 'Thimblerig Song' "My gentlemen so quick and nimble"
22. (Dorothy, Bellringer, Bobstay) Trio 'Little We've Found Out'
23. (Alice, Whitt) Duett 'Again! Again!' "Again! Again O tell me"
24. (Ensemble) Finale 'At Last I Hope' "At last I hope my self-willed daughter"

Revivals : Mansion House (Concert version), 28 June 2000; Bloomsbury Theatre, 21 Mar
2005
France : Chatelet, Paris (as Le Chat du Diable), 19 Oct 1893

INTIMIDAD
or, The Lost Regalia
Royal Strand Theatre (Mrs Swanborough), 8 Apr 1875, closed 12 June 1875

Olla Podrida (Village Innkeeper) - Mr Edward Terry ● Latherero (Barber, Money-Changer)
- Harry Cox ● Intimidad, A Guerilla Chief - Mons. Marius ● Frutti-Porto (Lieutenant of
Intimidad) - Mr Turner ● Capitaine D'Ossy (of the French Silver-Greys) - Mr Harry St
Maus ● Flor-Fin (Daughter of Intimidad, secretly married to Captain Tric-Trac) - Angelina
Claude ● Pablo (A young Guerilla) - Marie Stevens ● Bergamette, Mousseline (Sous-
Officers in the Silver-Greys) - Miss Barber and Miss Williams ● Cachucha (Waitress,
betrothed to Olla) - Lottie Venne ● Dona Squabosa (Cachucha's Aunt) - Mrs Raymond
● Trabucio, Zamorra (Guerilla Scouts) - Miss Grahame and Miss Holmes ● Absinthe,
Pompon (Buglers in the Silver Greys) - Miss Matthews and Miss Hubert ● Giglampez
(Junior Lieutenant of Intimidad) - Ethel Prescott ● Regalia, Infant child of Flor-Fin - Miss
Lowther ● Guerillas of Intimidad, Hussars, &c., &c.
Dir. Mr W. H. Vernon and the Author; MD Mr Harry Reed; sc. Mr H. P. Hall; cos. M. &
Mme Alias
Musical Numbers not known

CHILPERIC
"The Musical Spectacle, in Three Acts and Seven Tableaux." With additional music by
Hervé.
Alhambra Theatre (J. A. Cave), 10 May 1875, closed Fri 13 Aug 1875

Chilperic (King of the Gauls) - Charles Lyell ● Fredegonda (A peasant girl) - Lennox Grey
● Dr Senna - Harry Paulton ● Siegbert (Chilperic's brother) - Mr J. H. Jarvis ● Brunhaut
(Siegbert's wife) - Emma Chambers ● Galswinda (Castilian Princess) - Katherine Munroe

• Don Nervoso (a needy Noble) - Mr W. Warboys Fatout - Frank Hall • Combert - Mr Clifton • Landry Adelaide Newton • Divitiacus (The Arch Druid) - Mr G. T. Penna • Alfred (the Pet Page) - Alice Hilton • Upwards of 200 chorus and ballet.   The Grand Barbaric Ballet with Mdlles Betty Rigl, Pertoldi, Sidonie, M. Jousset
Dir. J. A. Cave; MD. Mons G. Jacobi; sc. Alfred Calcott; cos. Alfred Thompson.
Musical Numbers not known

THE ANTARCTIC
or, The Pole And The Traces
Musical Farce
Royal Strand Theatre (Mrs Ada Swanborough), 27 Dec 1875, closed 5 Feb 1876
Paletot (A fashionable Parisian Taylor) and Ultramarine (A South Pole navigator) – Edward Terry • Old Bastille (An ex-Detective) - Harry Cox • Amadis de Batignolles (Fire Insurance Company agent) - Mons. Marius • Verpillon (Farmer at Pommes Frites) - Mr Turner • Eusebe (Valet to Old Bastille) - Mr H. Carter • Flo (Daughter of the real Ultramarine) - Angelina Claude • Madeleine Bastille (Paletot's Bride) - Lottie Venne • Phrosine, Delphine (Two of Flo's Schoolmates) - Miss Ethel Prescott, Miss Westfield • Ca-y-est, On-y-va (Two extra Waiters)   Miss Lizzie Williams and Miss Holmes • Schoolgirls &c., &c.
Dir. W. H. Vernon and Mrs Swanborough; MD Mr Harry Reed; sc. Mr H. P. Hall; cos. M. and Mme Alias (Miss Price)
Musical Numbers :
Chorus of Waiters   "Clean the glasses, wipe theplates"
Entranbce of Bridesmaids
Trio   "All is joy, doubt is past"
Duet   "Confide in me my dearest friend"
Chorus   "So aloud should discover all his errors ere he wed"
Trio   "How do you feel yourself son-in-law ?"
Chorus   "Oh a boarding school is lovely, and a boarding school is gay"
Song (Flo)   "Cocoanuts are nature's wonder"
Finale Trio   "If we're to have such floods again"
Slate Pencil Chorus   "Tick, tickety, tick, tickety, tick / Our lesson now we take"
Song (Amadis)   "Whenever I get hold of something nice"
Quartette   "Of one thing I am sure, its almost safe there'll be a row"
Finale   "Has anyone seen, has anyone marked, a litle tiny dog ?"
Song (Madeleine)   'You look only on the surface'   " 'Tis nice to saunter by the river"
Finale   "Now our story's done"

THE SOUL OF HONOUR
No Record of Performance
Published : (T. H.) Lacy's acting edition of Plays, etc. vol. 104. [1850, etc.]

BEAUTY AND THE BEAST
Theatre Royal, Manchester, 24 Dec 1875
Dividendia (the evil Spirit of wealth)- Margaret Cooper • Nuptilaina (the good Spirit of the wedding ring) - Miss Lily Gifford • Cupid (the little God of Love) - Nelly Bouverie • Baron Contango (The British Merchant of the olden time) - John Rouse • Cast included J. Furneaux Cook, but remainder of large cast not known.
Scenes and Musical Numbers

Scene 1   A dark look-out in the Emma Mine (painted by shareholders)
        Choral Dance   "Yes ! lets be gay where fortunes have been won"
        Song (Cupid)   "Not so fast ma'am pray"
        No. 2 (sic)   Quartette
Scene 2   The Crystal Flowers of Purity and Home of Nuptialina
        Ballet of Snowflakes
Scene 3   Back Parlour in Baron Contango's House
        No. 3   Trio
        No. 4   Song   'Beauty's first dream of love'   "Baron ! we ask her hand !"
        No. 5   Finale and Dance
Scene 4   Deck of the Rotten-tubber at Sea
        No. 6   Chorus of Sailors   "Ah me! Good morning! How d'ye feel Old Tar?"
        No. 7   Lurching Song and Chorus
        No.8   Reefers' Dance
        No.9   Concerted Piece and Chorus   [Climax of Cyclone]
Scene 5   By the Sad Sea Waves
        Melodrame   "A life on the ocean deep"
        Finale - Concerted Piece
Scene 6   The Haunted Jungle
Scene 7   The Enchanted Garden of the Castle Bruin
        Music   'The Roast Beef of Old England'
        No.   Drimking Song
        No.   Song and Chorus (Beast)   "Now that you are competely at your ease"
        Melos - Air of Beauty's Song in Sc. 3
        Finale
Scene 8   Poor Kitchen or Garret
        No.   Song (Beauty)   "My children ! Ah ! My father – jubilation !"
        Duettino (Beauty and Baron)   "What like the prince - pa?"
        Finale and Dance
(Scene 9   Front door of HRH The Beast) - whole scene scored through
Scene 10   Throne Room of Palace of HRH The Beast
        Chorus
        Grand Duo (Beauty and Beast)
        Procession March   -   Grand Ballet
Scene 11   Room in Baron's House
        Love Song (Beauty)
        Finale
Scene 12   Grotto in Beast's Ground
        No.   Solo and Chorus   "She's here ! and yet I tremble"
        General Chorus

MADAME L'ARCHIDUC

Opera Comique, composed by Jacques Offenbach, libretto A. Millaud
(Bouffes Parisiens (Salle Choiseul) 31 Oct 1874)
Opera Comique (Charles Morton), 13 Jan 1876

Marietta (Madame L'Archduc) - Emily Soldene ● Fortunato (Captain of the Household Troop) - Kate Santley ● The Archduke - W. T. Hill ● Giletti, a Waiter, husband to Mariotta – Felix Bury ● The Count, a Mysterious Nobleman - E. Connell ● The Countess, his wife – Violet Granville ● Ricardo (a faithful Attendant on the Count) - Clara Vesey ● Pontefiasconi, Frangipanno, Bonaventura, Bonardo (Conspirators against the Archduke) - W. G. Bedford, C. Campbell, B. R. Pepper, W. S. Penley ● Pianodolce, Andantino, Chi-lo-sa, Tutti Frutti (Ministers of State) - Messrs Johnstone, Lawson, Fraser, Nolan ● Polenta, an

Innkeeper - C. F. Parry ● Beppino, Giacometta (Servants at the Inn) - Messrs Paris, A. Palmer ● Waiters, Servants, Dragoons, Pages, Courtiers, Ladies, &c.
Dir. Miss Emily Soldene and Mr R. Barker; MD ; sc. T. Grieve & Son.

Musical Numbers :

Act I
1. "Dark" Chorus. MNADMNAD. "I hear from certain information / Mum is the word"
2. Bridal Song and Chorus Chorus "Home now from church the bride we're bringing"
   Song "Here comes the bonny bride"
3. Honeymoon Song (Marietta) "One has to run off after marriage"
4. Lament of the Aprons "We courted her never, nor kissed her"
5. The Kissing Quartet and Catching Song (Marietta, Countess, Giletti, Count) "Now, my love, let me be repeating"
7 (sic) Song and Chorus (Fortunato) "Who am I? just ask the Morning Post ?"
8. German Bouffe Duett (Le Com, La Con, + Cho) "Kennst du Bismarck, Herr von Moltke"

Act II
1. Chorus of Retainers - Song Introduced [presume referring to next number]
2. Laughing Duett (Gil, Mar) "Oh! Marietta, is it you?"
3. Song (Fort) 'Two's Company' "A shadow lingers when I'm near you"
4. Alphabet Sestett (Gil, Mar, Sce, Them, Lycur, [sixth not named but may be Frang])
5. Chorus and Song (Archduke) "Hail! the Archduke this way is coming"
   Song 'Original' "Original, Original, I am an old Original"
6. Rustic Song and Chorus (Mar + Cho) 'Where I Come From' "We'll dance tonight"
7. Chorus and Scene " 'Tis the Ducal bell a tinkling"
   Scene (Arch, Fort, Mar, + Cho) "I, Peter the Little, Archduke of that name"
   End of Scene (Mar, Gil, + Cho) "The road! the road! the road!"

Act III
1. Chorus 'Song of the Watch' "While like a raven swoops the darkness down"
   Song (L'Arch, Fort) 'The Sleepy Sentinel' "One eye open, the other sleeping"
2. Morceau D'Ensemble, Air, and Polka "Right you are, right you are!"
   Chorus 'The Arrest' "How now, how now? What is the matter?"
3. Duett (Fart, Mar) "My lady speak. 'Tis the man, yes 'tis the same"
4. Song (Mar) 'Not That' "Silk and satins arrayed in / A poor village maiden"
6 (sic) Finale (Mar + Cho) "Now farewell to high station"

Australia ● Prince of Wales, Melbourne, 26 May 1877

PIFF PAFF
or, the Magic Armoury
A Fairy Musical Extravaganza in Five Scenes after Le Roi Matapa by Clairville and Gastineau, music arranged by Michael Connelly
Criterion Theatre (Alexander Henderson), 31 Jan 1876, closed 13 Apr 1876

Prince Glamour (Heir apparent of Glamourie) - Lydia Thompson ● King Gramerci XXXVII (Impecunious sovereign) - Lionel Brough ● Cattivo (his generalissimo) - George Beckett ● Sir Radcliffe, Sir Huyvé (the Army of Gramerci) - Messrs Martin and Appleby ● Oldest Inhabitant - Mr Bunch ● Cherub (Buttons of Prince Glamour - Willie Edouin ● Haut-vol (Chief Falconer) - Camille Dubois ● Houp-la (Chief Verderer) - Pauline Markham ● Banjeau (Court Minstrel) - Ella Chapman ● Queen Folichonne (Gramerci's second wife) - Miss Ewell ● Finette, Minette (Princesses, daughters of Glamour) - Misses N. Claremont, Lina Merville ● Parfait Amour (Pet Page) - Rozie Lowe ● Jaconde (a Goatherdess) - Violet Cameron ● Hortense (wife of Cattivo) - Miss Davis ● Pages and Maids of Honour.

153

Stage Manager Lionel Brough; MD Michael Connelly; sc. Julian Hicks; cos. Alfred Thompson.

Musical Numbers :
1. Moonlight Quartette (Haut, Houp, Min, Fin) "Low sighs the night wind"
2. The King's Song (King) "Boys, your King is growing old"
3. Chorus (Maids of Honour) "At the dawn of day"
4. Song (Glamour) "When the season's done"
5. Song (Jaconde) 'Simplette' "He was high born"
6. Duet (Glam & Jac) "Now if you'll come"
7. Finale Sc.1 (Tutti e coro) 'Time's Up'
8. Dancing Song (Glamour) 'Apple of my Eye'
9. Gobble Duett (Glam, King, and coro) "There's naught so nice as pickin' "
10. Trio and Chorus (Glam, King,Cattivo, e coro) 'Follow, Follow'
11. Duett (Houp-La and Haut-Vol) "Lo! the mighty minstrel ponders"
12. Melange (Banjeau) 'Down South' : Finale Sc.2
13. The Fright Chorus (Pages) "How we tilli-tilli-tremble"
14. Procession Chorus (Tutti) 'All Hail! Our Royal Master'
15. Legend "Piff Paff" (Glam and coro) "A sorcerer once made a gun"
16. Waltz Song 'PTO' (Houp & coro) "PTO? What the meaning of those signs may be"
17. Finale Sc.3 'Poor Little Man' (Tutti e coro) "Alone ! I stand against the lot"
18. Chorus (Pages) 'Maid of my Soul'
19. Finale Sc.4 (Glam, King, Cattivo & Cherub) "Something's up ! That I am sure of"
                  Nonsense Rhymes for the Times   [Finale Sc.4]
20. Wash Tub Chorus (Pages & Maids of Honour) "Here are we all in washing tub"
21. Finale (Tutti e coro) "Time's up ! the curtain's due"

America : Eagle Theatre, New York, 21 Nov 1877

ROULETTE

Burlesque. Bought by John Hollingshead at the Gaiety, Spring 1876, but never produced.

ROBINSON CRUSOE
Prince's, Manchester, 7 Oct 1876
Folly Theatre, 11 Nov 1876

Robinson Crusoe - Lydia Thompson ● Jim Cocks - Lionel Brough ● Will Atkins – George Barrett / Phillip Day ● Wai-ho - W. Forrester / Harry Collier ● O-pop-o-nax - Emily Duncan ● Gig - Topsy Venn / Lina Merville ● Latitat - Mr Bunch ● Friday - Willie Edouin ● Polly Hopkins - Violet Cameron ● Angelica - Ella Chapman ● Ylang-Ylang - Emily Vining ● Christopher (a Hullite) - Miss E. Vernie ● Deb (his wife) - Miss Honiton / Miss Deacon ● Tib (his daugher) - Miss Leslie ● Slider (Pirate bow-oar) - Miss P. Vernie ● O-wy-o-wy (Indian lyrical aspirant) - Miss Brougham ● O-were-o-were (Indian lyrical aspirant) – Miss C. Morgan ● The two Obadiahs - Messrs Martin and Appleby ● Townspeople of Hull,
Ferocious Pirates, The Indian Tribe of the Nyummy-Nyums, &c
Dir. J. C. Scanlan & Lionel Brough; MD Michael Connelly

Musical Numbers are listed in the Lord Chamberlain's copy as type of song and the characters singing it, but without titles or first lines. The following were introduced :

      The Two Obadiahs
      Put it in the Bag

America : Wallack's Theatre, New York, 12 Sept 1877; Eagle Theatre, New York, 12 Dec 1877; Park Theatre, New York, 9 Jan 1879

NELL GWYNNE
Comic Opera, composed by Alfred Cellier.
The Prince's Theatre, Manchester,
16 Oct 1876, closed 5 Nov 1876 (24 performances)
Nell Gwynne (an actress, and foster sister to the Lady Clare) - Pattie Laverne ● Lady Clare (a country heiress and ward of Charles II) - Alice Cook ● Marjorie (Maid of all work in Rat Castle) - Marie Williams ● Talbot (Chief page to Charles II, cousin to Lady Clare) – Kate Aubrey ● Jessamine (Niece of Old Weasel, in love with Falcon) - Kathleen Corri ● Rochester (In disgrace at court; landlord of the "Kings Head Inn") - Alfred Brennir ● Buckingham (also exiled from court; waiter at the Kings Head - Richard Temple ● Falcon (A strolling player) - W. H. Courtenay ● Weasel (Village usurer and pawnbroker) - John Furneaux Cook ● Amen Squeak (Beadle and parish clerk) - J. H. Ryley ● Charles II - Mr G. Shelton ● Gilleflower (Drawer at the "Kings Head") - Miss A. Randolph ● Hodge, Podge (Two rustics) – Messrs Muddiman and Hayes ● Madge, Junkett (Their wives) - Mrs Lanbauch, Miss Lynch ● Villagers, Drawers, Royal pages, The Watch, etc.

Musical Numbers :

Act I - The Happy Village of Curds-super-Cream

1. Concerted Number
    a. Drinking Chorus
    b. Rustic Dance
    c. Scene for Buckingham
    d. Coda
2. Buffo Duet   (Roch & Buck) 'The Model British Waiter'
3. Quartette (Jess, Roch, Buck, Weasel) 'O Lucky day! '
4. Ballad (Nell) 'Her Heart' "A slighted maid once said"
5. Quartette (Nell, Lady Clare, Roch, Buck) 'Be kind to the poor girls, pray!'
6. Pillory Chorus 'Into the stocks -Into the stocks!'
7. Song and Chorus (Amen Squeak & coro) 'Shove 'em in the Stocks'
8. Grand Duo (Jess and Falcon)
    a. 'O hear my vow' (Tenor solo)
    b. Balcony scene   (Sop & Ten)
    c. Ensemble   "O fate that severs heart from heart"
9. Finale Act I (Tutti e coro)
    a. Chorus
    b. Scene (Falc, Amen, Weas, Jess)
    c. Entrance of Nell and Clare en Paysanne, Rustic Song
    d. Soli, ensemble, and coda
        Act II - Interior of Rat Castle
10. Pawn Chorus (STB) 'When Money's Scarce'
11. The Sob Song (Jess) 'He Promised to Come'
12. Ballad (Roch) 'Maids and Mice'
13. Fortune Teller Sestette (Jess, Nell, Clare, Roch, Buck, Weasel) 'Come now! the cards'
14. Air and Refrain a tre (Nell, Clare, Jess) 'Two faces 'neath a hood'
15. Romance (Falcon) 'We're I the Light'
16. Finale Act II (Tutti e coro)
    a. Chorus
    b. Scene (Weas, Nell, Clare, Roch, Buck), and repetition of Stocks Song
    c. Andante a la Serenade

d. Quintette (Nell, Clare, Roch, Buck, Weas) 'Heart and Pulse'
e. Rataplan, Tutti e coro, and Lantern March
Act III - The Trusting Tree
17a. The "Tryste", Rustic Movement and Dance
   b. Chorus of Old Women (SS)
18. Ballad (Lady Clare)'My Love is all My Own'
19. Duettino (Nell & Clare) 'Love's Confession'
20. Song (Nell) 'Oh! Cupid is a Madcap'
21. Chorus (SSTB) 'Come from Bar, and Field, and Street!'
22. Finale (Tutti e coro) 'Nell Gwynne is a Madcap'

HOT WATER
Farcical Comedy in three acts from La Boule by Meilhac and Halévy.
Criterion Theatre (Alex Henderson), 13 Nov 1876, closed 3 Feb 1877
Chauncery Pattleton - Charles Wyndham ● Sir Philander Rose - Edward Righton ● Martin (of the New Inn) - C. Trition ● Corbyn (of the Middle Temple) - H. Standing ● Moddle - J. Clarke ● M'Lud - H. Ashley ● Clerk of the Court - J. Anderson ● Stage Manager - J. Francis ● Pietro- Mr Ridley ● Tim - Master Rivers ● Mr C. Pattleton - Fanny Josephs ● Madame Mariette - Nellie Bromley ● Lady Rose - Miss Eastlake ● Mrs Pitcher - Miss M. Davis ● Jane - Miss Edith Bruce ● Nina - Miss Myra Holme
Acting Manager - Mr H. J. Hitchins ● MD - Mr J. Fitzgerald
Revival : Criterion Theatre, 15 Aug 1894

RETAINED ON BOTH SIDES
Operetta in one act, composed by Charles Lecocq, from Deux portières pour un cordon,
libretto by Hippolyte Lefebvre and M. Lucian.
Published : Metzler & Co., (Opera Bouffe Series), London, 1875
Sandown, IoW, 4 Sept 1876
Sugden (a briefless barrister) - Mr Newton Bayliss ● Araminter (his wife) - Liebe Konss (Mrs Newton Bayliss)
Prince's Theatre, Manchester, 13 Nov 1876
Sugden - Mr Albert Brennir ● Araminter - Miss Kathleen Corri
   Musical Numbers :   Overture
   1. Song (Aram) 'Folk Want No Law' "Folk want no law, 'tis most distressing"
   2. Song (Sug) 'The Lawyers Creed' "I can't engage ... or to speak plainer"
   3. Duet 'What a Temper' "What a temper, what a passion"
   4. Finale 'Reconciliation' "If again quarrels shall come ever"

SINDBAD THE SAILOR
or, Harlequin Old Man of the Sea,
and the Diamond Fay of the Enchanted Valley of the Roc!
Pantomime
Prince's Theatre, Manchester 19 Dec 1876, closed 2 Mar 1877
Sindbad - Marie Williams ● Koh-i-noor - Kathleen Corri ● Ali-el-Ektro - J. H. Ryley ● The Hadji - John Rouse ● Hafiz and Yussouf (Two of Hadji's Parlour Boarders - Misses M. Lucette and Miss Alice Cook ● Zuleika (Koh-i-noor's maid) - Miss Julia Bullen ● Fiz (Buttons) - Miss Nellie Kennedy ● Sultan Hubble-Bubble XXXVII - Mr A. Brennir ● Bags (Captain of the good ship 'Sultan of Mocha') - Miss A. Wood ● The Diamond Fay – Emma Toms ● Discord (The Demon Fiend) - Mr G. Shelton ● Bim and Bom (Private Band of the

Sultan) - J. Caufield and H. Booker ● The Sleepy Cabin Boy - Mr G. Lewis ● The Fat Believer - Mr Lawrence ● The Sheriff of Bassorah - Mr H. J. Roberts ● Kibob (Captain of the Sultan's Pages) - Miss A. Randolph ● Kismet (Middy on board the "Sultan of Mocha") - Miss Josy Corri ● Tarboosh (of the Hadji's Academy) - Miss Greenwood ● Maids of Honour, Circassian Slaves, Reefers, Pages, Market Girls, Sailors, Turks, &c.
Dir. H. B. Farnie
Musical Numbers not known

OXYGEN
or, Gas in A Burlesque Metre
Burlesque, in collaboration with Robert Reece
Folly Theatre (Alex Henderson), 31 Mar 1877
Prince Fritz, Crown prince of Virgamen - Lydia Thompson ● Hanser and Otto (His fellow students) - Emily Duncan and Marie Williams ● Doctor Ox (Professor of Chemistry at Gottingen) - Philip Day ● Van Tricasse (Burgomaster of Keekendone) - Lionel Brough ● Niklausse (Leader of the Council) - R. Nelson ● Franz (His son, betrothed to Suzel) – Willie Edouin ● Tarantula (Manager of the Opera House) - Ella Chapman ● Clerk to the Council - Mr Bunch ● Suzel. (The Burgomaster's daughter) - Violet Cameron ● Gretelein and Lottchen (Her friends) - Misses Merville and Rosie Lowe ● Hermance (Her Governante) – Harriet Coveney ● Citizens, Citizenesses, Councillors, Pages, Students, &c.
Dir. Farnie and Reece; sc. Messrs Grieve & Son; cos. Draner of Paris, executed by Mrs Wilson and Mr Harrison of Bow Street; Chorus mistress Mrs Johnson..
Musical Numbers not known

THE GOLDEN BUTTERFLY
Extravaganza - revised version of Piff Paff
Crystal Palace, Easter, Mon 1 Apr 1877
King Gramerci - Lionel Brough ● Queen Hannah - Maria Davis ● Joconde - Violet Cameron ● Cattivo - Philip Day ● Prince Glamour - Edith Bruce ● Buttons of Prince Glamour – Willie Edouin ● featuring the Majiltons (les trois Diables), &c.
Dir. Charles Wyndham; sc. Julian Hicks
Musical Numbers not known, but probably the same as for Piff Paff.

THE CREOLE
(La Créole)
Comedy-Bouffe, composed by Jacques Offenbach, libretto by Albert Millaud (Bouffes Parisiens, 12 Feb 1857)
Adapted in collaboration with Robert Reece.
Brighton, 3 Sept 1877
The Folly Theatre (Alex Henderson), 15 Sept 1877, closed Sat 15 Dec 1877
Zoe (Creole, ward of the Commodore) - Katherine Monroe ● Rene (of the Mousquetaires Rouges, Nephew of the Commodore) - Nellie Bromley ● Antoinette (Commodore's daughter) - Violet Cameron ● The Commodore Palatras (of the Frigate "La Blague") - John Howson ● Frontignac (A briefless advocate) - Dudley Thomas ● Gargotte and Babillard (Notaries, advisers of the Commodore - Messrs Bedford and Charles Ashford ● Sabord (Bosun and servant of the Commodore) - Mr Mitchell ● Tribord and Beret (Quartermasters of "La Blague") - Charles Lascelles and Clavering Power ● Paul (Cabin boy of "La

Blague") – Josie Corri ● Yvonne and Jacqueline (Maids to Antoinette) - Julie Evans and Adelaide Barton ● Lolotte and Berthe (Maids in the Estaminet "Aux Pecheurs Fideles" - Misses Imms and Angel ● Yogarita (Zoe's attendant) - Kate Poletti ● Casserole (Cook of the Admiral's villa) – Clara Grahame ● Fishermen, Fisher Girls, Peasants, Sailors, the crew of "La Blague", &c., &c.

Conductor Mr J. Fitzgerald; sc. Julian Hicks; cos. M & Mme Alias; Chef du Chant Mrs Johnson; Acting Manager Mr J. C. Scanlon.

Musical Numbers :
Chorus of French Peasants 'At our guns and bastions scoffing'
Song (Rene) 'You have felt that way yourself'
Trio (Antoinette, Rene, Commodore) 'Now, Consorts, close the line'
Bridal Chorus 'With bouquets, jewels, songs and dances'
Ballad (Rene and Chorus) 'Gran'Pa'
Finale to Tableau 1 (Tutti e coro) 'Ever mine own'
Song (Antoinette) 'Whispered in kisses'
Ballad (Zoe) 'Memorie'
Recit & Air (Zoe) 'Sit close to me and murmur low'
Duo (Zoe and Rene) 'Zoe, Zoe, witching and beautiful Zoe'
Chorus (Peasants) 'Not in the least do we wonder'
(Two Notaries and Coro) 'The Lay of the Chicken'
Creole Song (Zoe and Coro) 'The Mango Tree'
Finale to Tableau 3 (Coro) "Hark, Commodore, the signal shot"
Recit "Very good, very good"
Air (Zoe) "And so you think"
Recit & Ballad (Antoinette, Zoe, Rene, Frontignac, Tribord & Beret) "There
    was an old hunter you're aware"
Song and Chorus (Commodore and Coro) 'The Warbling Cobbler'
Quartette (Zoe, Antoinette, Frontignac & Rene) "The Commodore is fast asleep"
(Zoe) -Lullaby-
Finale - Reprise of Creole - Refrain

THE SEA NYMPHS
Musical Romance written in collaboration with Robert Reece; music by Charles Lecocq from Ondine au Champagne, libretto by H. Lefèbvre, Pelissie and Merle (Folies Marigny, 5 Sept 1866)
Published : Cramer's Opera Comique Cabinet No.7, J. B. Cramer & Co., London, 1874
Brighton, 3 Sept 1877
Folly Theatre (Alex Henderson), 15 Sept 1877, closed 21 Nov 1877
Coralie and Pearline (Two Sea Nymphs) - Kathleen Corri and Violet Cameron Sea-Fern, Silver-Sand, Murmer-of-the-Shell, Twinkle-Fin, Posphorine, and Anemone (Sea Nymphs) - Jessie Bailie, Ethel Montaigne, Julie Evans, Kate Grahame, Adelaide Barton, and Daisy Angel ● Smith and Jones (Engineers) - Messrs C. H. Drew and Bedford ● Kraken and Torpedo (Submarine monsters) - Charles Lascelles and Clavering Power ● Neptune - Charles Ashford

Musical Numbers :
    Overture
 1. Yawning Chorus (Sea Nymphs) "Of water we're getting weary"
 1A Melodrame - Entrance of Kraken and Torpedo
 2. Proclamation Chorus (Krak, Torp, Sea Nymphs) "Now you know"
 3. Valse Rondo (Coralie) 'Ah Dearest Earth'

158

4. Quartette (Cor, Pear, Krak, Torp) 'Accept the Pair' "Accept the pair of us"
5. Song & Chorus (Pear & Nymphs) 'The Ladies Brigade'
5A Chorus (Nymphs) 'Ah, What Funny Thing'
6. Ballad (Jones) 'The Siren of Greenwich' "Once to famous Greenwich town"
7. Romance (Smith) 'What Time the Ices'
7A Melodrame
8. Quartette (Cor, Pear, Smith, Jones) 'Can It Be'
9. Duettino (Krak, Torp) 'A Rashly Daring Mortal'
10. Chorus & March (Guards & Nymphs) 'Hither Comes Our Neptune Great!'
11. Finale (Tutti, Choro) 'Champagne Song' "Ere we do the sea abandon"

UP THE RIVER
or, The Strict Kew-Tea
Musical Comedietta, in collaboration with Robert Reece; composed by Hervé.
Folly Theatre (Alex Henderson) 15 Sept 1877, closed 15 Dec 1877
Tom - Mr. Bedford ● Maria (his wife) - Miss V. Granville ● Pier Keeper - Mr. Clavering
Power

Musical Numbers ● Overture
1. Cavatina (Maria) 'Where Shall I Go' "My love is vain, My life is dismal"
2. Ballad (Tom) 'My Love's a Maid of Lowly Race'
3. Duet (Maria & Tom) 'Ah! Thou Perfidious'
4. Trio (Maria, Tom and Slack) "Through my veins joy is flowing"
5. Finale (Tutti) "All who'd go up the river"

CHAMPAGNE
or, A Question of Phiz.
Burlesque, written in collaboration with Robert Reece.
Strand Theatre (Mrs Swanborough), 29 Sept 1877, closed 22 Dec 1877
Clicquot (Count of Champagne) - Mr Harry Cox ● Rum-ti-tum (The Family Minstrel) – Mr
W. S. Penley ● The Chevalier de la Mayonnaise - Mons. Marius Mousseline, Comptesse
Clicquot - Mdlle Camille Clermont ● Vanilla (My Lady's Page) - Camille Dubois
● Bobinette (My Lady's Maid) - Lottie Venne ● Dodolphe and Popaul (Pages) - Miss La
Feuillade and Laura Carthew ● Fichu and Panier (Two more from downstairs) - Gwynne
Williams and Miss Hewitt ● Madame Haricot (Cuisiniere) - Miss Gwynne Williams ● The
Count's household, &c., &c.
Stage Man. Horace Wigan; Stage Dir. Henry Carter; Acting Man. Arthur Swanborough;
MD. Henry Reed; sc. H. P. Hall; cos. M and Mme Alias.

Musical Numbers :
Chorus "We are pages of the Count"
Duet (Chev, Van) "Some ladies lend kind glance on me"
Song (Bob) "If you should ever want a barber"
Mail-bag Chorus "Here's the mail so ope' the bag"
Song and Chorus "Who would not be a soldier bold"
Duet (Count, Rum) "My faithful vassal now you see"
Trio (Van, Chev, Count) "This page and that Chevalier"
Finale to scene "Hail to the brave who fight for native land"
Concerted Piece "Oh set your bells a ringing"
Concerted Piece "Yes, now the old imposter's off, let's all be very gay"
Song 'Weasel Asleep' "I'm a child of innocence"
Finale to scene "Oh I think I see him falling grandly", with music and dancing

Duet (Chev, Count) "Oh pretty Countess deign to let me kiss that lily hand"
Processional March ~ Finale

RUSSIA
or, The Exiles of Angara.
Written in collaboration with Robert Reece, from a novel by Prince Lubermirski, Tatiana, or, the Conspiracy.
The National Theatre "late Queen's Theatre, Long Acre" (Alex Henderson) 27 Oct 1877, closed 23 Nov 1877

The Emperor - Mr F. De Belleville ● Schelm - Hermann Vezin ● Palkine - Mr Dolman ● Muller, a German Adventurer - Arthur Stirling ● Count Vladimir Lanine - Mr E. H. Brooke ● Harry L'Estrange - John Billington ● Corporal Flannigan - Shiel Barry ● The Cossack Captain - Mr Vollaire ● Gronitz - Mr Field ● Ferryman of the Angara - Mr Astor ● Olga - Miss Carlisle ● Tatiana - Henrietta Hodson ● Madame Dugarey - Eleanor Bufton ● Guests, Attaches, Ambassadors, Staff and Escort of the Grand Duke, Soldiers, Bridesmaids, Conspirators, Police.
Dir. H. B. Farnie; Asst Stage Man. Mr C. Morell; MD. Mr Mallandaine; sc. Julian Hicks, H. P. Hall, &c.; cos. Mrs May, Mrs Corgan

HESTER GRAY
or, Blind Love
Drama, written in collaboration with Robert Reece, "expressly for Miss Wallace"
Prince's Theatre, Manchester (G. H. Browne), 27 Oct 1877

Mark Gray (Blacksmith, late Farrier in Stanley's Dragoons) - Mr A. D. McNeill ● Tercel Deane (Colonel in the Fusiliers) - Edward Compton ● Hugh de Baskerville (Captain in his regiment) - Mr G. Robinson ● Peter (Apprentice to Gray) - Mr T. F. Doyle ● Rev. Samuel Jones - Mr E. G. Osborne ● Muggins (Landlord of the "Fisherman's Rest") - Mr Lester Barrett ● Joseph (Travelling Showman) - Mr C. H. Stephenson ● Hester Gray (Mark's Wife) - Miss Wallis ● Minnie (their child) - Miss Banks ● Widow Gray (Mother of Mark Gray) – Mrs Charles Pitt ● Gwendoline Deane (sister of Tercel Deane) - Miss Emma Toms ● The Queen of the Air (wife of the Original Salamander) - Miss E. Inman ● Junkett (Hester's Maid) – Miss Ethel Hope ● Journeymen Blacksmiths, Soldiers, Mountebanks, Convicts, Servants, &c.

SHOOTING STARS
New versionof L'Œil Crevé by Hervé
Folly Theatre (Alex Henderson), 22 Nov 1877

Dindonette - Katherine Monroe ● Alexandrivore - Violet Cameron ● Fleur de Noblesse – Miss L. Beaumont ● The Marquis de Tra-la-la - Mr C. H. Drew ● Pouf (his Factotum) – John Howson ● Palisandre - Charles Ashford ● The Mysterious Carpenter - Mr F. Mitchell ● Chavassus and Copeau (of the Archer Guards) - Clavering Power and Mr Bedford ● Eclosine - Julie Evans ● Mariette and Françoise (her Gossips) - Adelaide Barton and Miss R. St. George
MD John Fitzgerald; sc. Julian Hicks; cos. M & Mme Alias; Chef du Chant Mrs Johnson; Acting Manager J. C. Scanlon.

Musical Numbers :
1.   Rondo   'My Lover is an Archer Bold'

2. Idyll 'Marquis and Shepherdess'
3. Duett 'I long for the Archery meeting'
4. Finale 'Rouse! each gay Toxophilite'
5. Ballad 'If perchance my Lover'
6. Finale 'All in, and may the best man win'
7. Valse Rondo 'A Joiner's Calling'
8. Chorus 'The Brave deserve the Fair'
9. Septuor & Chorus 'Who's this, Archer, so grim?'
10. Finale 'Run him in'
11. 'The Song of the Sentry'
12. Romance 'Here, through my Prison Bars'
13. Duett 'Oh, What joy to behold'
14. Chorus of Doctors
15. Song 'Affectations of the Heart'

BABES IN THE WOOD
or, the Demon Colorado, the Blighted Tuber
and the Harlequin Baron of the Whoa Emma Mine.
Pantomime
Prince's Theatre, Manchester 18 Dec 1877

The Baron de Bœuf (otherwise the cruel uncle) - John Wainwright ● Arthur and Agnes (the Babes) - Janet Banks and Pauline Banks ● Emma Winslow (their Nurse) - Mr J. L. Shine ● Bill o'th'Irk (a villain) - Mr E. G. Osborne ● Tommy O'Angel Meadow (a decent blackguard) - Mr T. F. Doyle ● Jack o'Lantern - Nellie Bouverie ● Prince Hilarious - Lizzie Coote ● Wild Rose (Barmaid at the "John Barleycorn") - Florence Smithers ● Mabel (a village gossip) - Nellie Kennedy ● King Eagle (of the Piping Times of Peace) - Mr B. Sloman ● Professor Pandy (schoolmaster to the babes) - George Skelton ● Grand Chamberlain (Controller of the Baron's Household) - Mr R. A. Roberts ● Macaroon (Chief Page to Prince Hilarious) – Miss Randolph ● Caramel (Chief Page to the Baron) - Miss Carthew ● Colorado - Mr G. Hamblin ● The Silver Fern Fay - Emma Toms ● Jo King (The Prince's Fool) - Harry Collier ● Ernest and Augustus (Two cheeky pages) - Misses Lambert and Barnett ● Prince's Pages, Baron's Pages, Millers, Brigands, Peasants, Wateau Shepherds and Shepherdesses ● Nursery Heroes and Heroines by Gilbert Juvenile Troupe
Musical Numbers not known

WILDFIRE
Spectacular, fairy, musical and pantomimic extravanganza, written in collaboration with
Robert Reece.
Published : Walter Smith, London, 1877
Alhambra Theatre (Charles Morton) 26 Dec 1877, closed 23 Feb 1878

Kit, the Cobbler (Village politician and a very bad husband) - Harry Paulton ● Daisy (his very meek spouse) - Lennox Grey ● The Baron Hey Derry Downe (Lord of the Manor) - Mr J. H. Ryley ● The Baroness (his termagant Wife) - Pattie Laverne ● Azurine (his stepdasughter) - Lizzie Robson ● Wildfire (a Tricksy Spirit) - Emma Chambers ● Babblina (a Village Gossip) - Adelaide Newton ● Pomposa (Chief of the Baronial Police) - Clavering Power ● Pontino (Grand Chamberlain) - Frank Hall ● Prince Sigismund (affianced to Azurine) - Mr Nordblom ● Bitts (The Baroness's Coachman) - Mr R. Marchant ● Tootle (the Village Choirmaster) - Mr Ross ● Masher (Chief Page to the Prince) - Miss F. Montague ● Crasher (Chief Page to the Baron) - Miss Imms ● Peasants, Flower Girls,

Valets, Pages, Maids of Honour, Cobblers, Millers, Witches, Hunters, &c. by the Ladies and
Gentlemen of the Chorus. The Pantomime action by the celebrated Rowella Troupe.
SM. Mr Roberts; MD. Mr G. Jacobi; Chorus Master Mr Hobson; sc. A. Callcott; cos.
Grevin, Draner, Wilhelm Faustin &c. and Miss Fisher, Mr May, and M. Alias
Ballets invented and arranged by M. Bertrand.
Musical Numbers :
Act I   Sc.1   The Village
Lantern Chorus of Villagers (Tutti)   "We village maidens all too bold"
Sc. 2   A Hall in the Baron's castle
Chorus of Affrighted Servants (Tutti)   "Oh! what a row, a scandal and a clatter"
Song (Baroness)   "Never was a lady of rank and position so bothered as I"
Mock Operatic Quartette (B'ness, Azur, Pomp, Baron)   "O! rage and despair"
Finale to Sc. 2 (Tutti e coro)   "No! we servants here can no longer stay"
Sc. 3.   The Public Square in the Village
Grand Sabot Ballet
A Topical Song (Kit)
Chorus of Village Gossips   "Here we simple villagers"
Duet and Chorus (Daisy, Babblina)   "When at the altar they gave me away"
Ensemble   "Goodness me, she seems to like it"
March and Chorus 'The Village Choir'   "He's a coming"
Duettino (Prince and Azur)   "Nearer to me and nearer Come"
Finale to Sc. 3 (Tutti e coro)   "If any thing goes wrong today"
Chorus of Spirits   "Deep draught of slumber Let each take"
Act II   Sc. 1   Kit's Establishment
Ballad (Kit) 'Love Me?'   "Wind sighing in the lea"
Trio (Kit, B'ness, Wild)   "Ah! maiden once enthralling"
Song and Chorus   (Pomp and Police)   "Of evil doers we're in constant terror"
Finale (Tutti e coro)   "Goodbye, Mister Cobbler, 'tis your turn now"
Sc. 2.   The Boudoir of the Baroness
Chocolate Chorus   "Now to our lady waking"
Song (Daisy)   "Everything is so new and droll"
Duet (Prince and Azur)   "Down by the brook 'tis sweet to rove"
Chorus   "She will but little mercy show"
Duettino (Kit and Daisy)   "Yes, you see in me a martyr"
Ensemble   "Oh! mustn't it have been merry?"
Chorus   "This wedding day let's happy be"
Romance (Prince)   "Fly rosy hours, away be winging"
The History of Ladies Dress - from Paradise down to the present.
Chorus   "To the Ball! to the Ball"
Sc. 3   An Ante-chamber of the Castle
Song (Baron)   "I can't exactly understand what's happened to my wife"
Dancing Duet and Chorus (Baron and Daisy)   "Since the polka's danced again"
Sc. 4.   The Lamp-lit Gardens of the Castle
Grand Military Ballet ~ Dresden China Minuet by Children ~ Fife and Drums Cortege
Inserted number "Here Stands a Post", words Clement Scott, music W. C. Levey

MADCAP
(La Chaste Susanne)
Bouffonerie Musicale in One Act and Two Tableaux, written in collaboration with Robert
Reece.
The Royalty Theatre (Kate Santley) 7 Feb 1878

Mons Pommefrittes (Proprietor of the Brasserie Alsaciennes, Paris) - Lionel Brough ● Artaxerxes Cocatine (Milliner and Bonnet Maker) - Mr F. Mervin Flageolet (Tenor and Music Master at a Ladies' Boarding School) - Walter H. Fisher ● Captain Pompom (of the National Guard) - Mr J. E. Beyer ● Bock (his Orderly) - Mr Bunch ● Mlle De Grenadine (otherwise Madcap! - the Ward and Plague of M. Pommesfrites) - Kate Santley ● Madame Nini (the young and romantic wife of Pommesfrites) - Rose Cullen ● Josephine (her Dame du Comptoir) - Eugenie Nicholson ● Mme Minerve (Principal of the Ladies' School at Passy) - Miss Ewell ● Pupils, Waitresses, Soldiers of the National Guard, School Girls, &c.
Dir. Mrs W. H. Liston and the authors; MD. Mr A. J. Levy; sc. Julian Hicks; cos. M and Mme Alias.
Musical Numbers not known

LES CLOCHES DE CORNEVILLE
Comic Opera
Composed by Robert Planquette, libretto by Clairville and Charles Gabet (Théâtre des Folies-Dramatiques, 19 April 1877)
Adapted in collaboration with Robert Reece.
Published : Joseph Williams Ltd., London, 1878
Folly Theatre (Alex Henderson) 23 Feb 1878, closed 24 Aug to transfer to the Globe Theatre 31 Aug 1878, closed 20 Mar 1880 (704 performances)
Reopened 15 May 1880 to 26 June,
transfer to Olympic 28 June, closed 14 Aug 1880
Serpolette (A Waif) - Katherin Monroe / Emma Chambers ● Germaine - Violet Cameron ● Manette - Lily Beaumont ● Gertrude - Annie Randolph ● Susanne - Laura Carthew ● Catherine - Clara Graham ● Marguerite - Ethel Barrington / E. Barrett ● Jeanne – Maggie Archer / Kate Percival ● Nanette - Clara Sidney ● Henri, Marquis de Cornville - Mons. Loredan / John Howson ● Gaspard (A Miser) - Shiel Barry ● The Bailie - Mr W. J. Hill ● Grenicheux - Mr F. Darrell / Mons. Loredan ● Gobo (The Bailie's shadow) - Charles Ashford ● Christophe (A Cadet) - Miss C. Delisle ● Peasants, Naval Officers, Sailors, &c.
Dir. H. B. Farnie; MD Mr Edward Solomon; sc. Ryan; cos. Alias
Musical Numbers :   Act I
1.a Chorus "All who for servants"
   b Air and Chorus "They Say"
2.   Rondo (Serp) "I may be Princess"
3.   Barcarolle (Gren) "On billows rocking"
4.   Duet (Germ & Gren) "Twas but an impulse"
5.   Legend of the Bells (Germ & Cho) "Yes, that Castle old"
6.   Valse Rondo "With joy my heart"
7.   Finale to First Tableaux "Such conduct is quite sad"
8.   Song "Tho' they may not pursue me"
9.a Chorus "Come farmers small" (Sur le marché)
   b Chorus of the Servants "Than us you will not find better"
   c Coachman's Chorus "Who are drivers wanting"
   e Finale "Tell me, Girl, what may be your name"
        Act II
10.a Chorus "Let our torches light up the gloom"
        Air 'By his side' "From pallid cheek you may be telling"
    b Trio "I'll shut my eyes"
    c Song "Not a ghost at all"

11. Buffo Song "Oh dear! Oh dear! That riot"
12. Song and Chorus "Oh! see their good brands notched in battle"
13. Song and Chorus "Marchioness● how astounding"
14. Duet "Tis she! a happy fate
14 (bis) 'Yea or Nay' "When he bargains at a fair"
15. Quintett and Chorus "Ah! he's looking somewhat pale"
16. Finale "Love, honour, happiness"

Entracte   Act III

17. Song of the Beggars "Aye! aye! aye! the good old times"
18. Chorus and Song "There she goes with horses prancing"
19. Cider Song "Normandy pippins good all over"
20. Rondo Valse "That night I'll ne'er forget"
21. Duet "My Lord! my Lord!"
22. Finale "Old man I pardon thee!"

Revivals : Provincial Tour 1878; Globe, 15 May 1880; Globe, 4 Sept 1880; Globe, 10 Sept 1881; Haymarket, 11 Nov 1886; Opera Comique, 17 Feb 1890; Prince Edward, 16 Mar 1931; numerous provincial and amateur productions; BBC Broadcasts, 15 July 1927, 6 Mar 1935, 1-2 Mar 1938.

America : Metropolitan Casino, 31 Oct 1881 [There were many rival versions]

Australia : Academy of Music, Melboourne, 23 Nov 1878

STARS AND GARTERS

Written in collaboration with Robert Reece, from Leterrier and Vanloo "L'Étoile", "with music from the most popular sources"

The Folly Theatre (Alex Henderson) 21 Sept 1878, closed 12 Oct 1878

Lazuli - Lydia Thompson ● King Jingo XIX - Lionel Brough ● Zadkiel (his astronomer) - Harry Paulton ● Zamio (Head of Police) - Edith Blande ● Princess Laoula (Daughter of the King next door, and betrothed to Jingo) - Annie Poole ● Porcupino (Ambassador) – Alfred Bishop ● Aloes (his young fiancée) - Rose Cullen ● Piquet (Chief of the Royal Pages) – Miss Denman ● Esbronfette (Maid of the "Jingo Arms") - Inez d'Aquilar ● Trop and Tard (Police) - Messrs Nolan and Smith ● Schmick (Hereditary Headsman) - Mr Bunch ● Pages of the Household, Maids of Honour, Cavaliers, Populace, &c., &c.

MD. Michael Connolly; Acting Manager J. C. Scanlon; sc. Mr Ryan; cos. Braner, M & Mme Alias

Musical Numbers not known

CARMEN, OR, SOLD FOR A SONG

Burlesque, written in collaboration with Robert Reece

Folly Theatre (Alex Henderson), 25 Jan 1879

Carmen - Lydia Thompson ● Don José - Lionel Brough ● Escamillo (the toreador) – John Howson ● Michaela (cousin and fiancée of Don José) - Adelheide Praeger ● Frasquita and Mercedes (waiting maids at Pastia's Pub) - Jessie Greville, Lia Rohan ● Il Dancairo and Il Remendado (smugglers) - George Giddens, W. Bunch ● Zuniga and Morales - Annie Forbes, Miss Thorrington ● Lillas Pastia (proprietor of the original bodega) - Edith Blande ● Pablo, Inez and Luisita (young people of the district) – Miss K. Percival, Edith Barnet, Daisy Angel ● Cigarette girls, outlaws, matadors, soldiers, &c., &c.

Dir. H. B. Farnie; M.D. Michael Connolly; sc. E. Ryan; Cos. Madame Gilpin.

Musical Numbers not known

MADAME FAVART

Opera Comique, composed by Jacques Offenbach, adapted from libretto by
H. Chivot and A. Duru (Folies Dramatique, Paris 28 Dec 1878)
Published : Cramer & Co., London, 1880
Strand Theatre (Mrs Swanborouh), 12 Apr 1879,
closed 28 Aug 1880 (502 performances)

The Marquis de Pont-Sablé (Military Governor, under the Maréchal Saxe, of Artois) –
Henry Ashley ● Hector de Briopréau (Employé in the Gendarmerie, and subsequently
Lieutenant of Police at Douai) - Walter H. Fisher ● Major Cotignac (of the Dauphiné
Musketeers) – Mr Lewens ● Biscotin (Proprietor of the Arras Tavern, the "Grand
Monarque") - Harry Cox ● Le Sergent - Mr Delange ● Charles Favart (Dramatic Author
and struggling Manager) - Mons. Marius ● Justine Favart (his wife, an actress) - Florence
St John ● Suzanne (Daughter of Major Cotignac, subsequently wife of Hector Briopréau) -
Violet Cameron ● Joli-Cœur (of the État-Major, Camp of Saxe) - Miss Randolph ● Sans-
Quartier (of the État-Major) – Ethel Barrington ● Vivandieres, Buglers, Travellers, Guests.
Dir. H. B. Farnie; MD. John FitzGerald; sc. H. P. Hall; cos. M & Mme Alias;

Musical Numbers :

Act I

1. Chorus & Solo (Bisc) 'The Coach is Come'
2A Trio (Suz, Hect, Cot) ' 'Tis He'
2B Air-Valse (Suz) 'It was not at rout or ball'
3. Song (Fav) 'The Calendar of Bacchus'
4A Chorus 'Now for dinner'
4B Air (Mme Fav) 'Over mountain, through valley'
4C Solo & Chorus 'Tho' I believe him not'
5. The Novice's Song (Mme Fav) 'Ave! My mother'
6A Ensemble 'After Marching' "After marching all the long day"
6B Rondo (Mme Fav) 'The Artless Thing!'
6C Strette 'We Drink' "We drink! for so your will is"
7. Comic Trio (Suz, Hect, Fav) 'Farewell! Suzanne'
8A Ensemble 'Now the coach is waiting'
8B Air (Suz) 'No, you will never'
8C Coach Scene & Finale 'This Match'
8D Quintett "Onward speeding through the night"

Act II

9A Song (suz) 'The Débutante' "O Madame looks lovely"
9B Chorus 'O Madame Looks Lovely'
9½ Romance (Hect) 'The Two Eves' "I know 'tis an old, old story"
10. Song (Mme Fav) 'Puff!' "From the oven hot and vasty"
11A Chorus 'The Ladies' Pet' "Great man in peace"
11B Air (Pont-Sab) 'Yes! I date from the xivth Louis,'
12A Dramatic Scena 'Ah! 'Tis too bad'
12B Quartett 'Now we have laid our heads'
13A Air & Duo (Mme Fav) 'Conjure not up a glittering vision'
13B Bell Chorus 'We hope this cold collation'
14. Vocal Minuet (Mme Fav) 'An old woman's dream'
14 bis Chorus 'Something's wrong'
15A Finale (Tutti & Chorus) 'Now then, my Marshall Saxe,'
15B Solos & Chorus 'Rataplan' "Tambours are beating"

165

Act III
16. Drill Chorus & Vivandiere's Song 'Right! Left!'
17A Chorus 'The Great Favart'
17B Duo (Suz & Fav) 'I faint! I die!'
18A Chorus 'See, up the hill ascending'
18B Tyrolienne Duet (Mme Fav & Hect) The Pedlar's Song
19. Air (Suz) ' 'Tis not in numbers peril lies'
20A Duet 'Yes! be brave'
20B Chorus 'Long Live the King!'
21. Duet (Mme & Mons Fav) 'One Loving Kiss,' "I'm braver now"
22. Chorus 'Bravo! Well done!'
23. Finale Chorus 'Now all is over'
Revivals : Avenue, 11 Mar 1882; Avenue, 20 Apr 1887
America : Haverly's Fifth Avenue Theatre, New York, 19 Sept 1881
Australia : Theatre Royal, Sydney, 17 Sept 1881

THE BARBER OF BATH
(Apothicaire et perruquier)
Operetta, composed by Jacques Offenbach, libretto by Elie Frébault (Théâtre Bouffes
Parisiens (Salle Choiseul), Paris, 17 Oct 1861)
Published : J. B. Cramer & Co., (No.3 in Cramer's Opera Comique Cabinet), London,
1874
The Olympic Theatre (Fanny Josephs), 18 Dec 1879
(Previously performed in the provinces and by amateurs but no details available.)
Master Gilbert (A Retired Tradesman) - Mr W. S. Penley • Curlew (A Hairdresser and
Barber) - Mr F. Charles • Sylvester (An Apothecary) - David Fisher, Junr • Gertrude
(Gilbert's Daughter) - Miss F. Hastings
Musical Numbers : Overture
1. Romance (Gilbert) 'I Never Knew the Joys of Love'
2. Romance (Curlew) 'Angel of Beauty'
3. Duett (Gert & Curl) 'Is it a Dream'
4. Quartett (All) 'I Soon Would Quit'
5. Duett (Curl & Sylv) 'Pray be Calm'
6. Ballad (Gert) 'The Unsophisticated Girl'
7. Quartett Finale (Tutti) "For life we soon will be united"

ROTHOMAGO
or, The Magic Watch
Grand Christmas Musical Fairy Spectacular in four acts and seventeen tableaux adapted
from the French féerie. Music by Edward Solomon (Act 1), Procida Bucalossi (Act 2),
Gaston Serpette (Act 3) and George Jacobi (Act 4)
Alhambra Theatre (Charles Morton) 22 Dec 1879
closed 17 Apr 1880 (98 performances)
Rothomago (a Sorcerer) - Harry Paulton • Young Rothomago (his son) - Constance Loseby
• King Impecunioso XIX - Louis Kelleher • Surplus (Chancellor of Impecunioso's
Exchequer) - Clavering Power • Dodo (a Rustic Lout) - E. J. George • Princess Allegra
(betrothed to Rothomago jnr) - Mlle Julic • Fairy Angostura (A bitter, bad Fairy) – Annie
Bentley • Fairy Anisette (A sweet little Fairy) - Hetty Tracy • Fracasse (Young Noble-in-
Waiting) - Knight Aston • Frolique (Soubrette to the Princess) - Emma Chambers • Forget-

166

me-not - Rose Stella • Sylph - Carrie Braham • King of the Bears - Mr Vaughan • Arab devotee - Felix Bury • Scholar - Master F. Marchant • The Grand Vintage Ballet danced by Mlle Theo de Gilbert (Champagne), Mlle Rosa (Cognac) with Mlles Anna, Katy, Phillips, Taylor, &c • Memnon, a Grand Egyptian Ballet danced by Mlle Pertoldi (Ibis), Matthews (Ismael), Miss Denevers (Cleopatra), Mlles Anna, Katy, Phillips and Taylor (Priestesses) • Grand Ballet Céramique danced by Mlle Roselli (China), Mlle Rosa (Watteau), Miss Matthews (Geni), Miss Owen (Dresden), Miss Bryan (Sèvres), Miss Braithwaite (Nankin), Miss Coveney (Chelsea), &c
MD. Georges Jacobi; ch. Mons Bertrand; sc. A. Callcott & F. Lloyds; cos. Wilhelm
Musical Numbers not known

FORTY THIEVES
or, Striking Oil in Family Jars
Pantomime, written, invented, and music selected by H. B. Farnie
Gaiety Theatre, Glasgow and Prince's Theatre, Manchester, Dec 1879
Gaiety Theatre, Glasgow (Mr G. Bernard)
Ganem (Ali Baba's son, a Woodcutter) - Emily Soldene • Ali Baba (Small Coal and Potato Merchant) - Mr Richard Tabra • Casim Baba (Rich brother of Ali) - Mr G. K. Maskell • Hassarac (Lieutenant of the Forty Thieves) - Mr W. Mackintosh • Abdallah (His Captain) - Clara Vesey • Run-'em-in (Sergeant of the Bagdad Police) - Thomas Tabra • Sergeant Cop'um - Richard Leggett • Aziz (Bagdad Exquisite) - Anita Lemaistre • The Cadi (Impartial Oriental Judge) - Frederick Carville • Mustapha (Turkey Cobbler) - Harry Booth • Amber (Daughter of Cassim) - Kate Lovell • Cogia (Wife of Ali) - Miss Landri • Morgiana (Her Maid of All Work) - Fanny Wentworth • Brittania - Eveleen Trevor • Fatima (Laundress in Cogia's establishment) - Miss Thinner • Fairy Finance - Flora Ashton • Repudiation (A prevalent but bad Spirit in Ottoman Circles) - Miss E. R. Gwynne • Thieves, Palaquin-Bearers, Circassian Beauties, Policemen, Ladies of Bagdad, Peasants, Woodcutters, Musselmans, etc. • El Moko (Ali's Donkey) - Signor Mulecatto • Ballet of All Nations
Prince's Theatre, Manchester, (Charles Bernard)
Written and invented by Mr H. B. Farnie and Produced under his immediate direction
Ali Baba - Mr Wyke Moore • Ganem - Lottie Verona • Casim Baba - Robert Brough • Hassarac - John • Wallace • Abdallah - Myra Rosalind • Run-'em-in - Mons Bruett • Aziz - Lottie King • The Cadi - Sydney Harcourt • Mustapha - Mr T. D. Hicks • Amber – Lizzie Beaumont • Cogia - Miss Landri • Morgiana - Mlle Riviere • Fatima - Miss Thinner • Fairy Finance - Angela Tulloch • Repudiation - Fanny Clarke • Thieves, Palaquin-Bearers, Circassian Beauties, Policemen, Ladies of Bagdad, Peasants, Woodcutters, Musselmans, etc. • El Moko (Ali's Donkey) - Signor Mulecatto
Musical Numbers not known

THE NAVAL CADETS
Der Seekadett
Opera in three acts, composed by Richard Genée, libretto by F. Zell (Camillo Walzel)
(Theater an der Wien, Vienna 24 Oct 1876)
Published : J. B. Cramer & Co., and Joseph Williams, London, 1880
Royal Globe Theatre (Alex Henderson), 27 Mar 1880, closed 14 May 1880

Inez-Maria-Estrella (young Queen of Portugal) - Violet Cameron ● Dona Dolores (confidant of the Queen) - Miss St Quenten / Emma Chambers ● Cerisette (Singing soubrette of the "Théâtre des Alienations Musicales" at Paris) - Selina Dolaro ● Don Florio (Captain of the Fleet and Favourite of the Queen) - Mons. Loredan ● Don Miguel, Don Luis, Don Pedro, Don Pascal (His friends, Officers of the Marine) - Messrs Wilson, Hill, Savidge, and Reeves ● Januario (A Peruvian Exquisite) - Mr W. E. Gregory ● Garlic (Servant of Don Florio) – Mr Mitchell ● Don Mauritio (A young Scapegrace, Nephew of the Governor of the Brazils) - Denbigh Newton ● Paz (Bourgeois Bridegroom) - Mr Baron ● Vaz (Best Man) - Mr Morganti ● Don Prolixio da Frutti-Porto (Tutor of the Queen - Harry Paulton ● Guava (Indian Page to Januario) - Katie Abrahams ● Sebastiano (Page to the Queen) - Miss Harwood ● Gomex and Gonzalves (Pages to Don Florio) - Misses Kate Poletti and Montelli ● Carlos (First Naval Cadet) - Clara Graham ● Vasquez, Ferdinand, Vespuccio (His Comrades) - Misses Ruth Avondale, M. Sharp, and Kate Chorley ● The School pupils, Maids of Honour, Courtiers , Soldiers of the Watch, Sailors of the Fleet, &c.
Dir. H. B. Farnie; MD. Edward Soloman; sc. Ryan, Spong, Hann; cos. M & Mme Alias.
Musical Numbers :

Act I

1.a	Chorus of Officers	"Long live Don Florio"
b	Recitative and Scene Don Prolixio	"Fair gentlemen, I give you greeting!"
c	Air and Coro Don Florio	"Yes, fortune's but a woman"
2.	† Duet	"My love, my own"
3.	Vocal Waltz	"Masks and Faces"
4.	Bolero	"I am Don Januario"
5.	Quartette	"Ah, you are there"
6.	Duet	"Thee I adore" and Indian Hammock Song
Finale	"A most terrible mystery", Indian Hammock Song & Cadets Chorus	

Act II

8.	"To the deuce with all our books"	
9.	Song (Dolores)	
10.	Chorus	"Let us hold High Fête"
11.	Sextuor	"Her glance away"
12.	Romance (Queen)	
12½	"Impulsive Girls"	
13.	Romance	"Woman's War"
14.	Duettino	"What Courage!"
15.	Couplets	"Poor old Pro"
16.	Finale	Tutti "Let our mariners all a welcome shout"
Septet and Chorus, Finale continued.		

Act III

17.	Chorus and Dance	"Wake now love-song"
18.	Chorus and Solo	"We come with a crying complaint"
19.	Duel Quintette	"Now Gentlemen"
20.	Duo and Air	"And thou wilt be my bride"
21.	Duettino	"Here we are! This the place"
22.	Quartette and Chorus	"This must be"
23.	Finale reprise Cadets Chorus.	

LA FILLE DU TAMBOUR-MAJOR

Opéra comique, composed by Jacques Offenbach, libretto by Henri-Charles Chivot and Alfred Duru (Théâtre des Folies Dramatiques, Paris, 13 Dec 1879)
Alhambra Theatre (Charles Morton), 19 April 1880, closed 18 Dec 1880 (211 performances)

Stella (La fille du tambour-major) - Constance Loseby ● La Duchesse Della Volta – Fanny Edwards ● Claudine (Vivandiere) - Edith Bland ● The Abbess - Miss Turner ● Theresa (wife to Clampas) - Sallie Turner ● Bianca - Miss Claris ● Lorenza - Miss C. Devine ● Monthabor (the Tambour-Major) - Mr F. Mervin ● Capitaine Robert - Mr W. Carleton ● Griolet (the little drummer) - Fannie Leslie ● Le Duc Della Volta - Fred Leslie ● Le Marquis Bambini - Mr L. Kelleher ● Clampas (an Innkeeper) - Mr C. Power ● Gregorio (Gardener to the Convent) - Mr R. Sweetman ● Sergeant - Mr Redman ● Major Domo - Felix Bury ● Antonio (a peasant) - Mr Burgess ● French soldiers, Officers, Pupils at the Convent, Italian nobles, Pages, Notaries, Brigands, Peasants, etc.

MD Mr N. D. Jacobi; Cos. M. and Mme Alias

Musical Numbers :

Act I

1.a   Convent Chorus   "Oh! At the call of duty"
  b   Recitative
  c   Couplets 'Forbidden Fruit' "Here they are! golden, russet, dapple"
2.a   Soldiers Chorus 'After dusty highway tramping'
  b   Air 'Honour and Glory'
3.   "To mercy you will be inclined"
4.   Complaint 'Cold as the snow' "Cold as the Alp snow in summer"
5.a   Dinner Chorus (and Song) "Now then for the leg of lamb"
  b   Recitative
  c   Song 'Italia! Land of song' "Italia! Italia! land of song"
6.   'Hark, Hark, The Distant Bugles'
7.   Entrance of Pupils and Soldiers
8.a   Recitative "But who will sing"
  b   Camp Song 'Princess and the Recruit' "There was once a Princess"
9.   The Confession 'Ora pro me' "I own 'tis rather odd for a maid"
10.   Finale to Act I 'Enough, enough, now let's be gone'

Act II

11.   Quartette 'The Billet-Paper' "It is a billet-paper clear"
12.   Song 'One! Two! ' "I know brave comrades that you'd never"
13.   Vocal Waltz and Score 'Stella' "Stella! then we wait"
14.   Duet 'It must be now'
15.   Couplets 'A Jewelled Throng' "A jewelled throng of ladies fair"
16.   Finale Act II
        a. Chorus. 'Lo! The Notaries'
        b. Septet and Chorus   "Here where the noblest of Italy gather"
        c. Air 'When soldiers marched' "When soldiers marched my window by"
        d. Stretti "Faith, Sirs, she puts it so prettily"

Act III

17.   'Hush! Here is the place'
18.   Tarantella 'By chance we had' "By chance we had our billet"
19.   Song 'The Little Jehu' "I am a little Jehu, as you all may know"
20.   Quartette 'Once again' "Once again! once again!"
21.   Duet 'Oh, what a strange feeling'
22.   Finale to Act III. 'What is that music stealing'

Revivals : Connaught Theatre, 10 Jan 1881

THE GUV'NOR

Farcical Comedy

Vaudeville Theatre (D. James and T. Thorne), 23 June 1880

Mr Butterscotch (Retired Confectioner) - John Maclean • Freddy (His Son, of Ilex Rowing Club) - Thomas Thorne • Theodore Macclesfield (Boat Builder at Putney) - David James • Theodore (His Son, Student at Guy's) - Mr W. Herbert • Jellicoe (Retired Pickle Manufacturer) - Mr W. Hargreaves • Gregory (a Yorkshire Groom - out of livery) - Mr J. W. Bradbury • The MacToddy (a Gentleman from Glen-mutchin) - Mr D. B. Stuart • Cantle - Mr L. Fredericks • Cab Driver No. 3407 - Mr A. Austin • Ullage - Mr Howard • Mr Vellum - Mr A. H. Roberts • Gunnel - Mr J. Welch • Aurelia (second Wife of Mr Butterscotch) - Marie Illington • Kate (His Daughter by First Marriage) - Miss M. Abington • Barbara (Housemaid in the Butterscotch Family) - Cicely Richards • Mrs Macclesfield (The Boat Builder's Wife) - Sophie Larkin • Carrie (His Daughter) - Kate Bishop

CROSS PURPOSES : A MISUNDERSTANDING
One-act Play
Published : Round Table (Annual) 1875
No record of production

SUMMER CLOUD
One-act operetta adapted from the play Cross Purposes (above)
Strand Theatre (Mrs Swanborough), 18 Sept 1880, closed 21 May 1881 (curtain raiser to Olivette)
Cyril Hargrave (Tenor), Phillis Daintree (Mezzo), Jack Freke (Baritone), Jenny Freke (Soprano) - Messrs H. Parry and A. Fenwicke, Mmes Vere Carew and Emily Duncan
Musical Numbers : Lord Chamberlain's copy in the British Library is marked in five places where musical numbers are to be inserted but no lyrics are written in.

OLIVETTE
(Les Noces d'Olivette)
Comic Opera in three acts, composed by Edmond Audran, libretto by Henri Chivot and Alfred Duru (Bouffes-Parisiens, Paris 13 Nov 1879)
Published : Chappell & Co., London, 1880
Strand Theatre (Mrs Swanborough), 18 Sept 1880, closed 3 Feb 1882 (467 performances)
Capitaine De Merimac (of the Corvette "Cormorant") - Mons. Marius • Valentin (Officer in the Rousillon Guards, - his nephew) - Knight Ashton • Marvejol (Seneschal to the Countess of Rousillon, and Mayor of Perpignan) - M. de Lange • Postiche (Barber and Innkeeper at Perpignan) - Mr H. Cox • Duc Des Ifs (Cousin and Heir-presumptive of the Countess of Rousillon) - Mr H. Ashley • Coquelicot (his Foster-brother) - Mr H. Parry • Olivette (Daughter of the Seneschal) - Florence St John • Bathilde (Countess of Rousillon) – Violet Cameron • Veloutine (The Seneschal's housekeeper) - Emily Duncan • Courtiers and nobles, Pages, Citizens, Wedding Guests and Sailors, Soldiers of the Guard, &c.
sc. Mr Ryan; cos. M and Mme Alias; Conductor Mr Hiller; Acting Manager Mr Arthur Swanborough
Musical Numbers :
Act I
1.   Gossip Chorus and Air   "Just fancy what is said ..."
     Air   'Timid and Graceful'   "Yes! Olivette marries today"
1.a 'The Convent Slept'   "The convent slumbered all save I"
2.   Marine Madrigal 'The Yacht and The Brig'
3.   Valse Song   'First Love'   "Oh heart! Wherefore so light"

4. Song   'O! Woman's fickle'
5. Couplets   'Bob Up Serenely'   "If in a state of exhilaration"
6. Serenade   'Darling, Good Night'   "In quaint and in mystic word"
7. Concerted Piece   "Your partisans, brave soldiers, handle"
8. Finale Act I   'Speak, Sir Captain'
   Scene   "But why so timid here ashore"
   Sob Song   'Oh My Father'
   Marriage Bells' Chorus   "Now my friends, we'll all be gay"
   Act II
9.a Chorus   'Soon the Bride'
 b Air   'The Matron of an Hour'
10. Quintette   'It is he'   "Yes! 'tis himself again"
11. Air   'Wayward Woman'   "When lovers around a woman throng"
12. Duet   'What! She your Wife'
   Ballad   'Leaf by Leaf the Roses Die'   "Think not my love"   (music Hervé)
13. Song   'Not Wife, Nor Maid'   "I do think Fate (upon my life)"
14. Duet   'I Love my Love So Well'   "O white-robed maid, who me remindest"
15. Finale Act II   'What Joy in Honeymooning'
   The Farandale   "The vintage over"
   Recitative   "Now signal to our band"
   Act III
16. Chorus and Song   "Hillo! hillo! just tumble up in an old caboose"
   'Jamaica Rum! A Grog-orian Chant'   "Give milk to babes, to peasants
      beer"
17. Romance   'Nearest and Dearest'
18. The Torpedo Song, or, 'The Torpedo and the Whale! A "Shell" of Ocean'
18½ Exit of Sailors - reprise of part of 18
19. Bolero   'Where Balmy Garlic Scents the Air'
20. Quartette   'No - No - Tis You!'   "No, no, 'tis you are the deceiver"
21. March Militaire
22. Finale   "All is ended comme il faut"

Revivals : Avenue Theatre, 13 Jan 1883; Provincial Tour, 1881
America : Bijou Opera House, New York, 25 Dec 1880, trans. to Fifth Avenue Theatre,
31 Jan 1881; Metropolitan Casino, New York, 10 Oct 1881, Fifth Avenue Theatre 15 Mar
1882
Australia : Theatre Rpyal, Sydney, 13 Aug 1881

LES MOUSQUETAIRES
(Les Mousquetaires au couvent)
Operetta, composed by Louis Varney, libretto by Paul Ferrier and Jules Prével, based on a
vaudeville 'L'habit ne fait pas le moine' by Saint-Hilaire and Duport (Bouffes-Parisiens,
Paris, 16 March 1880)
Published : Cramer & Co., London, 1880
Globe Theatre (Alex Henderson), 30 Oct 1880, closed 25 Jan 1881

Narcisse Brissac (Captain of the Red Musketeers) - Frank H. Celli ● Gontran de Solange
(his Comrade) - Henry Bracy ● The Abbé Bridaine (Ex-tutor of Gontran, and Visitor at the
Convent of Ursulines) - Harry Paulton ● The Compte de Pontcourlay (Governor of La
Rochelle) - Savidge ● Rigobert (Sergeant of the Red Musketeers) - Eugene Stepan
● Pompard (Landlord of the "Festive Cauliflower") - Charles Ashford ● Fracasse, Patatras
(two conspirators against the Cardinal Richleau disguised as Monks) - Messrs Hunt and
Martin ● Simone (Waitress at Poupard's Inn) - Alice May ● Marie de Pontcourlay (niece of

171

the Governor) - Mdlle Sylvia ● Louise (Her Sister, a Pupil at the Convent school) - Elsie Moore ● The Superior of the Ursulines - Maria Davis ● Sister Hannah (Her Coadjutor) – Clara Graham ● La Tulipe. Blavet (Petites Trumpettes in the Red Musketeers - Misses Emma Weathersby and Callaway ● Frontin, Beaujolais (Pages of the Governor) - Misses Vaccani and Gilchrist ● Trognon (a Flower Girl) - Emma Temple ● Nougat (a Candy Merchant) – Daisy Clive ● upils at the Convent school, Peasant Girls, Musketeers &c., &c. Directed by H. B. Farnie ; M.D. Mr M. Hiller; Incidental dances Mr John Lauri ; sc. Mr E. Ryan and Mr Spong ; cos. Mons. & Madame Alias ;

Musical Numbers

Act I

1. Chorus 'We're Men of War' "We're men of war and tillage"
   Flower Couplets and Chorus 'Of New Pluck'd Roses'
2. Chorus and Scene (Simone, Rigob, Chorus) 'How They Treat Us'
   Song (Simone & Chorus) 'The Grey Musketeers'
3. Chorus 'Good Morning' "Good morning, Mr Abbé"
4. Song (Brissac) 'A Woman and a Sword' "My latest love, close to my side"
5. Trio (Gont, Briss, Brid) "Own up! be a man"
6. Chorus and Villanelle (Simone & Chorus) 'Squeek Goes the Fiddle'
   Villanelle (Simone & Chorus) £When the simple peasant's daughter"
   Scene and Chorus (Sim, the Gov, Pich, Chorus) 'You'll Have to Stop'
7. Duet (Marie, Gont) 'Oh That We Might Fly' "+ to some distant shore"
8. Finale to Act I (Tutti & Chorus) 'Landlord, Fill Up'
   Rustic Song (Simone & Chorus) 'Should Robin at My Window Tap'
   Chorale 'Near Them' "Near them O let us gather"

   Act II

9. Chorus (Abbess and Pupils) 'The 'Ologies'
10. Scene (Pupils) 'Confess Our Faults'
    Romance (Marie & Ensemble) 'By Night, By Day'
    Two-Part Song (Pupils) 'O Father We Regret'
11. Concerted Piece (Marie, Louise, Abbess, Sister Hannah, Gontran, Brissac, Pupils) 'Draw Near' "Ah" draw near to me, timid maiden"
12. Two-Part Song (Pupils) 'Two and Two'
13. Ballad (Brissac) 'The Captive and the Bird' "Round the lone keep, where the sea birds are flying" (Introduced. Song, music by Planquette)
14. Valse Song (Marie) 'Ye Summer Birds'
15. Romance (Gontran) 'My Dream of Love'
16. Chorus 'Now Hear the Pilgrims Preaching'
    Couplets (Brissac & Ensemble) 'Love's Not a Science'
17. Finale (Tutti & Chorus) 'With Us Darling'

America : Fifth Avenue Theatre, New York 25 April 1882.

LA BOULANGERE
(La Boulangère a des écus)
Comic Opera, composed by Jacques Offenbach, libretto by Meilhac and Halévy (Theatre Variétés 19 Oct 1875)
Published : J. B. Cramer & Co., London, 1881
Globe Theatre (N. A. Burt), 16 Apr 1881, closed 8 July 1881
Louis XV the young King of France, masquerading as a Page named Ravennes - Maud Taylor ● Margot, a Bakeress - Mdme Amadi ● Toinette, Landlady of the "Au Berger Fidele" – Miss Wadman ● Jacqueline, her Waitress - Miss Evelyn ● Valpré, Delorme, Arnand, Varennes (Pages of the Regent) - Clara Grahame, Ruth Avondale, Miss K. Percival,

Camille Dubois • Agio - Miss Melnotte • Navette, Carotte (Girls in Margot's shop) - Misses Percy and Julie Gompertz • Bernadille (Fashionable Hairdresser) - Mr F. Celli • Flam (Head Detective) - Harry Paulton • Muffle (His Apprentice) - Mr C. Ashford • Coquebert - Mr Mansfield • Captain to the Watch - Mr Stepan • Commissary - Mr G. Temple • Stock Exchange men, Robbers, and Thieves, Market People, Pages, Courtiers, Bakers, Maids of Honour, &c., &c.

Musical Numbers : Overture

1a. Chorus of Robbers 'Lo! now the tranquil hour'
1b. Song (Ravanne) 'The Fancy Bazaar' "Light fingered gentlemen"
2. Scene & Melos (Rav, Robbers & Pages) 'For your good hint'
    Melos "Everyone to his post"
2½ Melodrame. Detectives' Music
3. Duet (Toin & Bern) 'So, Sir you are here'
4a. Chorus of Speculators 'Here around'
4b. Stockjobbers Song 'Once a lady's heart'
5a. Chorus 'Bakeress Margot'
5b. Song (Margot & Chorus) 'My sisters and myself''
6. Ballad (Toin) ' 'Tis so good to have a sweetheart'
7a. Chorus & Scene 'What's this we hear'
7b. Quintett & Chorus (Tutti) 'All Right ! All Right! All Right!'
7c. Song & Chorus (Bern) 'We Drank It Once'
8. Finale to Act I (Tutti & Chorus) 'You Are Free'
            Act II. Entr'acte (Instrumental)
9a. Chorus & Air 'Here are bargains'
9b. Song (Rav & Chorus) 'Sweet Jam tart'
10. Romance (Toin) 'Far Apart' "If you tell me he is in danger"
11. Idyll in Black and White (Margot) 'The Coalman and the Miller'
11½ Chorus 'Exit of Detectives'
12a. Chorus 'The Men of Dough'
12b. The Baker's Song (Bern & Chorus) "An 'arrangement' we're in white"
13. Quintett & Chorus (Tutti) 'Be off ! my men'
13½ Chorus Exit 'Gentiles, do not forget'
14. Air (Bern) 'Yes ! you are free' (Music by A. Cœdes)
15. Finale to Act II (Tutti & Chorus) 'In us you see a court'
            Act III. Entr'acte (Instrumental)
16. Melodrame. End of First Tableau
17. Second Tableau. Watteaux Chorus and Dance 'There is a perfume'
18. Romance (Toin) 'Parted' " 'Tis the rose-realm of pleasure"
19a. Chorus 'We now shall have occasion'
19b. Æsthetic Song (Margot & Chorus) 'Dado-ism'
20. Valse Lente (Bern) 'The Dream Is Over'
21. Finale (Tutti & Chorus) Reprise of Market Marseillaise "Some mirth"

PARADISE VILLA
One-Act Comedy
Strand Theatre (Mrs Swanborough) 15 Oct 1881, closed 12 May 1882
Mr Bilberry - Harry Carter • Fitz-Greene Bilberry - Lytton Grey • Temple Figtree – Mr Charles • Flora Bilberry - Millie Turner / Miss Rivers • Mrs Nagglethorpe - Eleanor Bufton • Jane - Miss Vere Carew
Revivals : Comedy Theatre, 17 Jan 1883

THE MASCOTTE
(La Mascotte)
Operetta in three acts, composed by Edmond Audran, libretto by Henri Chivot and Alfred Duru (Bouffes-Parisiens, Paris 29 Dec 1880)

Adapted in collaboration with Robert Reece.

Brighton 19 Sept 1881

Comedy (Alex Henderson) 15 Oct 1881, closed 15 Apr 1882, transferred to Strand Theatre 13 May, closed 29 July 1882 (271 performances)

Laurent XVII (Duke of Piombino) - Lionel Brough • Pippo (A Shepherd) - Mons. Gaillard • Prince Fritellini (Crown Prince of Pisa) - Henry Bracy • Rocco (A Farmer) - Mr T. P. Haynes • Matheó (An Innkeeper) - Mr W. Bunch • Parafante (A Sergeant) - Mr St Albyn • Bianca, Tito (Bohemians) - Misses Ada Wilson and K. Abrahams • Guiseppe (A Peasant) - Mr C. Hunt • Princess Fiammetta (Laurent's Daughter) - Minnie Byron • Bettina, A Country Girl, "La Mascotte"- Violet Cameron • Royal Pages, Maids of Honour, Courtiers, Peasants and Soldiers.

Dir, H. B. Farnie; MD, sc. W. Perkins, T. E. Ryan, T. W. Grieve; cos. Alias.

Musical Numbers :   Overture
1A   Chorus   "Now the merry vintage closes"
1B   Air   "Wine's the Friend of Wit'   "Wine's the friend to wit and gladness"
2A   † Legend (Pippo & Chorus)   'The Mascotte'   "One day a gnome
2B   Melodrame "Now the merry vintage closes" [reprise]
3A   Scene   'Nay, Stay! Dear Charmer'   "Nay, stay dear charmer!"
3B   Song (Bettina)   'Hands Off'   "Hands off! you saucy creatures!"
4A   Hunting Chorus   'Now Sport is O'er'
4B   Song (Laurent)   'Wise folk have always noted'
4C   Melodrame   "Now sport is o'er" [reprise]
5   Arietta (Fiametta)   "Give me the Swain'
6A   Duet (Bettina & Pippo)   'Glou, glou!'   "When in your eyes I look"
6B   Melodrame [music over dialogue]
7   Finale   'The Bell! The Bell!'
   Act II   Entracte
8A   Pages' Chorus   'Oh, She's Charming'
8B   Pages' Song   'Forgive a burning hearts effusion'
8C   Melodrame   "Oh! she's charming" [reprise]
9A   Scene (Bettina & Laurent)   'Let me alone'
9B   Song (Bettina)   'Oh! give me back'
10   Chorus   'Now for laughter'
11A   Saltarella (Pippo)   'Let the nautch-dancers'   "Great nobles! we are come"
11B   Melodrame [music only]
12   Duet (Bettina & Pippo)   'This silk attire'
13   Song (Fritellini)   'Love is blind'   "Were I ask'd to describe a saint"
14   Finale   'Here comes the bridegroom'
   Act III   Entracte
15   Soldiers' Chorus   'Fill the Can'   "Fill the can, for were victorious"
16   Recit & Drum Song (Fritellini & Chorus)   ' 'Tis the tap of the drum'
17A Scene   'Artists you are'
17B Song (Fiametta)   'Love is blind' or 'The Attractive Girl'
18B Wedding Chorus   'Yonder in the Holy Wood'
19 Quartett   'Dost thou linger'
20 Finale   'Now all is safely over'

Revivals : Comedy, 23 May 1884; Comedy,4 Apr 1885; Prince of Wales's, 1886; Royalty, 23 Jan 1888; Gaiety, 1891 (Florence St John's Benefit); Gaiety, 9 Sept 1893

MANOLA
(La Jour et la nuit)
Comic Opera, composed by Charles Lecocq, libretto by Albert Vanloo and Eugène Leterrier. (Nouveautés, Paris, 5 Nov 1881)
Published : J. B. Cramer & Co., London, 1882
Strand Theatre (Mrs Swanborough) 11 Feb 1882, closed 12 May 1882

Dom Brasiero - Mr H. Ashley ● Miguel (Equerry to Dom Brasiero) - Mons. Desmonts ● Pablo (Servant to Bravo and Dom Calabazes) - Harry Charles ● Stefarno (Aide-de-Camp to Dom Brasiero) - Eugene Stepan ● Don Calabazes (Prince of Villa Viciosa) - Mr W. J. Hill ● Manola (a Creole Girl, betrothed to Miguel) - Rosa Leo ● Beatrix (Contessa d'Asti Spumanti) - Irene Verona ● Tessa (Maid to Beatrix) - Maud Branscombe ● Sanchita (Landlady of the "Lovers' Rest" Posada) - Vere Carew ● Pages of Dom Brasiero, Bridesmaids to Beatrix, Lackeys at the Tras-os-Montas, Muleteers, Soldiers, Notaries &c.
sc. Ryan; cos. (after Wilhelm, Faustin & Dramer) M & Mme Alias; Cond. Mr Hiller

Musical Numbers :
Act I. Moorish Hall in the Castle of Tras-os-Montes
1a. Chorus 'Let's Have a Look' "Let's have a look at the bridal trousseau"
  b. Couplets (1st Page and Chorus) "The brides physique we know but dimly"
2. Lady's Maid Rondo (Mig & Maids of Honour) 'You'll Do'
3. Exit Chorus (Mig & Chorus) "What shall we do?"
4. Couplets (Manola) "Like trembling dove that, shaken from her nest"
5. Couplets (Caleb) 'Women' "Of that dread tyrant Cupid Rex"
6a. Ensemble (Chorus) "Now the bride is here!"
  b. Scene (Cal, Mig, Man) " 'Tis now my turn to greet Madame"
  c. Air (Manola & Cho.) 'My Lady' "Yes! I am! I am 'my lady' "
7. Duet (Man, Mig) "Let us die! let us die!"
8. Couplets (Beat) 'Taken For Another' "Yes! it must be pleasant I own"
9. Finale to Act I
  a. Trio (Man, Beat, Mig) 'Invocation to Cupid' "Little God of Love"
  b. Chorus "The notaries are waiting, Parchment and pen in hand"
  c. Song (Manola) 'The New Moon' "Ah, I remember long, long ago"
Act II. Gardens of the Castle
10. Pages Serenade (Tutti) "To life and light the world is springing"
10½ Exit of Pages (Tutti) "But if in slumber still thou'rt laid"
11. Song (Bras) 'Procrastination' "I've long observed, though still in manhood"
12. Couplets (Manola) 'Had I Only Known' "By Jove! She's delightful!"
13. Two-Part Song (Man, Beat) 'The Two Birds'
14a. Chorus "To furnish forth the Prince's luncheon"
  b. Ensemble (Man, Beat, Mig) "Ah! what prospect charming"
  c. † Song of the Onion (Caleb & Cho) "Onions are like an April day"
15. Snake Song (Manola) "Lo! that coil of gold and jewel, see it glide!"
16. Exit of Calabazes to Pigeon House (Man) "Maï a maï a"
17a. Scene Ensemble and Chorus "Who's that calling? Cho. "Pretty pigeon"
  b. Postillion's Song (Man, Mig) "Careless muleteers we be"
  c. Scene Ensemble and Chorus "Now my cloak, and my sword, and my hat"
    March "When she's led off whom you adore"
Act III
18. Bolero (Solo & Chorus) 'The Castagnette' "The castagnette were I describing"

19. Ballad (Sanch & Chorus) 'The Lovers' Rest'
20. Exit Chorus "Alza Alla"
21. Duet (Man, Mig) "We're lovers of good degree"
22. Drinking Song (Mig & Chorus) "Shall we our glass of wine forego"
        (Introduced - Music by L. De Wenzel)
23. Song (Bras) 'Say It Again' "I am by nature atrabilious"
24. Quartette (Man, Beat, Mig, Bras) 'Dark and Fair'
25. Finale to Act III. (Tutti & Chorus) "I my husband at length have won"

America : as Manola, or, Blonde and Brunette : Fifth Avenue Theatre, 6 Feb 1882
Australia : Opera House, Melbourne, 26 Dec 1882

BOCCACCIO
Operetta in three acts, composed by Franz von Suppé, libretto by F. Zell and Richard
Genée based on a play by Bayard, de Leuven and Beauplan
(Carltheater,Vienna 1 Feb 1879)
Adapted in collaboraton with Robert Reece.
Published : Boosey & Co., 295 Regent St., London. 1882
Comedy Theatre (Alex Henderson), 22 Apr 1882, closed 12 Oct 1882

Boccaccio (Student, Romancer and Satanist) - Violet Cameron ● Pietro (Prince of Palermo)
- Mr J. G. Taylor ● Lotteringhi (a bibulous Cooper) - Louis Kelleher ● Scalza (Court
Barber) - Mr C. Hunt ● Leonetto (a Student and Boccaccio's Chum) - Mr W. S. Rising
● Checco (a blind Beggar) - Mr Truro ● The Major Domo of the Grand Duke - Mr Brook
● The Chapman - Mr H. Perry ● Fresco (Apprentice to Lotteringhi) - Mr Lankey
● Lambertuccio (an Olive Grower) - Lionel Brough ● Fiametta - Alice Burville ● Peronella
(wife of Lambertuccio) - Miss Carlingford ● Beatrice (Daughter of Scalza) - Nellie Maxwell
● Isabella (wife of Lotteringhi) - Kate Monroe ● Tofano - Daisy Angel ● Cicisbro - Ruth
Avondale ● Students and friends of Boccaccio, Bouquetières, Olive gatherers, Pages of the
Prince of Palermo, Ducal Maids of Honour, Citizens, Coopers, Nobles of the Court, The
Florentine Patrol and Ducal Guard, &c., &c.
Dir. H. B. Farnie; sc. Mr T. E. Ryan; cos. M & Mme Alias (after designs by Wilhelm &
Faustin); MD. M. van Bienne.

Musical Numbers :
1a. Scene and Chorus (Checco & Chorus of Beggars) 'Hark to the Bells!'
  b. Tarantella (Chorus) 'Hither Girls and Boys' " 'Tis the day, so fresh, so gay"
  c. Chorus 'Ho! Fellow Students' "Ho! Fellow students, let's be merry"
2a. Scene and Chorus (Chapman & Chorus) 'Good Folk a Moment'
  b. Morceau D'Ensemble 'Every Arrow' "Every arrow hits its mark!"
3a. Serenade Bouffe (Scalza, Lamber, Lotter) 'From Thy Placid Slumber'
  b. Duel Scene and Ensemble 'Hark! They Come!'
4. Rondo (Bocc & Chorus) 'Let Me Relate' "Let me relate a short romance"
5. Duet (Fiam, Peron) 'Love and Piety' "The bells are ringing soft and low"
6. Volkslied (Fiam, Bocc) 'Young Love' "Young love is like a lily"
7. Duet (Fiam, Bocc) 'The Alms of Love' "A blind and helpless beggar"
8. Finale to Act I (Tutti & Chorus) 'Citizens! In Just Fury Rise'
      Act II
9. Rondo (Bocc, Leon, Prince) 'Onery, Twoery' "Oh! Pleasure's a treasure"
10. Serenade (Bocc, Prince, Leon) 'My Soul, My Star!'
11. Coopers Song (Lotter & Chorus) 'Bumpty-Rap-a-Ta'
12. Letter Trio (Fiam, Isab, Peron) 'A Letter! and Addressed to Me!'
13. Song (Isab) 'Flirtation' "Yes; a girl may start in life"

14. Kiss Chorus (Coopers & Olive-Gatherers) 'O, Take Care'
15. Yokel Song (Bocc) 'I'm But Country Bred' "Oh! Sir, I am but Country bred"
16. Otett (Bocc, Fiam, Isab, Peron, Leon, Prince, Lambert, Lotter) 'Quick, Quick"
17. Finale to Act II (Tutti & Chorus) "My business is to take with me"
    Act III
18. Chorus and Dance 'The Menuet Lesson'
19a. Recit. (Capt & Chorus) 'Now Pages All' "Now pages all, fall in"
  b. Chorus 'The Ladies' Own' "Now then, all in time, Like a flowing rhyme"
20. Ballad (Bocc) 'Forget Not to Forget' "We're parted, yet I know not why"
21. Exit (Bocc, Leon, Isab) 'Onery, Twoery' (reprise)
22. Duett (Fiam, Bocc) 'When First These Eyes'
22a. Duett (Bocc, Leon) 'O Mountains Blue' "O mountains blue in air"
23. Septett (Beat, Isab, Peron, Bocc, Lotter, Scalza, Lambert) 'You Silly Dolts'
24. Finale (Tutti & Chorus) "Wit is the weapon of wisdom"

Australia : Opera House, Melbourne, 2 Sept 1882

RIP VAN WINKLE

Comic opera in three acts and five tableaux by H. B. Farnie, Ludovic Meilhac and Philippe
Gille, composed by Robert Planquette.
Comedy Theatre (Alex Henderson) 14 Oct 1882,
closed 27 Oct 1883 (328 performances)
Theater an der Wein, Vienna, as 'Rip Rip' 22 Dec 1883
Théâtre des Folies Dramatique, Paris 11 Nov 1884 as 'Rip !'
Cast at Comedy Theatre, London

Rip Van Winkle (a village good-for-nothing) - Fred Leslie • Derrick Von Hans (the village
lawyer and Rip's rival) - W. S. Penley • Peter Van Dunk (Burgomaster of Sleepy Hollow) -
Louis Kelleher • Diedrich Knickerbocker (village schoolmaster and local poet) - Mr E.
Wilmore • Capt Hugh Rowley (of the British Army) - Fred Storey • Nick Vedder (landlord
of the "George III" Inn) - Lionel Brough • Gretchen (wife of Rip Van Winkle) – Violet
Cameron • Sara, Jacintha (two of her gossips) - Clara Graham and Constance Lewis
• Katrina (a village flirt, Daughter of Nick Vedder) - Sadie Martinot • Little Hardcase
(clerk to Derrick) - Madge Milton • Hans (his nephew) - Miss Effie Mason (in Act III
played by Mr F. Darrell) • Alice (Rip's little daughter) - Miss Alice Vicat • Tom Tit
(Bugler to Rowley's Company) - Rose Moncrieff • Gape (Waitress at the "George III") -
Grace Hawke • Leedle Jan (Katrina's brother) - Master Gallop • Dutch girl friends of
Katrina, Dutch lads, friends of Rip, Peasants of Sleepy Hollow, English Soldiers, &c.
Principal dancer - Ada Wilson.
Dir H. B. Farnie; MD Auguste van Bienne; ch. John d'Auban; sc. W. R. Beverley; cos.
Faustin & Wilhelm.
Musical Numbers :
    Act I
1a Chorus "Far and Near Our Cry be Heard"
 b Scene "On this Solemnity right royal"
 c Wheedling Duett (Gret & Kat) "You'll be kind, I can see"
2 Exit of Peasants "Yes! it is a common thing"
3 Air (Rip) "Oh! where's my girl of whom I'm fond?"
4 Canoe Song (Gret & Rip) "Where floweth the wild Mohawk river"
5 Chorus of Cowards "Can't you see we're coming?"
6 Legend of the Kaatskils (Gret & Cho) 'Oh! Beware!' "From deep forest hoary"
7a Trio (Rip, Alice, Hans) "Ere the marriage contract is drawn"

177

b   Air (Rip)   "These little heads, now golden"
8   Rondo (Kat & Cho)   'The Village Well'   "Tis the hour we girls ne'er fail"
9   Finale Act I (Tutti & Coro)   "When I come back 'twill be no more to roam"
    Act II   (a) Entracte (b) Melodrame
10a   Lantern Chorus   "By the thicket path we are trudging slow"
  b   Scene (Gret, Kat, Coro)   "Where is Rip's wife?"
  c   Ballad (Gret & Coro)   "Now the twilight shadows are stealing"
11   Exit   "Our search is vain, lets home again"
12   Patrol Chorus   "The night is dark and lowering"
13   Trio (Gret, Rip, Derrick)   "Now won't you come along with me?"
14   Echo Song (Rip & Coro)   "Ho! ho! (no echo) Friends, echoes, why do ye fail"
15   Melodrame
16a   Scene & Chorus) (Hudson, Rip, Coro)   "You're very good, and friendly"
  b   Sea Song   'Blow High, Blow Low'   "Hendrick Hudson I am called"
17   Serenade (1st Lieut & Coro)   'My Pipe'   "I've had ladye-loves in my day"
18   Pas de Fascination
19   Finale Sestett & Chorus (Tutti & Coro)   'Slumber Mortal'
    Act III
Sc.1   Chorus of Woodcutters (Kat & Coro)   "Before our broad axes, Lo! they fall"
20a   Election Chorus   "Whatsoever may be won"
  b   Couplets and Ensemble   "Ladies cannot sit in Congress"
21   Rondo (Kat & Coro)   'Yes, No, and nothing at all'
22   Letter Song (Alice)   'True Love from O'er the Sea'   "I dare not break the seal!"
23   Hammock Song and Chorus (Lt Van Slous & Coro)   'Rock'd Upon the Billow'
23½   Melodrame
24   Song (Rip)   'Truth in the Well'   "The thirsty sun burns on the noon-tide brink"
25   Trio (Alice, Van Slous, Rip)   "I know you not! My father's dead!"
26   Air & Chorus   "Some say now that the voting is done"
27   Finale (Tutti & Coro) "From deep forest hoary" [Reprise - Legend of Kaatskils]
Revivals : Comedy Theatre 6 Sept 1884; Théâtre de la Gaîte, Paris 18 Oct 1894
America : Standard Theatre, New York, 28 Oct 1882
Australia : Opera House, Melbourne, 1 Jan 1884

FROLIQUE
Written in collaboration with H. J. Byron,
music selected and arranged by John Fitzgerald.
Published : Chappell & Co., London, 1883
Strand Theatre, 18 Nov 1882, closed Wed 17 Jan 1883

The Duke of Chartres - Mr F. Mervin ● Prof Polybius Pompon - Mr T. P. Haynes ● Comte de Clut Tourelles - Mons. E. Desmont ● Capitaine Frousac - Mons. F. Gaillard ● Pierre Coquillard - John S. Clarke ● The Duchess - Mdlle Sylvia ● Mirabelle - Miss Vere Carew ● 1st Page - Miss la Feuillade ● 1st Maid of Honour - Miss Huspeth ● Pages, Cooks, Maids of Honour in the Palais Royal, &c.

sc. Mr Ryan; Cos. M & Mme Alias; MD. John Fitz-Gerald; SM. Arthur Swanborough
    Musical Numbers :   Overture
    1.   Chorus of Masks   'To the Ball Tonight'
    2.   Chorus   'What's This Noise'
    3.   Chorus of Masks   Exeunt "To the ball tonight ... "
    4.   Melodrame (Pomp & Pierrot)
    5.   Melodrame   'The Reading of the Letters'
    6.   Duet with Chorus off (Duchess & Mira)   'What joy to be a simple lady'

7. Quintette (Duke, Aide, Duchess, Mira, Pomp) 'What a Form'
8. Finale Scene 1
  a. Ensemble "What's all this trouble now? "
  b. Duet (Duchess, Mira) "O brave sir, two ribald men pursue us"
  c. Song with Chorus (Capt) 'The Ladies Own' "The soldier's glory in the fray"
9. Melodrame Entrance of Duchess and Pierrot
10. Song (Duchess) 'What Could I Say' "At the mask'd ball he came courting me"
11. Chorus of Waiters 'Supper and Champagne'
12. Trio & Drinking Song (Duchess, Duke, Pierrot) 'The Tête à Tête'
13. Melodrame Entrance of Captain and Soldiers
14. Song (Capt) 'On Gaily On to the Scaffold'
15. Melodrame & Chorus (Maids of Honour, Pages) 'Up All Night'
16. Song & Chorus (Mirab, Maids & Pages) 'Silver Bell'
17. Melodrame Entrance of Pierrot and Guard
18. Melodrame Entrance of Capt, Guards, Pages, &c.
19. Ensemble with Solo for Capt 'Let us Guard'
20. Song & Ensemble (Aide, Duke, Duchess, Mirab, Pomp) 'The Monogram'
21. Finale (Tutti) "Now happy all trouble's done"

LA VIE
(La Vie parisienne)
Opera B ouffe, composed by Jacques Offenbach, libretto by Henri Meilhac and Ludovic
Halévy. (Palais-Royal, Paris 31 Oct 1866)
Published : Boosey & Co., London, 1883
Brighton, 17 Sept 1883
Avenue Theatre (Alex Henderson), 3 Oct 1883
The Baron von Gondremarcke - Lionel Brough ● Hon. Tom Splinterbarre - Herbert
Standing ● Lord Guy Silverspoone - Mr Forbes Drummond ● Snip - Mr A. Wheatman
● Knobstick - Mr R. J. Waldegrave ● Mr Muggins - Mr C. Hunt ● Blucher - Ernest Palmieri
● Joe Tarradiddle - Arthur Roberts ● Gabrielle Chevrette - Mlle Camille d'Arville ● Lady
Catherine Wyverne - Miss C. Gardiner ● Flounce - Clara Graham ● Trixie - Aimée Perin
● Baby Greene - Ivy Warner ● Taunto Torrington - Miss Fairfax ● Victor Emanuel Jonas -
Agnes Lyndon ● Capt Fluker - Josephine Clare ● Countess of Sevendials - Maud de Vere
● Miss Slyboots - Lily Harcourt ● Mrs Muggins - Bessie Bell ● Christine von
Gondremarcke - Lilian la Rue
Dir. H. B. Farnie; MD. G. Jacobi; sc. W. Spong & T. Rogers; cos. Alias after Faustin,
Wilhelm & Phil May.
  Musical Numbers :
    Act I
1. Station Chorus "Employees are we all on the South Eastern line"
2. Rondo (Lady K) 'The Lady's Art of Fascination'
3a. Chorus "The heavens low'r Here comes a show'r"
  b. Scene (Trixie, Greene, Splint, Silv) 'Trixie's Here'
4. Duettino (Silv, Splint) "Such brazen conduct saw I never"
5. Song (Joe) 'The Trout' "It needs no glass binocular" (Interpolated.
      Words by W. Pink. Music by F. Musgrave)
5½ Trio (Chris, Baron, Splint) "I'm a model Cicerone"
6. Romance (Chris) 'Shall We E're Meet' "I own that gaiety but grieves me"
7. Finale to Act I.
  a. Chorus "Guards and porters, now the time for hurry"
  b. Yachting Song (Solo & Chorus) "Now float our honoured Club Bargee"

179

    c. Ensemble & Chorus "Near and far, Here they are"
        Act II
8. Song (Splint) 'Lost Lovers' "Grave Lalage, daughter and aide of my tutor"
9. Duet (Gab, Blucher) "Bootmaker I, and you glove-maker sweet"
10. Romance (Chris) 'Dreaming and Waking' "I've dreamt a dream"
11. [missing]
12. Duet (Chris, Joe) "You haunt a maiden's happy dream"
13a. Baccarat Chorus (Chris, Splint, Baron, Chorus) "Short and long,"
    b. "The Baron as Banker gives the punters two cards"
14a. Table d'Hote Chorus (Gab, Bluch, Splint, Baron & Chorus) "Here we come£
    b. Song (Gab) 'The Colonel's Widow' "Ah! an air of daring divine"
15. Song (Joe) 'For Thee, My Love, For Thee' Interpolated. Words by W. Pink (not
               printed in vocal score). Music by F. Musgrave.
16. Finale to Act II
    a. Scene 'Now Ladies' "Ladies, gentlemen, dinner's served"
    b. Air & Chorus "Next to a band from Fatherland"
    c. Tyrolienne "Auf de Berliner Brück, Tra, la, la"
        Act III
17. Housemaids Chorus 'Get All Ready' "Ev'ry lounge and chair be rubbing"
18. Romance (Chris) "Our hearts will meet - where hands have met"
19. Chorus À La Gavotte 'Let England' "Now welcome, England Old"
20. Gavotte 'Among the Lilies'
21. Bouffe Song (Joe) [words not printed in vocal score]
22. Polka Chantée (Chris, Gab & S.S.T.B.) " 'Tis the hour of rapture,"
23. Chorus and Waltz (S.S.T.B.) 'He Is Tight' "We regret to say he's tight"
24. Finale to Act III 'On, Dance On' "Merrily, merrily, foot and toe"
America : Bijou Opera House, New York, 18 April 1883
Revivals : Provincial Tour 1883-84
America : Bijou Opera House, New York, 18 Mar 1884

FALKA
(Le Droit d'aînesse)
Comic Opera, composed by F. Chassaigne, libretto by Eugène Letterier and Albert Vanloo
(Théâtre des Nouveautés, Paris, 27 Jan 1883)
Published : Alfred Hays, London, 1883
Comedy Theatre (Alex Henderson), 29 Oct 1883, closed 26 Feb 1884 (158 performances)
Kolback (Military Governor of Montgratz) - Harry Paulton ● Tancred (His Nephew) – Mr
H. Ashley ● Arthur (Student - Son of a Rich Hungarian Farmer) - Louis Kelleher ● Lay-
Brother Pelican (Door-keeper of the Convent) - Mr Penley ● Konrad (Captain of the
Governor's Pages) - Miss Vere Carew ● Tekeli (Sergeant of the Patrol) - Mr Vaughan
● Boboky (Tzigan Scout) - Rose Moncrieff ● Boleslas (Chief of the Tzigani) - Mr W.
H. Hamilton ● The Seneschal (Kolback's Steward) - James Francis ● Falka (Niece of
Kolback, at the Convent School) - Violet Cameron ● Edwige (Sister of Boleslas) - Miss
Wadman ● Alexina de Kelkirsch (A young Heiress) - Louise Henschel ● Minna (Her Maid)
– Clara Graham ● Janotha (Landlady of the Inn) - Miss E. Nicholls ●Pages of the Governor,
Maids of Honour, Bridesmaids, Soldiers of the Household &c., &c.
Dir. H. B. Farnie; sc. Spong, Callcott, Grieve; cos Alias after Wilhelm & Faustin
        Musical Numbers :   Overture
    1a. 'Patrol Chorus' "While all the town is sleeping"
    b. Scene 'Whatever's the row?'

    c. Couplets 'Govenor Kolback' "Try to match him were vain"
2. Air and Refrain 'I'm The Captain', or, 'Tis the Captain Boleslas'
3. Nocturne 'There Was No Ray' "There was no ray of light"
4. Rondo Duet 'For Your Indulgence' "For your indulgence we are hoping"
5. Trio 'Now Then Hurry Scurry'
6. Finale (Act 1) Tutti e coro "More new sensation"
7a. Chorus 'Tap, tap'
  b. Couplets "P'raps you will excuse me staring"
8a. Chorus 'Now Comes Our Chief' "Now comes our chief this way"
  b. Couplets 'The Boarding School Girl!' "Uncle you're looking splendid"
9a. Bohemian Chorus 'Cradled Upon the Heather'
  b Air 'To the Greenwood'
10. Trio 'Oh Joy! Oh Rapture!' What the words that he said unto me"
11. Finale (Act 2) 'What's this Rumour'
12a. Bridal Chorus 'Rampart and Bastion Gray'
  b. Hungarian Rondo and Dance 'Kiss Chorus' "Catchee, catchee"
13. Exit Chorus 'Catchee, Catchee'
14. Romance 'At Eventide' (Introduced - music Planquette)
15. Duetto 'With a tear in our Voice'
16. Duo Berceuse 'Slumber! Oh Sentinel'
17. Marriage Bell Chorus 'There the Bells Go'
18. Trio 'Nunky Darling'
19. Marriage Bell Entrance 'There the Bells Go'
20. Finale 'And Now a Long Goodbye'

Revivals : Comedy Theatre, 30 Aug 1884 to launch provincial tour; Avenue, 19 Sept 1885; numerous provincial and amateur productions; BBC Broadcasts, 10 May 1924 and 24 July 1925
America : Casino Theatre, New York, 4 Apr 1884; Wallack's, 12 July 1886; Wallack's, 11 June 1887; American Theatre, 10 Mar 1900
Australia : Opera House, Melbourne, 24 Apr 1886

A MARRIAGE NOOSE
No Record of Production
An Original Comedy written expressly for Drawing Room acting. Dick's Standard Charades and Comedies for Home Representation, No. 488 - Jargonelle and A Marriage Noose written respectively by Mrs H. Parker and H. B. Farnie

NUMBER 157B
Drawing Room Charade
An original Charade in three scenes written expressly for Drawing Room acting.
Published in Bow Bells, 4 Dec 1867. Dicks Standard Charades and Comedies for Home Representation No. 492. Number 157B and Lovely written respectively by H. B. Farnie and H. P. Grattan. London. 1883

NELL GWYNNE
Revised 1876 libretto, with new lyrics, composed by Robert Planquette.
Avenue Theatre (Alex Henderson) 7 Feb 1884, transferred 28 April 1884 to Comedy
Theatre, closed 22 May 1884 (86 performances)
Nell Gwynne, actress at the King's Theatre (and disguised as, Lady Falbala, a supposed country dame, Joan, Cook at the "Dragon", and Zaphet, the Gipsy, a fortune teller) –

Florence St John ● Clare (Ward of the King) - Agnes Stone ● Jessamine (Old Weasel's niece) – Guilia Warwick ● Marjorie (Weasel's servant) - Victoria Reynolds ● Buckingham (exiled from Court - Landlord and Waiter at the "Dragon") - Michael Dwyer ● Rochester - Llewelyn (Lyn) Cadwaladr ● The Beadle - Lionel Brough / Louis Kelleher ● Weasel (Village pawnbroker and usurer) - Arthur Roberts ● Talbot - Cecil Crofton ● Falcon (Strolling player - Jessamine's lover) - Henry Walsham ● Hodge, Podge (Two Hampshire rustics - D. St John, C. Hunt ● Peregrine (Buckingham's page) - Agnes Lyndon ● Charles II - Augustus Wheatman ● Prue, Sue (Two village gossips - Bessie Bell, Lily Richards ● Waiters at the "Dragon", Village Girls, &c., &c.

Dir. H. B. Farnie; MD Georges Jacobi / Rubini A. Rochester; ch. Katti Lanner; sc. T. E. Ryan & W. Grieve; cos. Phil May, Arthur Fredericks, Wilhelm

Musical Numbers :

Act I

Chorus 'No Heel Taps'
Scene 'He Brings Our Score'
Air 'To You Ladies'
Duo Bouffe (Buck & Roch) 'The British Waiter'
Rondo (Nell) 'Only an Orange Girl'
Quartette (Jess, Roch, Buck & Weas) 'Oh Heart! My Lover's Near'
Song 'Once Upon a Time' "If to a Princess royal" (Buckingham)
Quartette "O'er Their Young Hearts" (Nell, Clare, Buckingham & Rochester)
Chorus "Clubs and Cudgels"
Beadle's Song ' 'Tis I' "Who's the greatest power local" (Beadle & Chorus)
Exit of Peasants
Serenade "Sweet Heart If Thou Be Nigh" (Falcon)
Finale "Oh Surprise" (Tutti & Chorus)

Act II Entracte

Pawn Chorus "About the Middle of the Week"
Rustic Rondo "Ah! Work-a-day, Life's Hard" (Nell Gwynne)
Song of the Clock "Tic Tac" (Jessamine)
Gipsey Duett 'Maid of the Witching Eye' (Nell and Clare)
Sextuor "Now the Spell" (Nell, Jess, Clare, Roch, Buck & Weasel)
Romance 'First Love' "Troth is naught - and the world is grey" (Nell)
Duett "The Dappled Fawn" (Jessamine and Falcon)
Song 'Illusions' "Faith There's a Season" (Buckingham)
Duett 'Turn About' "Rochester, Ah! Buckingham here?" (Buck and Roch)
Finale " What's Passing Here" (Tutti & Chorus)

Act III Entracte

Hunting Chorus "The Eager Hounds"
Scene 'The Broken Cavalier' "The trumpet sounds, to saddle springs" (Nell)
Exit of Hunting Party "Ta ra, Ta ra, Ta ra,"
Romance 'The Trysting Tree' "Run little brook, run with thy silver feet" (Falcon)
Scene and Air 'The Ball at the White Hall' (Nell Gwynne)
Old Air 'Green Sleeves' "Thy smock of silk both fair and white" (Nell Gwynne)
Idyl "Happy the Lot" (Weasel and Beadle)
Quartette 'The Rendezvous' (Nell, Clare, Rochester & Buckingham)
Duett "Timid Bird" (Jessamine and Falcon)
Finale (Tutti & Chorus)

Continent : Théâtre des Nouveautés, Paris as 'La Princesse Colombine' 7 Dec 1885; German version Theaterverlag 'Prinzessin Pirouette' 1886

America : Casino Theatre, New York, 8 Nov 1884; Koster and Bial's Music Hall, New York, 6 May 1901
Australia : Opera House, Melbourne, 17 July 1886

CHILPERIC
"The Musical Spectacle, in Three Acts and Seven Tableaux",
in collaboration with Henry Hersee
Empire Theatre (Alex Henderson) 17 April 1884, closed 25 July 1884

Chilperic (King of the Gauls) - Herbert Standing ● Siegbert (Archduke of Neustria) – Henry Wardroper ● Divitiacus (The Arch Druid) - Westlake Perry ● Rigolboche (Court Jester) - Mons. Paulus ● Alvarez, Bim-bom-bo (Minstrels of Castille) - Les Frères Tacchi ● Brathvan, Taska (Gothic Warriors) - Felix Bury, Mr Lopresti ● Toc (Page in the Palace) - James T. Powers ● Sieur de Gruelle (Grand Factotum) - Harry Paulton ● Frédégonda (A Peasant Girl) - Camille D'Arville ● Landry (her Sweetheart) - Agnes Consuelo ● Cason (King of the Goths) - Clara Graham ● Fana (The Arch Druidess) - Katherine Gardiner ● Brunehart (Siegbert's wife) - Clara Douglas ● Navette (a Flower Girl) - Rosie Heath ● Don Nervose (a Spanish Exquisite) - Miss Mattie Wynne ● Dona Tuberosa (Duenna to the Princess) - Sallie Turner ● Galsuinda (Castilian Princess) - Madge Shirley ● Pages to Chilperic, Huntresses, Druidesses, Maids of Honour, Spanish Pages, Gothic Soldiers, Druids, Courtiers, Spanish Officials, Patrol, &c., &c.
Dir. H. B. Farnie; MD. John S. Hillier; sc. Ryan, Grieve, Hart & Bruce Smith; cos. Alias after Bianchini, Faustin & Wilhelm.
        Musical Numbers not known except :
        Butterfly Song
        Oh! Rarest Sport

THE GRAND MOGUL
(Le Grand Mogol)
Operetta in three acts, composed by Edmond Audran, libretto by Henri Chivot and Alfred Duru (Gymnase, Marseilles 24 Feb 1877;
version in four acts, Gaîté, Paris 19 Sept 1884)
Ferée Orientale in adaptation with additional music by Audran.
Comedy Theatre (Alex Henderson) Sat 15 Nov 1884, closed 15 Jan 1885

Ayala (otherwise Charlie Jones) - Fred Leslie ● Prince Mignapour (Heir to the Mogul Throne) - Henry Bracy ● The Capitaine Coquelnoche (French Envoy) - Frank Wyatt ● Jugginsee-Lal (now Grand Vizier elect to the Mogul Prince) - Arthur Roberts ● Djemma (Ayala's Cousin - English girl, travelling as a Snake Charmer) - Florence St John ● Sara (her English Maid) - Miss Farebrother ● Orissa (Tire-woman to the Princess Bengaline) - Clara Graham ● Patchouli (a Bayadere) - Rosee Heath ● Bengaline (Princess betrothed to Mignapour) – Berthe Latour ● Azem, Mirzaphia (Young Rajas of the Court) - Miss Clyde Howard, Minnie Howe ● Pages of Princes, Ladies of the Court, Attendants, Waiters, Courtiers, Market Girls, Tributary Princes, Soldiers, Rajas, Conspirators, &c., &c.
Dir. H. B. Farnie; sc. T. E. Ryan; cos. designed and executed Alias
        Musical Numbers :
            Act I
        1a. Market Chorus 'Hurry Up!' "Who would be buying?"
          b. Recit and Air (Aya & Chorus) 'My Name's Ayala'
        2. Nibble-Ungen Lied (Djemma) 'The Two Mice' "A Grey mouse loved"

3. Bouffe Scene (Jug) 'The Defaulter's Progress' "Ring the bell, the Roodee clear"
4a. Chorus "Place there! place for Bengaline"
 b. Air (Beng & Chorus) 'But a Woman' "Let all their homage pay"
4½ Exit Chorus "Place there for Bengaline" (Reprise)
5. Duet (Beng, Mign) 'Enshrined Within My Heart'
   Couplets (Beng, Mign) "Young men sin with women and wine"
6. Serpent Scene (Djem, Beng, Aya & Chorus) 'Snake-Charming Free!'
7. Finale to Act I (tutti e coro) "All hail! the youth that threw me flowers"
   Act II
8. Chorus ' 'Tis Our King's Wedding Day'
9. Song (Sara & Chorus) 'Legend of the Pearls'
10. Trio (Beng, Coq, Jug) 'Silence, Mysterie!'
10½ Song (Mign) 'Ah, Me! I Love'
11 Duet (Djem, Aya) 'What a Vision'
12 Song (Aya) 'Loving and Loved Again'
13 Nautch Scene & Song (Beng, Mign, Jug, Coq & Cho) "Lissome as the snake"
   Indian Song (Beng & Chorus) "Within the jungle creeping"
14 Anacreontic (Aya, Mign, Djem & Chorus) 'India Ale' "Well did the Prophet!"
15 Chorus (Djem, Aya, Mign & Chorus) 'Leave the Young King Alone'
16 Lullaby (Djem) 'Dream On' "Dream on, dream on, in fancy free"
16½ Melodrame - Changing the Pearls
17. Finale to Act II (Tutti & Chorus) 'He Has Fallen'
   Act III
18 Chorus ' 'Tis Hot on the Shimmering River'
18½ Exit Chorus 'It is in this same careful way'
19 Bouffe Song (Jug) 'The Dotlet of My Eye' "When folks are not the 'Upper Ten'"
20. Romance (Djem) 'A Thousand Leagues of Foam' "When from my home"
20½ Melodrame
21. Quartette (Djem, Sara, Coq, Aya) 'Here is the Horrid Thing'
22 Duet (Beng, Mign) 'The Bayadère! 'Twas I'
23 Finale (Tutti & Chorus) 'Never More, My Love'

Revivals : Provincial Tour
America : Bijou Theatre, New York in Farnie's version 29 October 1881 as 'The Snake Charmer'; Metropolitan Theatre, 28 August 1882; Star Theatre, 26 Sept 1887; Wallack's Theatre, 1887.

KENILWORTH

New Fairy Burlesque Extravaganza, written in collaboration with Robert Reece. Music selected from Suppé, Tosti, Felix Keston, Offenbach, Strauss, Métra, Audran, Mullocher, &c.

Published : J. B. Cramer & Co. (9542) 1886

Avenue Theatre (Alex Henderson) 19 Dec 1885, closed 17 Apr 1886 (129 performances)
Dudley (Earl of Leicester) - Violet Cameron ● Sir Walter Raleigh - Phyllis Broughton ● The Earl of Essex - Emma Broughton ● Tressilian - Marie de Braham ● Amy Robsart – Laura Linden ● Flibbertigibbet - Kate James ● Janet Foster - Fanny Wentworth ● The Good Fairy, Star One - Nelly Hardinge ● Queen Elizabeth - Mr J. J. Dallas ● Tony Foster - Mr E. J. Lonnen ● Giles Gosling   Tapster at the "Bear Inn" - Mr H. Carter ● Wayland Smith - Vokes ● Mike Lambourne - Sam Wilkinson ● Sir Richard Varney - Arthur Roberts ● Mine Host of Ye Shippe - Helen Massey ● Lord Sandwich (Captain of Leicester's Pages) - Beatrice Gordon ● Lord de Midge - Blanche East ● Ciss o' the Inn - Ruby Mc Neil Anonanonsir (Drawer at the Greenwich Inn) - Ruth Fowler ● Lady Letitia Tartlett - Nettie

Lefevre • Leicester Herald - Nellie Hardinge • Marquis of Roochee - Maggie Mackintosh • Hon Tattenham Corner – Miss Clyde Howard • Lord de Knavesmire - Miss Harrie Price • Lord Fitzplunger - Nellie Lisle • Lady Patty Butter - Mattie Wynne • Sussex's Pages, Leicester's Pages, Ladies of the Tabouret, Ladies-in-Waiting, Sailors on the Royal Yacht, Huntresses, Village lads and lasses, Falconers, Courtiers, Noble-ladies, Court Hair-dressers, The Royal Patrol, Mashers, Mummers, Spanish Ballerina, &c., &c.
The Spanish Figure in Act II danced by Mesdames Nettie Lefevre, Beatrice Gordon, Chrissie Mayne, and Lily Lavine.
Dir. H. B. Farnie; MD. Michael Connelly; sc. Ryan, Spong, Bruce Smith; cos. Alias after Besche.

Musical Numbers not known

LURLINE
A new Burlesque in Three Acts and Six Tableaux, written in collaboration with Robert Reece. Music original or selected from favourite composers; Incidental motifs from Wallace's Opera by permission of Messrs Hutchings & Romer.
Published : Cramer & Co., London, [1886]
Avenue Theatre (George Wood) 24 Apr 1886, closed 3 July 1886
Sir Rupert the Rapless - Arthur Roberts • Skraggestein - Mr E. J. Lonnen • Lord de Sophtroe - Gerald Moore • The Gnome Professor - Sam Wilkinson • The Baroness von Geyser - Ramsey Danvers • Grabwitz - Felix Bury • Onduletta - Phyllis Broughton • Rivuletta - Madge Shirley • Captain Crawley de Crayfish - Emma Broughton • Bob - Nelly Hardinge • Wolfgang, Fritz (Friends of Sir Rupert's) - Daisy D'Angeli, Ellen Massey • Annichen, Gretchen (Two Lady Friends) - Nellie Lefevre, Ruby McNeill • Lord Sopeworks – Clyde Howard • Rortypal - Beatrix Gordon • Lurline - Violet Cameron
Dir. H. B. Farnie; MD. Michael Connelly; sc. T. E. Ryan and A. Colcott; cos. M & Mme Alias.

Musical Numbers not known
Mr Arthur Robert's songs written by Mr Fred Bowyer.

THE COMMODORE
(La Créole)
Avenue Theatre (George Wood), 10 May 1886
Burlesque Opera, new version of The Creole, written in collaboration with Robert Reece, composed by Offenbach.
Published : J. B. Cramer & Co., London (JBC&Co.9580), 1886
Avenue Theatre (Mr George Wood) 10 May 1886 matinee (Violet Cameron Benefit), Thur 20 May 1886, followed by tour.
The Commodore - Mr Lionel Brough • Maitre Garble, Maitre Babble - E. John Lonnen, Sam Wilkinson • Sabord - Mr F. Mitchell • Beaupre - Mr Tomkins • Frontignac - Arthur Roberts • The Capitaine Réné - Violet Cameron • Antoinette - Madelaine Shirley • Zoe – Mdlle Cornelie D'Anka • Berthe, Lolotte - Misses Nellie Hardinge, d'Angeli • Yagarita – Violet Dashwood • Pierre - Clyde Howard • Paul - Beatrice Gordon • Yvonne - Miss Ruth Fowler • Naval Cadets, Peasant, Crew of the Flagship, &c., &c.

Musical Numbers :
Act I
1. Chorus 'Anchored in the Roadstead'

Solo (Beau) "Fear not that"
1½ Exit Chorus "Anchored in the roadstead yonder"
2. Song (Ant) 'First Lovers' "Yes, I grant you, maidens need ruling"
3a. Chorus (with Réné) 'The Capitaine Réné'
 b. Song (Réné & Chorus) 'Oh, France, Beloved France'
3½ Exit Chorus 'Oh, France, Beloved France' (reprise)
4. Trio (Ant, Réné, Comm) 'Up Helm' "Up helm, and tack down here"
5. Song (Front) 'So Shy' "I'm always in a dreadful fluster"
6. Finale to Act I (Tutti e coro) "The Commodore's to mate his daughter"
    Old Mans Song "Come dearest girl, a little nearer"
                Act II
7. Entr'acte
8. Song (Réné) 'When Lovers Fond' [mus. Emile Jonas]
9. Scene and Air (Zoe, Ant, Réné, Front, Comm) 'I Welcome You'
10. Duet (Zoe, Front) 'Make Love to Me'
11. Duet (Zoe, Réné) 'You Have No Right'
12a. Chorus 'Certain Are We' "Not in the least do we wonder"
 b. Rondo [words not printed]
13. Finale to Act II (Tutti e coro) 'Whom Do I Love?'
    The Despatch Song "Hurry on Board, your anchor trip"
                Act III
14. Entr'acte
15. Sleep Song (Réné) 'I Guard the Lonely Deck for Thee'
16. Sestette (Zoe, Ant, Réné, Front, the Notaries) 'Vengeance'
17. Exit Chorus (As 16) (?) 'Let Us Swear'
18. Capstan Chorus (Beau & Chorus) 'We're the Lads'
19. Hornpipe
20. Quatuor (Zoe, Ant, Réné, Front) 'The Commodore is Fast Asleep'
21. Finale (Tutti) "Well, Commodore, we've enjoyed our trip"
America : Casino Theatre, New York, 4 Oct 1886

GLAMOUR
Comic Opera, written in collaboration with Alfred Murray, story revised from Piff Paff
with new music by William M. Hutchison.
Theatre Royal, Edinburgh, 30 Aug 1886 to start No.1 tour ending 13 Nov 1886
King Impecunioso 100th - John L. Shine ● Fabian - Victor de Lore ● Hugo - Joseph Wilson
● Trip - Fred A. Gaytie ● Count Inferno di Penseroso - Wilfred E. Shine ● Prince Glamour -
Charles Conyers ● Angelo - Florence Dawnay ● Queen Palmyra Jane - Susie Vaughan
● Princess Cynthia - Emilie Holt ● Princess Irene - Annie Montelli ● Countess Allegra -
Augusta Thompson ● Daphne - Giulia Warwick
MD. Edward St Quentin
    Musical Numbers :
    1 a Chorus of Sentinels "Through night so dark and morn so cold"
      b   Recitative "The coast is clear, no more afraid";
                  Serenade "If thou art sleeping, princess fair";
                  Duet "I hear! I hear! She is coming to me";
                  Quartette "Low sighs the night wind love laden"
    2 a Chorus of Huntsmen.   "To the merry, merry hunting meeting"
      b   Chorus of Pages.   "Our gracious king, our sov'reign head"
      c   Song. 'I am King Impecunioso' "I'm a hungry monarch and very hard up"
    3   Romance (Glamour) "O sweet unknown, who to my longing breast"
    4   Song (Daphne) "He was high-born, and she a simple maiden"
186

5   Trio (Dap, Glam, & Trip)   "You don't believe it?"
    Tarantella 'Invocation to Humming Bird'
6   Chorus of Pages and Courtiers. "Come away, come away with the spoil"
    Chorus of Maids of Honour. " 'Tis a shame, and a shame that is burning"
    Scene. "A capital scheme"
7   Chorus and Scene. " 'Tis a stew ! 'Tis a stew ! ";
                Quartette "Let us take a little table";
                Song "O there's naught no nice as picking A little devilled bone"
8   Song (Glam) If a lass should me deceive"
9   Act 1 Finale. "The lsot code of Gramercie"
10 Chorus of Pages and Maids of Honour. "With footfall light and wary"
11 Duet (Glam & Dap) "Let me go ! Let me go !"
12 Quartette "What's to be done? How can we tell ?"
13 Conspiracy Quintette. "Raise your hand up to your lip"
14 Sneezing Chorus (Maids and Pages) "All hail, our royal master !"
    'The less said about it the better' Topical song written by Walter Browne.
15 Legend of the Guns (Glam) "A sorcerer once made a gun"
16 Chorus "Now then the brand !"
    Arietta (Dap) "Love is a minstrel's theme"
17 Act II Finale.
    a   Chorus. "See the shepherdess convicted !"
    b   Scene "Order my cab !"
    c   Air (Dap) "Ah, heed mu supplication !"
    d   Scene "The ordeal's wholy reversed"
18 Jeering Chorus "He's a dainty cavalier"
19 Maid of my Soul (Dap) "Maid of my soul ! wherever thou may'st be"
21 Sestet "Yes, there's something in the air !"
    Duet (King & Queen) "You're a beauty ! You are not !"
22 Tub Chorus. "Here we are all in the washing tub"
23 Song & Duet (Galm & Dap) "In one brief day my hopes are banished"
24 Concerted Piece "O what is this terrible tale ?"
24 Finale - Couplets to Air of Legend of the Guns "Our story is ended"
Revivals : Two month tour, 1887 with one matinee at Crystal Palace

INDIANA
Comic Opera, composed by Edmond Audran.
Published : Boosey & Co., London, 1886
The Comedy Theatre, Manchester, 4 Oct 1886
Avenue Theatre (Mr George Wood) 11 Oct 1886,
closed 18 Dec 1886 (70 performances)
Cast at Avenue ● Aubrey, Lord Dayrell - Charles Ryley ● Matt o' the Mill - Arthur Roberts
● Philip Jervaulx - W. T. Hemsley ● Peter - Sam Wilkinson ● Sir Mulberry Mullitt – Henry
Ashley ● Captain Happe-Hazard - Miss A. Harcourt ● Indiana Greyfaunt - Mathilde
Wadman ● Nan - Mary Duggan ● Annette - Clara Graham ● Maude Cromartie - Ruby
McNeill ● Lady Prue - Phyllis Broughton ● Madge - Jessica Dene ● Ruth - Mattie Wynne
● Belle – Mabel Antony ● Winifred - Rita D'Angeli ● Lord Turniptop - Ambrose Collini
● 1st Keeper – Leon Roche ● 2nd Keeper - Bruce Blackburn ● Cosmo - Lily Richardson
● Eric - Connie Edwards ● Eben - Emmie Graham ● Dickon - Clare Bernard ● Giles -
Clarence Hunt ● with chorus.
Dir. H. B. Farnie; MD John Crook; sc. T. E. Ryan & F. Storey; Cos. Lucien Besche.

Musical Numbers : Overture

Act I

1A   Chorus   'Today We'll Dance'
1B   Mill Song   'When Logs on the Ingle'
1C   Scene   'It Is Time'
1½   Exit   ' 'Tis a Gossip Too'
2   Bouffe Song   'Seek the Woman'   "A certain judge in France
3A   Duet   'Bah! He Must Think Me!'
3B   Air   'Poor Young Thing'   "You say your bride squints"
3C   Stretti   'I See His Game'
3½   Exit   "Ah! you have not far to go"
4   Melodrame   'The Ferry Boat' [music over dialogue]
5A   Recit   'Why In Wild Quest'
5B   Valse   'Love Will Guide'
6   Quintette   'Ah! Let Us See'   "Ha! ha! ha! ... Ah! let us see"
6½   Melodrame   'Entrance of Peasants' [music only]
7   Finale
7A   Recit & Scene   'The Change is Done'
7B   Scene   'Before Lord Dayrell'
7C   Ensemble   'Love Will Guide'

Act II

8   Entracte
9A   Yawning Chorus   'Pray Excuse Me'   "Ah! Ah! Pardon me yawning"
9B   Letter-Bag Ensemble   'Skirts are Fuller'
10   Canzonet   'Watch Always at Thy Lattice'   "In days of chivalrie"
11A   Scene   'In No Sweet Frame of Mind'
11B   Scene   'How Well You Look'
11C   Rustic Ditty   'Jasper's Jacket'   "Jasper the woodman's bought a jacket"
11½   Exit   'There Are Bet and Bell'
12   The Dancing Lesson [music only]
13   Melodrame [music only]
14A   Scene   'I Must Go'
14B   Ensemble   'Till on my Venture Bold'
15A   Scene   'The Lease Duet'   "The aforesaid Lord Dayrell"
15B   Ensemble   There, at the dreamy hour'
16A   Valse   'Good-night'   "Of yore the curfew bell rang out"
16B   Scene & Recit   'My Quest's No Earthly Use'
16C   Ensemble   'Stay, Oh Stay'
16D   Coda Finale   'My Lords and Ladies'

Act III

17   Entracte
18A   Aubade   'Hark the Trill'
18B   Air   'Alas! How Quickly'
19   Air   'O Sunny South'
20   Song   'Lowly the Lass'
21   Chorus   "Here by the ford we'll wait"
22   Song and Chorus   'Open the Shutters Wide'
23   Duet   'How Break My Word'
24   Finale   'All Complication Now is Ended'
Comic Song   'The Plain Potato Fable' (Music by John Crook)

Revivals : Avenue Theatre 13 June 1887, closing 1 July 1887 (17 performances)
America : Star Theatre, New York, 18 Jan 1887 followed by tour; Wallacks Theatre, New York 11 July 1888.

ROBINSON CRUSOE

Burlesque, written in collaboration with RObert Reece, music by John Crook.

Published : Wilcocks & Co., London, 1886

Avenue Theatre (George Wood), 23 Dec 1886,

closed Sat 16 Apr 1887 (120 performances)

Robinson Crusoe - Arthur Roberts • Captain William Atkins - Mr C. W. Bradbury Old Hopkins - Mr R. Harris • Rev. Winkey Fum - Sam Wilkinson • Friday - Charles Sutton • Tappe, Grabbe (bailifs) - Mr F. Storey, Mr J. Atkins • Ka-Fé, O-lé (canibals) - Mr R. Collins, Mr L. Roche • Vivasseur - Henry Ashley • Jenny Jones - Miss Wadham • Princess Bamboula - Mrs Mackintosh • Jam-Jam - Janette Stear • Omihi - Clara Graham • Gaff – Lydia Yeamans • Britannia - Miss E. Grahame • Polly Hopkins - Phyllis Broughton • Fairies, &c.

Dir. H. B. Farnie; MD. John Crook; sc. Albert Colcott, W. Keith, and F. Story; cos. M & Mme Alias after design by L. Beche; Dances by Paul Valentine.

Musical Numbers :

ACT I

Naiad Chorus : "Once again we'll set eyes on Crusoe's barque"

Barcarolle (Chorus) "Sing we a barcarolle"

Chorus "Tis our delight on a shiny night"

Ensemble "Begone dull care"

The Slap Duet "Taste that for a moment"

Pirate Chorus "Oh we're the pirate crew"

Launch Chorus "What is that the neighbours all do say"

Song and Chorus 'The Auctioneer' "Hallo he is alter'd"

Chorus Finale Act I "The wind is blowing fair off the shore"

ACT II

Indian Chorus "We are a lot of heathens"

Oracle Chorus "Who will her husband be?"

Song 'As Artful as a Wagon-load of Monkeys' "Oh! her hair it has the tint"

Song 'The Bird and the Snake' "When a bird is singing gaily"

Finale Scene 1 "Sound the horn and beat the drum"

Comic Song 'Taint Natural'

Finale Scene 2 'O What a Surprise'

Avenue Minstrel Scene 'Listen to the Mocking Bird'

Finale Act II "Things look like Murder!"

ACT III

Jungle Chorus "When the midnight dews are weeping"

Chorus - Concerted Number

Folie Dance Miss Phyllis Broughton

THE OLD GUARD

Comic Opera, composed by Robert Planquette

Published : Enoch & Sons, London 1887

Grand Theatre, Birmingham, 10 Oct 1887

Avenue Theatre (Henry Watkins) 26 Oct 1887, closed 20 July 1888

(275 performances), reopened 1 Oct 1888, closed 27 Oct 1888

Polydore Poupard (Maire of Vaudrez-les-Vignes, and landlord of the Big Sabot Inn) – Arthur Roberts • Monsieur de Volteface (Political Envoy of the Emperor Napoleon) - Malcolm H. Grahame • Gaston de la Roche-Noire (A Young Nobleman in hiding) - Joseph

Tapley ● Capitaine Marcel, Sergeant Caramel, Lieutenant Vigoreux (of the Imperial Guard) – Alec Marsh, Mr L. Roche, Clara Grahame ● Marquis D'Artemare (an Emigre Noble) - Mr J. J. Dallas ● Fraisette (maid of the Village Inn) - Marion Edgcumbe ● Murielle (Heiress ? Of Artemare) - Fanny Wentworth ● Patatout (Bugler of the Imperial Guard) - Henriette Polak ● Follow-the-Drum (Cantiniere in Marcel's Company) - Phyllis Broughton ● Maconnais and Maiconaises, Company of the Old Guard, A Tableaux of Ci-devants (Louis XVI), Peasants, Conscripts, Enfants de Troupe, &c., &c.
Dir. H. B. Farnie; MD. John Crook; sc. Messrs Watkins and Hicks, and T. E. Ryan; cos. Alias after Mons. L. Besche.

Musical Numbers :

Overture
1. Conscription Chorus "In there, our young men draw"
2a Chorus "Fraisette ! Just look alive"
 b Song (Fraisette & Chorus) "I've only one !"
2½ Exit - Chorus "Who will in the ranks quick fall?"
3. Waltz Song (Marcel) "Only a moment love was mine"
4. Diligence Chorus "From The coach"
5. Valse (Muriel) "For ever thine !"
5½ Exit - Chorus "That we further news may hear"
6. Duet (Frisette & Gaston) "All I have to give"
7. Air (Frisette) "Fare thee well ! my humble home"
8. Finale "Here they come !"
  Act II
9. Entr'acte
10. Recruiting Song (Patatoout & Chorus) "Now, Ladies !"
11. Romance (Marcel) "A life and a love"
12. Song (Murielle) "A lowly servant lass am I"
13. Ci-Devant Chorus "To the rabble rout"
13½ Melodrame
14a Chorus "Ah! she's very pretty"
  b Scene & Air (Fraisette, Marquis & Chorus) "I feel - I don't know"
14½ Exit - Chorus "Ah! she's very pretty"
15. Duet (Fraisette & Marcel) "Young, and divinely fair"
16. Valse Chantée "(Frais, Mur, Gast, Marc, Cho) " 'Neath the lamplight"
17 & 17½ Melodrame
18. Finale
  a Chorus "Hail ! the welcome danger"
  b Song (Fraisette & Chorus) "For our country, right or wrong !"
  Act III
19. Entr'acte
20. Chorus "Hang the kettle up !"
21. Song (Patatout & Chorus) "The short cut home !"
22. Duet (Marcel & Gaston) "Soldier ! Alert !"
23. Trio (Murielle, Marquis, and Marcel) "You give consent ?"
24. Rustic Air (Frais & Cho) "Myheart, my hand are now my own!"
25 & 26. Melodrame
27. Finale "Duty bids me march away !"
Interpolated numbers :
Maire's Song (Poupart and Chorus) "I am a most tremendous local swell"
When We Were Young ! (Marquis and Poupart) "It seems to me but yesterday" (lyric Mr J.
        J. Dallas, music John Crook)
The Dashing Militaire (Poupart) "At the first I was nervous"

The Lovers' Hour (Gaston) "The Lovers' Hour is nigh"
Australia : Princess's, Melbourne, 11 Apr 1891

PAUL JONES
(Surcouf)
Comic Opera, composed by Robert Planquette, libretto by H. Chivot and A. Duru (Folies
Dramatique, Paris, 1887)
Published : Hopwood and Crew, London. 1889
Bolton (Carl Rosa) 10 Dec 1888 + tour
Prince of Wales (Horace Sedger) - The Carl Rosa Light Opera Company - 12 Jan 1889,
closed 15 Jan 1890 (370 performances)

Paul Jones (the celebrated Nautical Hero) - Agnes Huntingdon ● Rufino de Martinez (a
Spanish Naval Officer) - Mr Templar Saxe ● Bicoquet (a St Malo Ship Chandler) – Henry
Ashley ● Don Trocadero (Spanish Govenor of the Island of Estrella) - Frank Wyatt
● Haricot (Servant to Bicoquet) - James Francis ● Kestrel (Skipper of a Yankee Privateer) –
Arthur Hendon ● Bouillabaisse (An Old Smuggler) - Harry Monkhouse ● Petit Pierre
(Fisher Lad of St Malo) - Albert James ● 1st Lieutenant - George Preston ● Yvonne (Niece
of Bicoquette) - Mathilde Wadman ● Chopinette (Wife of Bouillabaisse) - Phyllis
Broughton ● Malaguena (Niece of Don Trocadero) - Kate Cutler ● Guava (Malaguena's
Creole Maid) - Mimi St Cyr ● Captain Octroi - Jeannie Mills ● Delphine - Florence Wilton
● Nichette - Miss Fitzgerbert ● Mignonne - Miss Forbes ● Estelle - Gladys Knowles
● Ramez - Tom Shale ● Don Antonio - Mr Pearce ● Jeanne de Kerbec - Miss Stanford
● Coralie - Miss Dashwood ● Alva - Minnie Howe ● Fernando - Miss Gwynne ● Marbon
(Mario) - Mr Sefton ● Goujon – Robert Mason ● Don Riboso - Mr Bottrill ● Louise de la
Forte - Miss Bell ● Val de Penna – Miss Douglas ● Maroona - Lillie Levine ● Merlan - Mr
Feltham ● Fishermen, Privateersmen, Spanish and American Man-o'-warsmen, Lassies of
St Malo, Ladies of the Chateau, Spanish Officers, Pages, Creoles, &c.

The Bourree in the 2nd Act danced by the ensemble and Miss Phyllis Broughton.
Dir. H. B. Farnie; MD Frederick Stanislaus; ch. John D'Auban; sc. J. Robson and T. E.
Ryan; cos. Mons. and Mme Alias from designs by Lucien Besch.

      Musical Numbers :   Overture
           Act I

1A   Chorus 'Come - shop there!'
1B   Recit "My men, of your money first"
1C   Couplets 'Confidence' "Some are fools, and some are clever"
1½   Exit 'This here is by chalks'
2.   Melos 'American Chanty' Music Only
3.   Melos Music Only
4.   Trio 'Heave oh!' "Upon a Mayday morning"
5.   Romance 'The Lee Shore' "Upon a lee shore"
6A   Chorus 'Maidens of St Malo'
6B   Scene 'Well, Girls!' "Well girls, what did you see"
6C   Air 'The Merman's Cave' "When I look'd and found no other body"
6½   Exit 'Maidens of St Malo'
7.   Duet 'A little bird on weary wing'
8.   Finale 'So your boats and your nets'
           Act II Entracte
9A   Chorus 'Captain! Ola!'
9B   Solo 'You're welcome, friends'

9C   Serenade 'Lull'd by Waves'
10. Duet 'The Shipping News'
11. Chorus 'How Bright the Day' "Tra, la, la, how bright the day"
12A Lilt 'He'd Looked at my Sabots' "Thinks I 'a peasant I will be'"
12B Montagnarde Music Only
12C Bourée Music Only
12½ Exit Reprise 'How Bright the Day' "Lightly pass, upon the grass"
13. Romance 'Before the Altar'
14. Morceau d'Ensemble 'True to Thy Troth' "Ha! True to thy troth"
14½ Romance 'Ever and Ever Mine' "Parted for aye?"
15. Duet 'For Lack of Gold'
16. Stave 'The Lassies!' "I can heave the deep lead"
17. Finale Act II 'They Say the Pirate'
            Act III Entracte
18A Chorus 'For affairs of State'
18B Air Bouffe 'Open the Council'
18½ Exit 'Viva Trocadero' "Praise me, acclaim me"
19. Trio 'O'er Ocean Gleaming'
20. Chorus and Scene 'Till the Light Fades'
21. Duo Berceuse - Recit 'It Cannot Be' Duo, 'On My Heart'
22A Chorus 'King of the Mosquitos'
22B Indian Song 'Ah-wah-ik to-mani'
22½ Exit 'P'raps he will shock us'
23. Scene and Melos 'Arrest Him'
24. Finale Act III 'The Lovers United'

Revivals : BBC Broadcast (extracts) 6 Oct 1936
America : Broadway Theatre, 6 Oct 1890; Union Square Theatre, 20 Feb 1892; Harlem Opera House, 20 Feb 1892; American Theatre, 31 Jan 1898
Australia : Opera House, Melbourne, 27 Mar 1890

PRIMA DONNA

Opera Comique in three acts, written in collaboration with Alfred Murray, composed by
Tito Mattei
Published : Hutchings & Co. (4446), London, 1890
Avenue Theatre (Claude Marius) 16 Oct 1889,
closed 14 Dec 1889 (60 performances)

Leopold (Grand Duke of Nierstein) - Alec Marsh ● Prince Maximillian (Prince of,Hanau) - George Sinclair ● Baron Pippinstir (Envoy Extraordinary from the Elector of Hesse-Hausen) - George Capel ● Sigismund (Valet de Chambre to the Grand Duke) - Harry Grattan ● Ballard (Manager of a Troupe of French Players) - Albert Chevalier ● Florival (Tenor in Ballard's Company) - Joseph Tapley ● Rigolet (Low Comedian of Ballard's Company) - Mr H. Grahame ● Anselmo (Heavy Man of Ballard's Company) - F. Benwall ● Lebel (Leader of the Band of Ballard's Company) - Stanley Betjeman ● Margravine of Adelberg (Ward of Pippinstir) - Florence Paltzer ● Princess Mina (Sister to Maximillian) - Amelia Gruhn ● Otto (Page to Maximillian) - E. Gower ● Foligny (Soubrette of Ballard's Company) - Ida Liston ● Pastorale (Duenna of Ballard's Company) - Maud Brent ● Ninette (Prima Ballerina of Ballard's Company) - Alice Lethbridge ● Delia (Prima Donna of Ballard's Company) – Sara Palma ● and large chorus.
Dir. Claude Marius; MD. John Crook; ch. Willie Warde; sc. Richard Douglass and Fred Storey.

Musical Numbers :
Act I
1. Chorus of Courtiers and Scene (Sigismund) "Our salaries all in arrear are"
   Sig) "What means, if you please, this wild commotion"
2. Ensemble (Actors) and Solo (Delia) "A troupe of comedians are we"
3. (Delia) 'Brava! Bravissima!' "Talk not of the smiles by a people adoring"
4. Romance (Leopold) 'Their pity I would scorn to crave'
5. Duet (Delia and Flor) 'Sweet, do not dream I'll forget thee'
6. Trio (Marg, Flor, Pipp) 'Who the deuce are you, sir?'
7. Chorus of Guards and Pages; and Scene; and Song (Mina)
   a. Chorus "Not a gentleman-in-waiting"
   b. Scene "What a humiliating meeting"
   c. Air (Mina) "I'm not yet a stolid matron"
8. Finale Act I (Nanette & Chorus) 'Oh excellent device'
   Final Chorus & Principals "List to the bell so gay"
   Act II
9. Chorus 'Banish care!' "Banish care for fun and folly"
10. Song (Ballard) 'Behind the scenes' "On the stage at night"
11. Song (Marg) 'Flirtation' "You think a woman at the altar"
12. Quartette (Marg, Flor, Ball, Pipp) 'How charmed I am to meet you'
13. Song (Delia) 'Love me!' "Oh dearest! oh dearest! words could never tell"
14. Chorus "Princess, who art fairer than the flowers of spring"
15. Duet (Leo & Mina) 'Yes or No!' "When a trembling lover dareth"
16. Chorus "Marriage bells will soon be ringing"
17. Finale Act II.
    a. Ensemble 'I am shocked'
    b. Scene & Chorus "My offer of alliance you spurn with jeering scoff"
    Act III
18. Chorus & Dance "Come where the dance invites us"
19. Romance (Flor) 'Love Farewell !' "We twain must sever, we part forever"
20. Kissing Duet (Del & Flor) "You can forgive? Yes, and you too"
21. Song (Pipp) 'Stranger than fiction' "If a bushel of lies raises dust in your eyes"
22. Reprise of Song "Come where the dance", and solo dance
23. Song (Leo) 'The Cause of Liberty' "In Cupid's list, where lovers meet"
24. Finale (Principals & Chorus) " 'Tis over! 'Tis over!

ROMEO AND JULIET
Opera, Roméo et Juliette, composed by Charles Gounod, libretto by P. J. Barbier and M.
Carré, after Shakespeare
(Théâtre-Lyrique, Paris, 27 April 1867)
Farnie's version printed alongside the French (French verso, English recto) in a booklet for
sale in Royal Opera House for the season of Royal Italian Opera.
Published : J. Miles & Co., London, 1867
Court Theatre, Liverpool, Carl Rosa Opera, 15 Jan 1890 (9 performances during 8 week
season); Drury Lane 5 Apr 1890
Romeo - Barton McGuckin ● Mercutio - Mr. F. H. Celli ● Benvolio - Mr Ellis ● Tybalt –
John Child ● Friar Lawrence - Sig. Abramoff ● Capulet - Max Eugene ● The Duke of
Verona - Mr. Albert ● Paris - Mr. Somers ● Stephano - Kate Drew ● Gertrude - Annie Cook
● Juliet - Mdlle Zella de Lussan
Revivals : Covent Garden, 12 July 1905; BBC Broadcast 1927

THE BRAZILIAN
(La Brazilienne)
Theatre Royal, Newcastle 19 Apr 1890
The Brazilian, composed by F. Chassaigne, libretto by H. B. Farnie, Max Pemberton & W. Lestocq.
Published : Alfred Hays, London, 1890
Theatre Royal, Newcastle 19 Apr 1890 (copyright performance)
America : Casino Theatre, New York, 2 June 1890

NECTARINE
(La Cantinière)
Comic Opera in three acts, composed by Robert Planquette, adapted in collaboration with Henry Hersee
Joseph Williams, n.d. [1894] Entered at Stationers Hall
No record of production
Musical Numbers : Overture
        Act I
1 Market Chorus "Covent Garden, England's Pride"
2 Gossips Song and Chorus "She now treats her Lover"
3 Air à Due "Breezes of Morning" (Louis and Nectarine)
4 The Wages Duet "You'll find, my Friend (Lovelace and Baron)
5 Terzetto "Hands off, Sirs !" (Nectarine, Baron and Lovelace)
6 Chorus "What's About to Happen"
7 Song & Chorus "'Rustic Simplicity' (Lovelace)
8 Song "Ah ! Deceivers !" (Vivien)
9 Finale Act I "What Can this Mean ?" (Tutti)
        Act II
10 Entr'acte
11 Chorus "Now then, Look Sharp !"
12 Blind-Fold Song "Why Am I a Prisoner Brought (Nectarine & Chorus.)
13 Song & Clog Dance "Kiss, but Never Tell" (Nectarine and Bijah)
14 Duet "Fit Abode for Fairies" (Nectarine and Lovelace)
15 Trio ""Desist !" (Nectarine, Louis and Lovelace)
16 Song "I am Bess Bloxam !" (Bess & Chorus)
17 Finale Act II "What a Striking Surprise !" (Tutti)
        Act III   Entr'acte
18 Chorus "Fill Up the Glasses !"
19 Rondo with Chorus "Poor Bijah !" (Bess & Chorus)
20 Duet "I Read Your Eyes" (Nectarine and Vivien)
21 Song "With Rage nearly Choking" (Lovelace)
22 Romance "I dare not Speak" (Louis)
23 Song "Really, upon My Word" (Nectarine)
23½ Chorus "What means this Commotion ?")
24 Finale "Just like Youm in Sooth" (Tutti)

THE REHEARSAL
Koster & Bial's Music Hall, New York, 13 Feb 1893

V V
Kilburn Town Hall, Fri 27, Sat 28 May 1887

Mr Parry Cole wrote the music and thanked Farnie for permission to use the piece. Nothing else known.

THE MAGPIES
Les Bavards. Operetta in two acts. Libretto Charles Nuitter. Music Offenbach.
Original production : Ems, 12 June 1862.
Farnie Version : said to be "Popular in America" .

APPENDIX 2
SONGS BY H. B. FARNIE

The following list is intended to include only those songs written for concert hall, drawing room or music hall and not songs written for shows which have been listed in Appendix 1. But due to the practice of both managements and leading artistes of introducing songs into shows to freshen up a piece or simply because they liked them, some of these will have been inserted into a show after its opening. This is noted where known.

Absence. Original poetry by Compte A. Ségur, Music Ch. Gounod. Metzler & Co. [1889]

Adore, and be Still (Canticle) (Le ciel a visité la terre) Poetry by A. Segur, Music Ch. Gounod. J. B. Cramer & Co., London, 1877

Am I to Blame? Ballad. Music Felix Keston. Boosey & Co., London, [1886]

Among the Lilies! Reverie. "Among the lilies stray'd they twain forgetting" Adapted to the melody of the Stéphanie Gavotte, music Alphons Czibulka. Boosey & Co., London, 1883

Among the Water Lilies - Boat Song "We have drifted on the river, To the water-lily bay" Music Luigi Arditi [1871]

Amy Robsart "Deep fall the shades of night" Music Joseph Philip Knight. Duff and Stewart, London, 1870

Anita : song. "Thou dost not speak to me, mine own" Music Henry Brinley Richards. Cramer, Wood & Co., London. 1864.

At Eventide "'Tis eventide, the shades of night are falling". Music Robert Planquette. Alfred Hays, London, 1884. Introduced into Falka.

At Midnight "Tones soft and low" Original German by Prutz (Um mitternacht), Music Francis Berger. London [1866]

The Auctioneer. Music John Crook. J. B. Cramer, London [1887]

The Austrian National Anthem "God! to whom we low are bending". No.7 in Metzler's Standard Edition of Celebrated War Songs of the East. Metzler & Co., London. 1877

Beautiful Bells "The snow is crisp, the air is keen" Wm A. Pond, New York, 1868. In 'Spirit of Burlesque' series.

Beauty Sleep (celebrated L'Ardita) "O'er meadow and lea" Music Luigi Arditi. Cramer & Co., London, 1869

Bessie's Mistake. Music by F. Campana. Hopwood & Crew, London, 1870. Sung by Madame Trebellini-Bettini

Bethlehem - 18c. Carol "Cradled all lowly" Music Ch. Gounod. Metzler & Co., London, 1866. Later published as 'Cradled All Lowly', and in a revised version as 'The Shepherds' Nativity Hymn'

The Bird and the Snake "When a bird is singing gaily". Music Auguste Cœdès. Cramer [1889]

Bird of the Wild Wing "Bird of the wild wing, Bird of the foam" Music W. Vincent Wallace. London, 1864

The Black Watch. Music Brinley Richards. Cramer & Co, London, 1874

The Blucher Song – The great national German song. "What are the bugles sounding" Metzler & Co., London, 1870

Boat Song "adapted to the celebrated baritone air from La Forza del Destino" "Son pereda, son ricco d'onore" "Swiftly thro' the west the shadows dim are flying" Music by Verdi. Cramer, Wood & Co., London. 1864.

The Bridal Dream "Who knows what dreams" Music Hervé. London [1874]

The Brigand Chief "O! I am a brigand chief, That's to say a thief" From Ernani. Wm A. Pond, New York, 1868. In 'Spirit of Burlesque' series.

Brindisi. Music Lindheim. London, 1872. Introduced late into Genevieve de Brabant.

The Broken Tryst "He promised to come" Music Alfred Cellier. London, 1877

The Buccaneer "Swiftly flies my good bark from the land" Music Frederick Lablache. Cramer, Wood & Co., London. 1864. Composed for and sung by Charles Santley.

By Babylon's Wave: anthem (Près du fleuve étranger) "Here by Babylon's wave" Psalm 137 paraphrase. Music Ch. Gounod. Cramer & Co., London, 1866

Capstan Song "Yo-ho! Round with her boys, yo-ho! " Music Alberto Randegger. Cramer & Co., London, 1865.

The Captive and the Bird: romance "Round the lone keep" Music Robert Planquette. J. B. Cramer & Co., London, 1880. Introduced into Les Mousquetaires

The Cavalier's Steed "I'll throw my rein on my charger's neck" Music Joseph Ascher. Cramer & Co., London, 1864.

Chant du Départ. Metzler & Co., 1870

Charge, Chester, Charge! : Marmion's last war-cry "Upon the field a wounded knight" Music Henry Thomas Smart. Cramer & Co., London, 1865 (Also Novello, Ewer & Co., London, 1877)

The Child's Wish. Music Gounod..Pond, New York, n.d.

Christmas Morn (Noël) Poesy Jules Barbier, Music Ch. Gounod. J. B. Cramer & Co., London [1868]

Come In! : ballad "O well do I remember now" Music Frederick Stanislaus. J. B. Cramer & Co., London, 1877

Constancy. Music Ch. Gounod. Cramer [before 1879]

The Cossack's Farewell (The red sarafan) No. 2 in Metzler's Standard Edition of Celebrated War Songs of the East. Metzler & Co., London, 1877

Cradled all Lowly - see Bethleham

Danish National Song (Den-Tapre Landsoldat) "The trumpet-call to arms, I'll soon be in the fray" Music arr. T. M. Mudie. Cramer, Wood & Co., Aug 1864

David Singing before Saul : scena (David chantant devant Saul) Recit. : "I left my flock to stray upon the plain" Aria : "By thee no more the righteous sword is wielded" (from 1 Samuel XVI.23) Music Luigi Bordèse. Cramer & Co., London, 1865

David to Jonathan - Sacred Song "Weep Maidens" Music Henri Charles Antoine Gaston Serpette. London [1876]

Deep in My Heart (Il Tempietto del Core) "Deep in my heart! within this heart of mine" (Ho un tempietto) Poetry by G. S. Patuzzi, Music Andrea L. Traventi. Cramer & Co., London, 1875

The Deluded Bee, a doleful song. Music William Marshall Hutchison. W. Marshall & Co., London, 1884

The Dove and the Maiden "The maiden in her simple bow'r" Music Offenbach. J. B. Cramer & Co., London, 1873. In H. S. Leigh's 'Bridge of Sighs'

The Dove and the Raven "Tell us o dove with the rainbow breast" Music Michael William Balfe. Hutchings & Co., [1888]. Sung by Mr Brereton.

Dove of the Ark - Sacred Song "Though now on earth" Music Henri Charles Antoine Gaston Serpette. London [1876]

The Dreamer. Music Gounod. Pond, New York, n.d.

The Dream of Home (Il Bacio) "Brightly dawns" Music Luigi Arditi. London, 1864

Earth is no Lasting Place. Music Gounod. Metzler & Co., London, 1868 (Published in Bow Bells,9 Sept 1868)

Egyptian National Song. No. 3 in Metzler's Standard Edition of Celebrated War Songs of the East. Metzler & Co., London, 1877

England yet "Old England yet! the nation cries" Music Julius Benedict. Chappell & Co., London, 1868

Evening Bringeth My Heart Back to Thee - ballad "I am tired of the brightness of day" Music Fabio Campana. Metzler & Co., London, 1875. Sung by Adelina Patti

Ever or Never. Music Fabio Campana. Hopwood & Crew, London, 1880

Eyes. Music Fabio Campana. Hopwood and Crew, London, 1870

The Eye that Brightens When I Come - Ballad Written to the melody of Dan Godfrey's Belgravia Waltz. Chappell & Co., London [1867]

The Faded Bloom (Donne-moi cette fleur) Poesy de Leon Gozlan, Music Gounod. Choudens, Paris. J. B. Cramer & Co., London, also Metzler & Co., London [1889]

The Fairy Voyage. Music Ch. Gounod. Pond, New York, n.d.

The Fall of the Leaf "How softly comes the golden eve" Music George Alexander Macfarren. London [1864]

Fan, The [Farnie owned the copyright at the time of his death, nothing else known]

Farewell for ever "All night thro' thy slumbers" Music Michael Connelly. n.d. [Oliver Ditson, Boston, 1906]

Fatal Star. Music Gounod. London [1887]

The Fateful Bridge of Sighs - Barcarolle "Oh! tell me not" Music George Jacobi. London [1879]

The Fields of Paradise - sacred song "O'er the turf that wraps the lonely grave" Adapted to the 'Marche funebre' section of Chopin's piano sonata No. 2, Op. 35. Cramer & Co., London, 1866

The First Leaf (La premiére feuille) "Now the sun has made a clearance" (Enfin le soleil qui brille) Music C. Leofort. Metzler & Co., London, 1872

Flora Macdonald to Prince Charlie "Where dost thou wander" Music by Joseph Philip Knight. Sinclair & Co., London [1867]

Flow'rs from My Sweet (Envoi de Fleurs) "Who gave me" Poesy d'E Augier, Music Ch. Gounod. J. B. Cramer & Co., London [1877]

The Flower's Last Sigh. Music Gounod. Pond, New York, n.d.

The Flying Dutchman : legend "To storm and wind" Music Luigi Bordèse. Cramer & Co., London, 1879

For Lack of Gold He Left Me. "For lack of gold, or of flock in fold" Music Ch. Gounod. Cramer & Co., London, 1865. Sung by Mlle Theresa Titiens.

Forget Not to Forget "We're parted! yet I know not why" Music Alfred Plumpton. Boosey & Co., London [188-] Inserted into Boccaccio for Violet Cameron

The Forlorn Hope "They told us true 'tis perilous our post" Music Henri Charles Antoine Gaston Serpette. Metzler & Co., London, 1878 [Revised version of The Last Cartridge q.v.]

For Native Country Dying (Mourir pour la Patrie) Metzler & Co., London, 1870

The Free Lance "As off he rode, the trooper turn'd and gaz'd" Music Peter Joseph von Lindpaintner. Cramer & Co., London, 1866 (Companion song to The Standard Bearer q.v.)

Friendship. "O happy he" In 'Songs of the Rhineland' J. Cramer & Co., 1867

The Friend We Had at School. Music W. T. Wrighton. Metzler & Co., London, 1870

Gallant so Gay ! - ballad "Forth rode the knight" Music Robert Harold Thomas. Ashdown and Parry, London, 1866

The Galloping Snob of Central Park "As I go riding in Central Park" Wm A. Pond& Co., New York, 1868 (Spirit of Burlesque series)

Garibaldi : A National Song "Long the genius of Italy slumbered" Music Luigi Arditi. Cramer, Wood & Co., London. 1864

The German Fatherland "Where lies the German Fatherland?" (Was ist des Deutachen Vaterland) Music Edward Francis Rimbault. Metzler & Co., London, 1870

The German Rhine (Sie sollen ihn nicht haben) Music Edward Francis Rimbault. Metzler & Co., London, 1870

The Gift and the Giver - Sequel to the Stirrup Cup "The mandoline ceas'd" Music Luigi Arditi.

The Gipsy's Farewell. Music Robert Planquette. Alfred Hays, London, 1884. Introduced into Falka

Girl in the Eelskin Dress - comic song "The days are past of Crinoline" Cramer, 1877.

Gliding Down the River - Boat song "Strike the sail" Music Ch.Gounod (adapted to a movement in the Faust ballet music) Pitt and Hatzfeld, London, 1887 (Original words, not translated from any of the French versions by Christophe, Sédillot, or Barbier)

Glou, Glou! "O, who would pine in gilded hall" New words to The Shepherds' Duet from La Mascotte for solo voice and for the drawing room. Music Audran. London, 1881

Golden Dreams - Romance "O happy land" Music Hervé. London [1874]

The Gondolier's Last Good Night : A Legend of Venice. Music Luigi Arditi. Cramer & Co., London, 1864

Good Night! (Gute Nacht) "Now good night!" (Gute Nacht! Allen Müden) Words in English and German. In conjunction with L. H. F. du Terreaux. Music Alberto Randegger.

Good Night, Heaven bless you. Music Gounod. London [1870]

The Grape - drinking song "Oh! were I Norman" Music John E. Mallandaine. Cramer & Co., 1874. Introduced into J. Oxenford's drama *The Two Orphans*

The Greek National Air. Metzler & Co., London. 1877. No. 4 in Metzler's Standard Edition of Celebrated War Songs of the East.

The Guardian Angel "Still is the night low thro' the pine trees" Music Ch. Gounod. Metzler & Co., London, 1866

The Guards' Song "Weave garlands for the brave" Music Daniel Godfrey. Chappell & Co., London, 1864

The Happy Dawn of Day "The morn is coming from the hills" Written to subjects from Nicolai's overture to The Merry Wives of Windsor. Cramer & Co., London, 1864

A Happy New Year (La bonne année) "A time of revel, wine, and singing" Music George Lefort. Metzler & Co., London, 1872

Haul on the Bowline "O the bark is running" Music Odoardo Barri (Edward Slater). London [1877]

The Haunting Thought (Die verlegenheit) "When others jest and song awaken" (Ich möchte dir wohl etwas sagen) Music Alexander Reichardt. Cramer & Co., London, 1865.

The Hero of Magdala, or, England Yet "Old England yet! the nation cries" Music Julius Benedict. Chappell & Co., London [1873]

Hero to Leander "Now the world calm and still" Music Gounod. London [1865]

Hidden Flowers - Ballad "The woodland lane is dark" Music Charles Handel Rand Marriott. London [1876]

Hilda. Advertised on back cover of Olivette vocal score, 1881, nothing else known.

A Holy Calm, a Peace Divine (First line the same) (Companion song to Sweet Spirit Hear My Prayer q.v.) Music W. Vincent Wallace. Cramer & Co., London, 1865

Hymn of St Hilda's Nuns "While the sea bird's shrilly crying" Music Brinley Richards. Cramer & Co., London, 1866

Hymn to Night (Hymne à la nuit) "Lo! through the paling blue" Music Gounod. London [1877]

I Love Him So "I love my love, yet sometimes" Music Princess Kotschubey. Cramer, London, 1874. Introduced into Genevieve de Brabant

I Love You [American title of Language of Love (qv)]

If Love be All - Romance "O love, my love" Music Elizaveta V. Kochubei. London [1873]

In Sheltered Vale. Review of a concert in Dublin, Dec 1876. Nothing else known.

In the Time of Apple Blossom. Music by F. Campana. Hopwood & Crew, London [1880]

Into the Fold. Music G. Serpette. J. B. Cramer & Co., London, 1875

Is it yes? "They stood in the deep bay window" Music by Louis Engel. Metzler & Co., London, 1884. Sung by Madame Christine Nilsson.

Is it love, the spirit of beauty. Music Clément Philibert Léo Delibes. Metzler & Co., London, 1873. From La Cour du Roi Pétaud but not included in Fleur de Lys.

It Can Never Be (Je ne puis espérer) "A fate more sorrowful" Music Ch. Gounod. J. B. Cramer & Co., London [1877]

I've seen my fate today "Tonight ..." Music George Benjamin Allen. London [1866]

Ivy "My love is not like roses" Music Charles Handel Rand Marriott. London [1876]

Jesus Wept "Jesus wept! o hallowed tears" Music J. F. Barnett. Metzler & Co., London, 1868

Just After the Battle "Still upon the field of battle I am lying Mother dear". Metzler & Co., London, 1870

Just Before the Battle "Just before the battle, Mother". Metzler & Co., London, 1870

Keep Your Powder Dry - National song "Of all the lessons of the past" Music by Dan Godfrey. Chappell & Co., London, 1866

Land-ho - A four-part song. Music Henry David Leslie. Novello & Co., London, 1869

The Language of Love : A polyglot ballad "For 'love' each country has its own name". J. B. Cramer, London, 1873

The Last Appeal - Serenade "Maiden mine" Music George Alexander Macfarren. London [1864]

The Last Cartridge "They told us true" Music by Henri Charles Antoine Gaston Serpette. London [1875] Later revised as The Forlorn Hope q.v.

The Last Watch "The breath of the tempest has swept away" Music George Alexander Macfarren. London [1866]

The Lay of the Last Oyster "To tell my sorrows" Written and arranged H. B. Farnie. London, 1875 Sung by Lydia Thompson.

Leaf by Leaf the Roses Die - Ballad "Think not my love will soon be failing" Music Herve. London, 1880. Inserted into Olivette.

Leah's Song "For him I gave up all! " Music Brinley Richards. Cramer, Wood & Co., London, 1864

The Legend of the Nile "When Nile's fair waters first their banks o'erflowing" Music George Benjamin Allen. Metzler & Co., London, 1866

The Lesson of Youth. English words in collaboration with L. H. F. du Terreaux, Music Alberto Randegger. From 'Songs of the Rhineland' Cramer, Wood & Co., London, 1867

A Letter to say "Goodbye" - ballad "Yes mother" Music Henri Charles Antoine Gaston Serpette. London [1876]

Life's Curfew Bell. "At the fall of night there's a curfew rung" Composed by Luigi Arditi. Cramer & Co, London. 1865. Sung by Mr (Charles) Santley

Like a Tale that is Told "The forest was dark" Music by Odoardo Barri (Edward Slater). London [1882]

Lisette "Come to the wood" Music John E. Mallandaine. Cramer & Co., London, 1874

A Little Bird Told Me. Music J. P. Knight. Metzler & Co., London, 1868

The Little Gipsy. Music by F. Campana. Hopwood & Crew

The Live-long Day (Den lieben langen Tag, by Friedrich Slicher) "Thro' all the live-long day" English words in collaboration with L. H. F. du Terreaux, Music Alberto Randegger. No. 2 from 'Songs of the Rhineland'. Cramer & Co., 1870

Long Live the Czar, Russian National Anthem. No. 1 in Metzler's standard edition of celebrated war songs of the east. Metzler & Co., London, 1877

Longing. Music Gounod

The Lost Star : song. "With white hair streaming upon the wind" Composed by W. Vincent Wallace. Chappell & Co., London 1865.

Lo! the light-footed Spring. Music Gounod

The Loved Can Ne'er be Lost. Music A. Warlamoff. Cramer's Standard Russian Songs. 1874

Love in Youth (used in Genevieve de Brabant) : Ballad. "Youth has a wisdom". London, 1872

Love the Vagrant : the celebrated Havanera (sic) in Carmen. "Love is wayward like any bird" (from original text by Meilhac and Halevy) Music by Georges Bizet. Metzler & Co., London, 1878.

Love Ties. "How shall I keep my love by me". Music by F. Paolo Tosti. Composed for, and sung by Miss Violet Cameron in The Sultan of Mocha. Chappell & Co., [1886]

The Lover's Tryste. Music Louis Engel. Boosey & Co. [1886]

Mabel. Words put to a waltz by Dan Godfrey. Chappell & Co., 1865

Maid of the Silv'ry Mail. "The shepherd drives his flock". Music Frank Mori. London, 1865. In The River Sprite.

The Maiden's Prayer ('Madre pietosa Vergine' from La Forza del Destino) "Mother! mother, who art a virgin pure" Music by Verdi. Cramer, Wood & Co., London, 1864.

March of the Men of Harlech. "By green hill" Arr, by Edward Francis Rimbault. London [1873]

The Mariner's Welcome Home. "Oh past is our long night of sorrow" Composed by G. A. (Sir George Alexander) Macfarren. Cramer & Co., London, 1865

Marriage Bells. "There's music in an olden song". Arranged by Michael Connolly. J. B. Cramer, London, 1878

The Marseillaise. "At last hath broke the day of glory". Music Edward Francis Rimbault. Metzler & Co., London, 1870

Medjé. Chanson Arabe (Paroles de J. Barbier) Music Charles Gounod. J. B. Cramer, London, 1865

The Message from the Battle Field - An Incident of the War. Music John Pyke Hullah. Metzler & Co., London [1875]

Mignon. Music Charles Gounod. London [1877]

The Mill Wheel (Die Mühlenrad) "Beneath the cool mill river" (In einem külen Grunde) Written in collaboration with L. H. F. du Terreaux, Music Alberto Randegger (from Johann Ludwig Friedrich Glück) No. 3 from 'Songs of the Rhineland' Cramer & Co., London, 1870

Mizpah "Thou and I must know tomorrow" Music Odoardo Barri. J. B. Cramer & Co., London, 1872

The Musketeer - dramatic song "The donjon keep loom'd dark" Music Edmond Membrée. Cramer & Co., London., 1865

My Love is an Olden Story- (First line the same) Music (Carl Wilhelm) Adolph Schloesser. Cramer & Co., London., 1865

My Own Countrie. Music by John Crook. J. B. Cramer & Co., London [1889] Sung by Miss Wadman

My Star of Heaven, my Flower of Earth "When in the heaven" London, 1870. Sung by Mr John Rawlinson.

The Name Upon the Sand - ballad "Do you not recall the days" Music by J. R. Thomas. Metzler & Co., London. [186-]

The Nearest Way Home - ballad "Who does not remember the 'nearest way home' " Music Luigi Arditi. Duff & Stewart, London, 1868. Sung by Mlle Louise Liebhart.

Noël (Christmas Morn). Poesy de Jules Barbier. Music Ch. Gounod. Metzler & Co., London, 1889

Nom de Marie, Le. Parole de Cte A. De Segur "Our Lady of the Sea" Music Ch. Gounod. Metzler & Co., London, 1889

Not All Forgot "Soft from the valley" Music Charles Loret. Cramer & Co., London, 1865

O Bag - see Put it in the Bag

O Give Me the Song of a Maiden (First line the same) Written and adapted by H. B. Farnie. Cramer & Co., London, 1865

Oh! Ma Charmante - see Sweet Dreamer

The Old Home "Faint o'er the garden" Music Frank Mori. London, 1865

Old Love (Duet). Music Charles Handel Rand Marriott. London [1876]

The Old Minuet. No copy found earlier than 1951.

The Old, Old Song "How sweetly falls on heart and ear, A quaint and simple childhood's tune" Melody and Written by H. B. Farnie. Metzler & Co., London [1873] Introduced into The Bohemians.

The Old Organist "The organist was old and blind" Music by Ciro Ercole Pinsuti. J. B. Cramer & Co., London, 1877

On Thy Heart - berceuse "Sometimes my path is dreary" Music Offenbach. J. B. Cramer & Co., London, 1880

One Smile of Thine - an Arabian love song. Music by F. Campana. Hopwood & Crew, n.d.

One Summer Eve. Music Fabio Campana. Hopwood & Crew, London [1882]

Only last night. Music Gounod. Wm A. Pond & Co., New York, n.d.

O Star of Love [The Balcony Serenade] "No bow'r, sweet heart can I offer, No pomp nor pride of state" Metzler & Co., London [1873] Introduced into The Bohemians

O touch the ivory keys again. Music Luigi Arditi. London, 1864

Our Starry Home "When falls the red sun in the mere" Music J. Ascher. Chappell & Co., London, 1865.

O weary wandering star. Music Gounod. London [1880]

Pale from My Lady's Lattice - a serenade "Pale from my lady's lattice" Music Victor Massé. Cramer & Co., London, 1865

Parisian War Song (La Parisienne). Metzler & Co., 1870

Parted "'Tis the rose realm of pleasure" Music Robert Planquette. London [1881]

Parting in Spring "That I must leave thee" from Heinrich Esser (Scheiden im Frühling). London, 1866

Passion Flowers "Below the cross" Music Odeardo Barri (Edward Slater). London, 1877

The Path thro' the Corn - ballad. Music Robert Planquette. Chappell & Co., London, 1883

The Persian National Air (Arab song) No. 6 in Metzler's Standard Edition of Celebrated War Songs of the East. Metzler & Co., London, 1877

Pet Marjorie, ballad "There's one belov'd in ev'ry home" Music Frederick Lablache. Cramer Wood & Co., London, 1864

Philomela. Music Gounod. Wm A. Pond & Co., New York, n.d.

Picciola "In lonely cell I pine away" Music Brinley Richards. Chappell & Co., London, 1866

Pleasant Sleep and Happy Dreams "Well I know that fate is changeful" Music William Hayman Cummings. Cramer & Co., London, 1865. As sung by the composer.

A Poor Girl's Heart. Music J. Offenbach. Wm A. Pond & Co., New York, 1868. From the comic opera La Pericole.

Poor Jo! - ballad "My name's 'Poor Jo' a wagerbone am I" Chorus "Gents, if over my crossing you go" Music Charles Handel Rand Marriott. J. Scrutton, London, 1876 [reference to Bleak House]

The Post Horn "Fast along the mountain going" Music L. Koenig (Hermann Louis Koenig). Cramer & Co., London, 1866

Pretty Colette "A simple youth went courting" Written and adapted to a popular French air by Henry Farnie. Cramer, Wood & Co., London, 1864.

Primavera. Poesy Theophile Gautier. Music Ch. Gounod. Choudens, Paris [1870]

Proposing (Flirtation Song) "Once a pair of lovers by the river sat" Music by F. von Suppé. Joseph Williams, London [1880]

Pull Yourself Together "Some folks there be whose custom is". London, 1874. Sung by 'Jolly' John Nash

Put it in the Bag, A song for Sackbut (comic song) "O Bag! Creation owns thy use" Cramer, London, 1877. Sung by Lionel Brough.

Qui Vive! "'Twas the night wind's ghostly sound" Music by Leopold Amat. J. B. Cramer & Co., London, 1874

Red Jacket, a soldier's song "Where have you been, Red Jacket? " Music Fabio Campiana. J. B. Cramer & Co., London, 1878

Ring on Sweet Angelus, an evening song. Written by H. B. Farnie on themes from Gounod's opera 'Sapho'. Metzler & Co., London [1865]

Rovers Dream "Where droops the palm" Music L. Bordese.

The Sail is Spread, the song of the homeward bound. Music Henry Brinley Richards. London [1865]

St Peray! a favourite chanson-à-boire " 'Twas in the fair land of Champagne, upon a dusty summer's day" Music Offenbach. Cramer & Co., London, 1865.

The Scout : A Trooper's Ditty "Come! boor" Music F. Campana. Hopwood & Crew, London [1870]

The Secret. Music Fabio Campana. Hopwood and Crew, London, 1870. Composed for and sung by Mr Santley.

Servian National Song "Where the flow'r fields tempt the bee". Metzler & Co., London, 1877. No. 8 in Metzler's Standard Edition of Celebrated War Songs of the East.

Shall we our glass forego - Drinking song. Music Leopold de Wenzel. London [1882]

She Haunts Me Like a Happy Dream - ballad (First line the same) Music Frank Musgrave. Metzler & Co., London, 1877

She Talked in Her Sleep: serio-comic song "Robin loved little Rose" Music by J. R. (John Rogers) Thomas. Metzler & Co., London [186-]

The Shepherds Nativity Hymn - see Bethlehem

A Silent Pray'r for Thee! Music Joseph Philip Knight. London [1868]

Simplette - Ballad "He was high born" Music Decker-Schenck. London [1876]

A Sister's Love. Music Gounod. Wm A. Pond & Co., New York, n.d.

Sister Star! Music F. Gevaert. Metzler & Co., London, 1868

S'm other evening. Written and arranged by H. B. Farnie. Hopwood & Crew, London, 1887

Somebody that I like better : serio-comic song. Music Felix Keston. J. B. Cramer & Co., London [1887]

Songs of the Rhineland - 1. True Unto Death, 2. The Live-long Day, 3. The Mill Wheel, 4. Good Night!, 5. Friendship, Cramer, Wood & Co., London (1867-73) - see individual entries.

Speak to Me! "Why turn away when I draw near?" Music by Fabio Campana. M. Gray, San Francisco [1867-69], Hopwood & Crew, London, 1870. Sung by Signor Italo Gardoni, and Mr Tom (Thomas Theobald) Hohler.

The Spirit of the Bell "When I press my weary pillow" Chorus: "Soft the message that thou dost tell". Arranged to a melody by Ch. Gounod. Ashdown & Parry, London, 1867.

The Sprig of Eidelweis "On Alpine height" Music George Jacobi. Boosey & Co., London [1882]

In the Spring Time "In the time of apple blossom" Music F. Campana. 1873

The Standard Bearer. Companion song to The Free Lance (q.v.)

Star of my Night - serenade "Day is fading" Music John Baptiste Theodore Weckerlin. London [1874]

The Stirrup Cup "The last saraband has been danced in the hall" Music Luigi Arditi. Chappell & Co., London. 1863 Summer is Nigh. Music Julius Benedict. Cassells Choral Music, London, 1876

Sweet Dreamer (English version of 'Oh! ma Charmante') Music Arthur Seymour Sullivan. J. B. Cramer & Co., London, 1874

Sweet Spirit Hear My Prayer. Companion song to 'A Holy Calm , a Peace Divine' (qv)

A Tear (Eine Thräne) "With heavy tears life's dawning is opprest" (Thut man ins Leben kaum den ersten Schritt) Music Alexander Reichardt. Cramer & Co., London, 1864

That's the Way to Rule 'em "Whene'er the English find" Metzler & Co., London, 1873. Introduced into Fleur de Lys.

There's Thunder in the Air "Along the Rhine" Music Alfred Cellier. London, 1876. Introduced into The Sultan of Mocha.

Think sometimes love of me - Ballad. Music F. Von Suppé. J. B. Cramer & Co., London, 1887

Thou Art So Near and Yet So Far. Music Wilhelm Ganz. Wm A.Pond, New York, n.d.

Thou shalt not have it (The German Rhine) "Thou shalt not have it, craven!" (Sie sollen ihn nicht haben). Music Edward Francis Rimbault. Metzler & Co., London, 1870

Throned in the Stars - Barcarolle (Words from the Italian of Bazza) Music by Francis Berger. London [1866]

Time's Up! : comic song "Time's up! the horses neigh" Music André Rosenboom J. B. Cramer & Co., London, 1876

'Tis Vain With Hearts - Popular English Song "There may be eyes as brightly beaming" Music by P. Lacome. Dale & Co., Sacramento, California, n.d. Introduced and sung by Digby Bell in Madame Favart (America)

To a Young Girl (A une jeune Fille) Poetry by Emile Augier, Music Ch. Gounod. Metzler & Co., London [1868]

To Spring (Au Printemps) "Lo! The light-footed Spring" Poetry J. Barbier. Music Ch. Gounod. J. B. Cramer & Co., London, 1868

To tell my sorrows - see The Last Oyster

To the Nightingale (Au Rossignol) J. B. Cramer & Co., London [1868]

Tobias (Tobie, petit oratorio) Ch. Gounod Cramer, London, 1872

The Troubadour and the Water-butt - comic serenade (or, 'Waltzing round the water-butt) "My first love was romantic" Written with Harry Hunter. Francis Bros. & Day, London, [1885] Sung by Arthur Roberts in the 1885 revival of Nemesis, and by Harry Hunter

True Unto Death (Der treue tod) "The trumpet notes of war the knight arouse" (Der Ritter muss zum blut' gen Kampf kinaus) English version in conjunction with L. H. F. du Terreaux. Music Alberto Randegger. Cramer & Co., London, 1870. No. 1 from 'Songs of the Rhineland'

Turkish National Air "Wake! Islam, Wake!" Metzler & Co., London, 1877. No. 5 in Metzler's Standard Edition of Celebrated War Songs of the East.

Under the Hazel Tree - Ballad "I promised that I'd wait". Music P. D. Guglielmo. London, 1867

Up in a Balloon "I am as you know a Madison Belle" Written for use in America (original words by G. W. Hunt) Music by G. W. Hunt. Wm A. Pond & Co., New York, 1868. In 'Spirit of Burlesque' (Ed. Farnie) series. Sung by Miss Alice Dunning.

Vashti, scena "Still the banquet goes on!" Music Luigi Bordèse. Cramer & Co., London, 1865

The Vigil "A maiden watched" Music Julius Benedict. London, 1868

The Village Curfew. Music Gounod. Wm A. Pond & Co., New York, n.d.

The Vintage of Bordeaux "Pour out for me" Written and arranged H. B. Farnie. London 1873

A Volunteer Greeting "Neath the flag" Music Julius Benedict. London, 1867

Waiting "Here my darling, with song hath charmed the hours" Written and arranged by H. B. Farnie. London [1873] Introduced into Fleur de Lys. Sung by Miss Emily Soldene.

Waltzing Round the Water-butt - see Troubadour and the water-butt

The War of the Roses - ballad "Give Lancaster her spearsmen free" Music by J. R. (John Rogers) Thomas. Metzler & Co., London. [186-]

Warblings at Eve: song "With star on star for bridal dow'r" Music Brinley Richards. Robert Cocks & Co., London. 1866. Sung by Miss Stabbach.

The Watch on the Rhine. The great national German song, now being sung by the army of the Rhine. "A wild cry leaps, like thunder roar" Music Carl Wilhelm. Metzler & Co., London, 1870.

We have our Brave Hearts Still "So Britain's not so" Music David Braham. London, 1875

Weep Not, O Rose. Music F. Campana. Hopwood & Crew, London, 1870. Composed for and sung by Madame Sinico.

We Two "Who is unfaithful" Music Napoleon Henri Reber. London, 1868

What are the bugles sounding? - see The Blucher Song.

What do the Angels Dream of, Mother. Music Ch. Gounod, Metzler, late 1870s

When Golden Eve "When golden eve has lull'd my soul" Music W. H. Adams. Cramer & Co., London, 1865.

When in Heaven - see My Star of Heaven, my Flower of Earth.

When We Went a Gleaning - Ballad "When we went a gleaning" Music Wilhelm Ganz. Ashdown & Parry, London, 1866

Whispering Kisses - Ballad "When lovers fond go out a walking" Music Emile Jonas. Metzler & Co., London, 1877

Who's at my Window? Music George Alexander Osborne. Chappell & Co., London, 1867

Why Haunt'st Thou Me ? Music Warlamoff. J. B. Cramer & Co., London, ca.1875

Without Thee (Ce que je suis sans toi) Mélodie et paroles de L. De Peyre, Music Ch. Gounod. Choudens, Paris [1870]

Would that I could forget - Romance. Music Felix Keston. London [1887]

Yes! You are free. Music Auguste Cœdès. London [1881]

The Young Girl to Her Dove "Courtly Sir, in snowy ruffle" Music Ch. Gounod. Cramer & Co., London, 1865

APPENDIX 3
MUSIC

Songs for which Farnie wrote the music.

Apple of my Eye.
Beautiful Bells
The Brigand Chief (Ernani)
Kiss Kiss (Genevieve de Brabant)
The Language of Love
The Lay of the Last Oyster
Love in Youth (Genevieve de Brabant)
My Star of Heav'n, My Flow'r of Earth
O Give Me the Song of a Maiden
The Old, Old Song
O Star of Love
Pretty Colette ("adapted from popular French air")
Put it in the Bag
That's the Way to Rule 'Em (Fleur de Lys)
Time's Up
The Vintage of Bordeaux
Waiting
Yon Trembling Arch (melody by Farnie, accompaniment by Edward Salter)

SONGS USED IN THE MUSIC HALLS

Farnie's songs were written for the concert platform, the drawing-room and for his shows, and sometimes for particular artistes. A number came to be used in music hall and those identified are listed below, b y song, and then by artiste.

Artless Thing, The (from Madame Favart)	Florence St John
As Artful as a Wagon-load of Monkeys (from Robinson Crusoe)	Arthur Roberts
At Eventide	Maud Haigh
Buccaneer, The	Charles Santley
Dashing Militaire, The (from The Old Guard)	Arthur Roberts
Dotlet of my Eye, The (from The Grand Mogul)	Arthur Roberts
Evening Bringeth My Heart back to Me	Adelina Patti
For Lack of Gold He Left Me	Titiens, Theresa (Therese Tietjens)
Gend'armes Duet (from Genevieve de Barbant)	Felix Bury & Edward Marshall
Goodbye (Tosti)	Violet Cameron
Hero of Magdala, or England Yet	Charles Santley, Sims Reeves
I Love Him So	Emily Soldene
Is it Yes?	Christine Nilsson
Language of Love, The (from Nemesis)	Arthur Lennard, Edward Terry
Lay of the Last Oyster	Lydia Thompson
Life's Curfew Bell	Charles Santley
Marriage Bells	Emily Soldene
My Star of Heaven	John Rawlinson
Novice, The (from Madame Favart)	Florence St John
Old Organist, The	Signor Foli
Only an Orange Girl (from Nell Gwynne)	Florence St John
Previous Notice of the Question (from The Grand Mogul)	Arthur Roberts
Pull Yourself Together	'Jolly' John Nash
Put it in the Bag	Lionel Brough
Red Jacket	Signor Foli
Scout, The	Charles Santley
Secret, The	Charles Santley
S'm Other Evening	Arthur Roberts
Somebody that I like Better (from Kenilworth)	Violet Cameron
Tain't Natural (from Robinson Crusoe)	Arthur Roberts
Up in a Balloon (American version)	Alice Dunning
Waltzing Round the Water-Butt (from Nemesis)	Arthur Roberts
Watch on the Rhine	Natalie MacFarren
Yea or Nay (from Cloches de Corneville)	Violet Cameron

ARTISTES' REPERTOIRES

Artistes listed are those mentioned in the text and known to have used the material in the music halls or who are mentioned in Kilgarriff, Michael, *Sing Us One of the Old Songs*, O.U.P., London and New York, 1998

Brough, Lionel	Put it in the Bag

Bury, Felix (with Edward Marshall) Gend'armes Duet (Genevieve de Brabant)

Cameron, Violet	Good-Bye Somebody that I like Better (Kenilworth) Yea or Nay (Cloches de Corneville)
Foli, Signor	Old Organist, The Red Jacket
Haigh, Maud	At Eventide (Falka)
Lennard, Arthur	Language of Love, The (Nemesis)
MacFarren, Natalie	Watch on the Rhine

Marshall, Edward (with Felix Bury) Gend'armes Duet (Genevieve de Brabant)

Nash, 'Jolly' John	Pull Yourself Together
Nillsson, Christine	Is it Yes?
Patti, Adelina	Evening Bringeth My Heart back to Me
Rawlinson, John	My Star of Heaven
Reeves, Sims	Hero of Magdala, or, England Yet
Roberts, Arthur	As Artful as a Wagon-Load of Monkeys (Robinson Crusoe) The Dashing Militaire (The Old Guard) The Dotlet of My Eye (The Grand Mogul) Previous Notice of the Question (The Grand Mogul) S'm Other Evening Tain't Natural (Robinson Crusoe)
St John, Florence	The Artless Thing (Madame Favart) The Novice (Madame Favart) Only an Orange Girl (Nell Gwynne)

Santley, Charles	Buccaneer, The
	Hero of Magdala, or, England Yet
	Life's Curfew Bell
	Scout, The
	Secret, the
Soldene, Emily	I Love Him So (Inserted into Genevieve de Brabant)
	Marriage Bells
	Sleep (Genevieve de Brabant)
Terry, Edward	The Language of Love (Nemesis)
Thompson, Lydia	Lay of the Last Oyster
Titiens, Theresa (Therese Tietjens)	For Lack of Gold He Left Me

APPENDIX 5
POETRY

Some of Farnie's songs were published as poems before being set to music. There remain a few poems which might have been expected to be set to music but have not been found as songs.

This list does not include poetry which clearly was never intended to be a song.

Broken Reeds. The Orchestra, 23 July 1864

Cadet's Letter, The. The Orchestra, 10 Oct 1863

Heaven Our Home. The Orchestra, 5 Apr 1865, The Musical Monthly, May 1865

Last Watch, The. The Orchestra, 28 Nov 1863

Love's Belief. The Orchestra, 23 Jan 1864

Only a Ribbon. The Orchestra, 25 June 1864

Orat Qui Laborat. The Orchestra, 8 Oct 1864

Robin's Requiem, The.

Samphire Gatherer, The. The Orchestra, 19 Sept 1868

Rose, The. The Orchestra, 18 June 1869

Tell Us, O Dove. The Orchestra, 5 Nov 1864. This was described a a 'part song'.

INDEX
(To Chapters One to Nine and Notes)

219